MEATH

IRISH SEA

DROGHEDA

Boyne River

LOWER SLANE

UPPER SLANE

LOWER DULEEK

UPPER DULEEK

LOWER NAVAN

UPPER NAVAN

LOWER KELLS

LOWER DEECE

UPPER DEECE

RATOATH

DUNBOYNE

Ballyhoe
Innismott
Drumconrath
Loughbracken
Ford Bridge
Nobber
Michelstown
Syddan
Lobbins Town
Castletown
Kilpatrick
Killharveys
Mullog Cross
Dunkestown
Church
Killshine
Navan
Noble Newtown
SLANE
Dowth
Gerardstown
Clongill
Germanslough
Donaghpatrick
Rathberry
Dunmoe
Donaghmore
Fennor
Boyne
Dollardstown
Knockcommon
DULEEK
Ardbraccan
Athlumney
NAVAN
Follistown
Kentstown
Black Lion
Timole
Ardsallagh
Rataine
Dowdstown
Moatstown
Danestown
Lasmullen
Templecarn
Rathfeigh
Cullingstown
Piercetown
Macetown
Kildoon
Creekstown
Killbrew
Crookstown
Dunsany
Tryven
Killeen
Killeglan
ASHBOURNE
Scurlogstown
Batterjohn
DUNSHAUGHLAN
RATOATH
Donaghmore
Larach
Killtale
Galtrim
Derrypatrick
Knockmark
Rathregan
Grenoge
SUMMERHILL
Drumlargan
Kilmore
Rathbeggan
Black Bull
Killbride
Gallow
Killgoon
Raddonstown
DUNBOYNE
CLONEE
Ballyeagan
KILCOCK
Moyglare
To Dublin
MAYNOOTH

Mornington
Colpe
Painstown
Bellewstown
Donower
Newtown Platten
Baymore
Julianstown
Killsharvey
Ballygarth
Moorechurch
Clonalvy
Stamullen

The Landed Gentry & Aristocracy

Meath

(Volume 1)

Art Kavanagh

2005

Published by Irish Family Names
11 Emerald Cottages, Grand Canal St., Dublin 4

ISBN   0 9538485 4 X

Front Cover: Dunsany Castle (Courtesy Lord & Lady Dunsany)
Back Cover: Corballis Coat of Arms (Courtesy Corballis Family)

Set in Book Antiqua 11 pt.

Author's Acknowledgements

The Author is grateful to the following :- Kevin Mulligan for his research work on a few of the families, Lord & Lady Dunsany, Sir Reginald Barnewall, Lord Trimlestown, The Earl of Bective, Turtle Bunbury, the Staff of the National Library, Seamus Corballis, George Briscoe, Mrs. Charles Moseley, John Fowler, Mrs. A. Hamilton, Tony Coogan, Noel French, the Staff of Irish Architectural Archives, the Subscribers and the various authors mentioned whose works have been acknowledged in the book.

Subscribers

Lord & Lady Dunsany
The Corballis Family
Mr. George Briscoe
Mr. John Fowler
Mr. Michael Deegan
Mr. Fiachra Kavanagh

Contents

Map of Meath Showing the Locations of the Families

1. Aylmer of Balrath
2. Briscoe of Bellinter
3. Barnewall (Trimlestown)
4. Barnewall of Crickstown
5. Bligh (Darnley) of Clifton Lodge
6. Bolton of Bective
7. Conyngham of Slane
8. Corballis of Ratoath Manor
9. Everard of Randlestown
10. Fowler of Rahinston
11. Hamilton of Hamwood
12. Langford – Rowley of Summerhill
13. Plunkett of Dunsany
14. Plunkett of Killeen
15. Preston of Bellinter/Swainston
16. Preston of Gormanston
17. Taylour of Headfort
18. Tisdall of Charlesfort
19. Watson of Bect

Introduction

The place of the gentry and aristocracy in Irish History has never been properly understood. The landlords bore the burden of responsibility for the proper upkeep of their districts: they were the upholders of the law; they maintained the roads; they were the providers of educational opportunity and they were the initiators of improvement schemes for their tenants. Contrary to popular myth, propagated for political reasons in the 19th century, the landlords were in general very fair in their dealings with their tenants. Moderate rents were charged and in the cases where tenants experienced difficulties in paying the rent a great amount of leniency was shown. The amount of arrears appearing in the various account books that I have seen was staggering and would not be tolerated at all in modern times.

Unknowingly, the gentry and aristocracy were the vehicles that conveyed the people of Ireland from the tyranny of the Middle Ages into our modern democracy. Each generation of great lords and great landowners had to adapt to the changing circumstances of their time. The advent of the liberal ideas of Liberty and Equality that emanated from France in the 18th century hastened change. Many of the more enlightened of their number sought to bring about change in their own time. Lord Edward Fitzgerald rushed headlong to his own destruction driven by the fervor of his ideals. Others, just as enlightened but more cautious, worked behind the scenes, helping to bring freedom of worship and education to those who lived under their care.

In Co. Meath the presence of the great lords such as the Plunketts and the Barnewalls, whose roots in their native soil were very deep indeed, meant that the people of that county fared better than their neighbours in adjoining territories. Far sighted men such as William Burton Conyngham of Slane contributed enormously to the development of what is now our modern state. He was a most influential person in his time, who so impressed his peers, that Conyngham Road in Dublin was named after him. He sought to give employment on a large scale with the development of the Slane Mills and he helped enormously to preserve the antiquities of Meath.

As the 19th century came to a close and the tenants were given the opportunity to buy the lands they farmed, concern for their welfare inspired Horace Plunkett to found the first Co-Operative Society in Ireland. Since his death this inspirational movement has spread throughout the world bringing the benefits envisaged by its founder to people worldwide.

Horace's nephew, Edward Moreton Drax Plunkett was another exceptional man, whose enthralling stories, that found a wide audience during his lifetime, still captivate people today.

The descendants of many of the original founders of the dynasties mentioned in this book spread all over the world, where they became high achievers. The numbers of those who accomplished great things and rose to high office almost beggars belief. Ireland, and indeed the world, is indebted to those people of vision and enterprise. Their selflessness from which arose their greatness should not be forgotten.

List of Illustrations

Aylmer of Balrath
(Barons Aylmer)

During the reign of Henry VI, Richard Aylmer of Lyons, a Keeper of the Peace for both Dublin and Kildare, was appointed Sovereign of the Borough of Tassagard, a position that put him in charge of protecting the settler community from attack by the neighbouring O'Toole and O'Byrne septs. Richard's grandson Bartholomew served as High Sheriff of County Kildare in 1495 and married a daughter of the wealthy Meath magnate, Sir Christopher Chevers. The family subsequently rose to become one of the most prominent families in Meath and Kildare and, from 1530 onwards, key figures in the Dublin administration. By the close of Henry VIII's reign, the Aylmer's landholding extended from Kildare to Meath to Dublin.[1] Before the end of the 16th century they had established two independent branches at Donadea in north Kildare and at Dollardstown in County Meath. The first Aylmer of real significance, in terms of land acquisition, was John Aylmer who married Helen Tyrell of Lyons, an heiress, at the end of the 14th century and so the family acquired Lyons Manor. He may have been a successful merchant and was descended from

---

[1] Sir Gerald's brother-in-law, Sir Thomas Luttrell, Lord Chief Justice of the Common Pleas, was another beneficiary of the monastic spoils.

a family that had been prominent in the Lyons area since the Norman invasion.[2]

Thomas Cromwell patron of Sir Gerald Aylmer

In the 13th and 14th century, they intermarried not alone with the Tyrell family of Westmeath but with three major Meath families - the Petits of Piercetown, the Bathes of Dollardstown and the Chevers of Macetown. In the 15th century, the Tews of Dublin, Suttons of Kepok, Luttrells of Luttrellstown and Dillons of Fingal came into the fold.

The next two real achievers in the Aylmer family were Sir Gerald of Dollardstown and Richard Aylmer of Lyons who lived during the early and middle decades of the 16th century. Richard was the nephew of Sir

---

[2] Sir Richard Aylmer the 16th Baronet, a Canadian, in a lecture given at Donadea Church in 1992.

Gerald Aylmer[3] later of Balrath in Co. Meath who was Chief Justice of Ireland for a long period.[4]

Sir Gerald was a shrewd and ambitious man. He studied law in his youth and, catching the eye of Thomas Cromwell, was appointed Chief Justice of the Common Pleas. As a leading figure in the Dublin administration, Sir Gerald co-orchestrated the military campaign that defeated Silken Thomas. He personally commanded the force that burned Maynooth in 1534. When Silken Thomas and his five captured uncles were sent to London, Sir Gerald went as their escort. Initially Gerald was a keen supporter of Lord Deputy Leonard Grey and assisted him during the campaign against the O'Neills of Ulster. In 1539, Grey knighted him on the battlefield for his valour and granted him the manor and lordship of Dollardstown in County Meath, seized from Gerald's great-uncle, Attorney General Bathe, who was implicated in the Kildare Rebellion. Gerald's elder brother, Richard Aylmer of Lyons, chief sergeant of Kildare in 1535, also fared well in Lord Deputy Grey's loyalty payout, receiving the lucrative manor house of Donadea.

Indeed, Lord Leonard Grey's intimate circle divided the spoils so that the Earl of Ormond was granted Kildare's manor at Kilkea, Sir Thomas Eustace secured Kilcock, Thomas Cusack secured Ardmulgham and Grey himself, Maynooth. Richard's landholdings included 46 acres held by the glebe of Oughterard Rectory from the Abbot of Thomas Court Abbey in Dublin. He also held three gardens in Kill and the tithes of Fenaghes in the parish of Cloncurry. He was also in receipt of the tithes of Whitechurch and its glebe-land, the property of St John's Hospital in Naas. With the

---

[3] Sir Gerald's descendents include the distinguished 17th century naval officer Rear Admiral Matthew Aylmer and General Aylmer, Governor General of Canada from 1831 to 1835.

[4] In 1528 Fiant Henry VIII no. 25 Grant to Gerald Aylmer of the office of second justice of the Commons Bench

Fiant No. 38: 1534 Grant to Gerald Aylmer of the office of Chief Baron of the Exchequer to hold for life with a fee of £40 of silver.

Fiant 66 granted him extensive lands in Meath and Dublin

In 1541 Gerald now a knight and chief justice was granted a lease of valuable lands in Dublin city in St. Michan's parish.

In 1542 he was granted the site of the monastery of Friars Minors of Drogheda and other lands. He got other 'appurtenances' in Swords, Meath and Dublin.

dissolution of the monasteries, Richard was able to swiftly sweep these small outlying properties into his own estate.

However, he did not actually benefit from the break up of the large Kildare churches save for the short-term purchase of the Dominican house in Naas which he passed on to his brother-in-law Sir Thomas Luttrell within a few years.

Donadea Castle

Sir Gerald of Dollardstown found time to marry and had at least one son, Bartholomew Aylmer. Bartholomew had a lucky escape when he was part of a group that pursued some of the O'Tooles following a parley that failed. The O'Tooles turned on the pursuers who ran into a keep at Three Castles which was then set on fire by the Wicklowmen. The Palesmen surrendered and when they came out a Thomas Kelway, the constable of Rathmore, was killed. He lost his life for having hanged two servants of the O'Tooles whom he found 'eating meat within the English border'. The O'Tooles took many of the others prisoner including Richard Aylmer of Lyons but Bartholomew made good his escape.

Bartholomew's wife was Elinor Warren of Navan. He was appointed Clerk of the Peace for counties Kildare and Meath in 1553 and given the post of Clerk of the Crown. He died soon afterwards and was succeeded by his eldest son James, a minor at the time. James later married his second cousin, Anne, the daughter of Sir Richard Aylmer of Lyons and he inherited all his lands from his grandfather, Sir Gerald of Dollardstown who died in 1560. In 1569 James got letters patent from Queen Elizabeth 'of the manor of Dullardstown and all the lands attached to it' as well as Staffordston, Knockdromen and Luske Co. Dublin. He was quite active in the administration and he took part in a hosting against Shane O'Neill of Tyrone in 1566. James was a member of the group of Palesmen who travelled to London to protest against the Cess. Some of them were imprisoned in London and more in Dublin and it is reasonable to assume that James suffered too. He died in 1589. From him descended the Aylmers of Dollardstown.

Bartholomew's second son was Nicholas from whom descended the Aylmers of Balrath. Nicholas studied law and became Auditor General in Ireland. In 1583 he was granted leases on Church lands in nine counties. He was married to Margaret Plunkett the 3rd daughter and co-heir to Christopher Plunkett 7th Lord Killeen. Balrath and other lands came to the Aylmers because of this marriage.

Like his father, Christopher did not distinguish himself in any way and may in fact have died young, but not before he left an heir, Captain Gerald Aylmer of Balrath, who lived through the turbulent years of the Great War of 1641 and the even more turbulent times that followed when Cromwell left his indelible mark. Like many of his peers in Co. Meath, the Captain was a Royalist as was his son.

Captain Gerald married the widow of the 5th Lord Louth[5] and they had at least one son, his heir, Christopher. It would seem that he too was an active man during the disturbances of the 1640s-60s and he was knighted in 1662 by King Charles II. His wife was Margaret a daughter of

---

[5] This was Mary the daughter of Sir Richard Fitzwilliam of 'Merryon' in Dublin.

the 5th Lord Louth. She was in fact his step sister (as his father had married the widow of the 5th Lord Louth). They were married just before the start of the War of 1641. They had three sons and a daughter, Catherine who was married twice[6]. The eldest of the sons was Nicholas and from him descended the Aylmers of Balrath.

Balrath town and lands are in the parish of Ballymargarney in Co. Meath. In 1641 Balrath comprised some 232 acres 'but there is little doubt that a lot more land was inherited at the same time'. Nicholas had one son Christopher (1562-1614?) but it is his son, Gerald, a lawyer, who is most associated with the inheritance from Nicholas.

Gerald (1582-1662), the lawyer, was examined in relation to the outbreak of the war of 1641 in the Meath area and stated that his cousin James was appointed by the rebels as captain for Duleek. Death was the penalty for not joining.[7] This evidence was corroborated by Nicholas Dowdall of Brownestown Co. Meath who was examined before Sir Robert Meredith, Chancellor of the Exchequer. He is reputed to have said 'That a day or two after the slaughter of Englishmen at Jellyanstown, Meath, he went to Duleek to view the number of the rebels. He saw there James Aylmer of Dullardstown... he did not know if they had council with the Northern rebels. He himself went there because the rebels had taken prisoners some of his neighbours, including James Aylmer of Dullardstown and he was afraid of what they might do to himself. At a later meeting at Tarragh commanders were appointed for the barony of Duleek, Lord Gormanston, who nominated for captains under him, amongst others, James Aylmer of Dullardstown...James Aylmer was also present at the place of assembly for the assault on Drogheda. [8]

Prior to the rebellion, in 1604, Gerald had been admitted to Gray's Inn and was frequently mentioned in the Leinster Inquisitions as a trustee for the estates of the Aylmers, Nugents, Wellesleys, Cruises, Balfes, Dowdalls and Tuites.[9] He was employed as one of his counsel by Adam Loftus, Viscount Ely, Lord Chancellor of Ireland when that nobleman had been imprisoned by the Earl of Strafford.

---

[6] Her first husband was Sir Nicholas Plunkett of Dublin and her second husband was Michael Warren of Warrenstown, Co. Meath.
[7] Contemporary History of Ireland – Gilbert
[8] History of the Confederacy - Gilbert
[9] Inquisitions I. (R.S.) Leinster Vol. 1.

North Meath was overrun by the rebels in 1641 as they prepared for their attack on Drogheda. Balrath was probably directly in their path. Gerald, who was almost sixty years old and living in Dublin was allowed by the Lords Justices to go to Co. Meath to attend meetings between the landlords of the county and the rebels. Gerald was forced to agree to the decisions reached at the meetings and was told that if he did not his house would be burnt and his head cut off. In the event his house was occupied and probably looted. He and two others were appointed to advise the Confederates in matters of law. In addition he had to send one mounted man to take an active part, on pain of death.

When Ormonde came to Meath to oppose the rebels he offered pardon to those who surrendered. Gerald and some others including Sir John Netterville and James Bathe gave themselves up and were sent to Dublin and imprisoned. Gerald was kept in jail for more than a year and during that time his house in Dublin was ransacked, a servant was murdered, his goods were stolen and his wife and children mistreated. He was released in 1643 the same year that one of his sons was executed[10]. It is thought that Gerald later joined the Confederacy and fought against the Cromwellians and was outlawed during the period from 1649-1659. In 1660 letters patent were issued directing the Sheriffs of several counties to restore Gerald Aylmer of Balrath to quiet possession of his estates.

Christopher (1615-1671), his eldest son succeeded him. Father and son seem to have had a very strong disagreement with the father doing all in his power to dispossess Christopher. It may have arisen because Christopher was one of 100 who signed 'The Faithful Protestation and humble remonstrance' to the King, of the Roman Catholic nobility and gentry of Ireland.' In summary the lengthy document stated that 'they bring to light their wretched condition as Roman Catholics. They agree to accept the King's authority absolutely, repudiating that of the Pope against the King's power, and are willing to sacrifice their lives for His Majesty. They ask for protection against religious persecution for all who sign this petition. They only want freedom to worship in their own way and they ask for the repeal of the laws against Roman Catholics.'

---

[10] This was the man who was captured after the battle of Rathconell in 1643 when the Confederates were defeated by a force commanded by Sir Richard Grenville. – see Carte's *Life of Ormonde*

None of the other Aylmers would sign this document. Christopher was created a Baronet shortly afterwards. The Aylmer lands in Louth became the subject of protracted legal wrangling with Lord Massareene, who seems to have had some interest in them.

Christopher's son Sir Gerald, who succeeded his father in 1671 seems to have been the main beneficiary of his grandfather's will and was able to claim in the Court of Innocents for the lands in Meath, Louth and Dublin amounting to about 4500 acres. However he had considerable legal battles to fight during that two decade 1670-1690 in attempting to establish his rights to his estates. The lands mentioned in the legal documents were Balrath, Mullafin, Deanes, Thurstianstown, Thenshallstown, Rectory of Ballynagary, Higginstown, Sisley and O'Brienstown in Co. Meath. Other lands mentioned as being in Meath and Louth were Hyanstown, Reynoldstown, Gibstown, Shannon Park, Culeredan and Drumcowell. During the interim his finances deteriorated and his estate became encumbered necessitating the sale of some of the lands.

Prior to the arrival of King James in Ireland in 1690 Sir Gerald, a staunch Catholic, joined the Jacobite forces and was a captain in Lord Abercorn's cavalry. He was wounded and captured at the siege of Derry in 1689 along with Lord Netterville, Colonel Talbot, Major Butler and others. They were well treated and placed under house arrest and given medical attention. The besiegers however attempted to secure their release by rounding up over two thousand Protestants from the countryside around and herding them under the walls of Derry where they would die of hunger and exposure unless the prisoners were released. The defenders promptly declared that they would hang the prisoners immediately if the hostages outside the gates were not freed. A letter to this effect was sent to the commanding officer, who, after deliberating for a day with his fellow officers acceded to the request and allowed the Protestants to go free. Sir Gerald remained in captivity for two years and after the Battle of the Boyne in 1690 his house was looted. In the same year his brother Matthew, a Protestant petitioned to have the lands granted to him.

Sir Gerald was released in 1691 as part of a prisoner exchange and may have fought at the battle of Aughrim and the second siege of Limerick. He seems to have gone abroad after the Siege of Limerick and on the recommendation of his brother Matthew, an Admiral, was granted a pass to return to Ireland with his wife Emma Dillon and their servants in

1696. He died in 1702. Sir Gerald and Emma had four sons and six daughters.

Matthew the second son of Christopher of Balrath and brother of Sir Gerald had a very distinguished career in the English Navy and rose to the rank of Admiral. He was also a Colonel in a Cavalry Regiment. In a Naval battle off the coast of Cork in 1689 the English fleet was 'given a rough time of it' and George Aylmer, Matthew's younger brother was killed. Matthew was an M.P. for Dover during the first decade of the 18th century. In 1709 he was appointed Admiral and Commander-in-Chief of the Fleet. In 1718 he was created Lord Aylmer, Baron of Balrath. He died in 1720 and left the bulk of his estate to his son Henry and £500 each to his daughters Lady Norris and Mrs. Lucy Fortescue.

Matthew and Sir Gerald had one sister, Catherine, who married Sir Nicholas Plunkett the brother of the 1st Earl of Fingall and secondly Captain Michael Warren of Warrenstown, Co. Meath by whom she had three sons and two daughters. One of the sons was placed under the care of Admiral Aylmer and in time joined the Navy and rose to the rank of Vice Admiral.

Sir Gerald the 2nd Baronet had some of his estates returned to him. He was succeeded by his son, John, the 3rd Baronet who was born c.1670. It is not known if John took any part in the Jacobite wars.

John succeeded in 1702 to the title and estates but died in 1714 without an heir. In his will he left all his property to his wife[11] for her lifetime and then to his brother Andrew the 4th Baronet. Andrew may have been born in the 1680s. Andrew's wife was Catherine Hussey a cousin of the Earl of Beaulieu. In 1727 he and his wife restored the Balrath Cross in memory of some of the Bathe family. They were living at Mount Aylmer, near Balrath at the time. He died in 1740 and his will was not probated until 1755, because of legal difficulties. He was succeeded by his only son, Gerald the 5th Baronet. He died unmarried in 1745 and in his will left £1000 to Jervis Street Hospital. His executor was Ignatius Hussey. His will was further complicated by the fact that he attempted to disinherit his first cousin, Matthew Aylmer, whose father Patrick had become a Protestant.

---

[11] This lady went on to remarry a number of times. Her second husband was Dominick Meade of Tullyheady Co. Tipperary and her third partner was Thomas Lister of Athleague, Co. Roscommon. She may have been married a fourth time to Rev. Oliver Carter of Killala, Co. Mayo.

Finally most of the estates were divided amongst Sir Gerald's (5th) sisters Mabel, Margaret and Catherine. Mabel married James Strong of Balrath and got Balrath as part of her settlement. Margaret inherited a third of the estate and married twice. Her first husband was Robert Luttrell, a Dublin merchant and her second husband was Robert Netterville of Cruicerath. Catherine married John Malpas but had no family. Her portion of the estate was divided between the Strongs and the Nettervilles.

The Patrick mentioned above became a Protestant probably influenced by his uncle Admiral Matthew. He was the Patrick Aylmer who was a J.P. for Wexford in 1716. He married Williamza Hunt of Warwick in 1723 and they had one son Matthew mentioned above who became the landless Sir Matthew the 6th Baronet. When he died without an heir the line of Sir Gerald the 2nd Baronet came to an end. The baronetcy then devolved on a descendant of Admiral Matthew. He was Henry the 4th Lord Aylmer and 7th Baronet of Balrath.

His son, Matthew, the 5th Lord Aylmer and 8th Baronet of Balrath took his seat in the Irish House of Lords in 1800 and in the same year was voted an annuity by the government of £600 per annum. A year later he married Lady Louisa Anne Call of Whiteford, in Cornwall. He had been in the Army since 1787. He fought in the Peninsular Wars during the first decade of the 19th century. He was promoted to Major General in 1813. In 1814 he was appointed Adjutant General in Ireland and three years later he was granted the freedom of the city of Dublin. In 1819 he was appointed Governor of Kilmainham Royal Hospital. He was made Governor General of Canada in 1830.

He received further honours and was conferred with the Military Grand Cross of the Bath in 1836. He died in 1850 and was succeeded by his brother Frederick the 6th Lord Aylmer and 9th Baronet, (1777-1858) a Naval officer of distinction who attained the rank of Admiral. He was unmarried and his title passed to his second cousin once removed Udolphus a great grandson of Rev. John Aylmer the 4th son of the 2nd Lord Aylmer. The other descendants of the Rev. John Aylmer are too numerous to mention in this brief article and we will concentrate only on the men who inherited the title.

Udolphus, a Colonel in the Canadian militia, was succeeded by his son Matthew (1842- 1923) the 8th Lord Aylmer and 11th Baronet who served in the British Army in Canada, where he was born. He was involved in suppressing the Fenians there. He became Assistant Adjutant General at Canadian Headquarters. He retired as a Major General in 1907. He bought an estate in British Columbia and took up fruit farming. His wife was Amy Young of Montreal and they had three sons John, Kenneth and Basil and two daughters, Amelia and Florence who both married[12].

John, the 9th Baron of Balrath had no children and when he died in 1970 his title passed to his brother, Kenneth, then a rather elderly man of 87. Like his brother, Kenneth had no children either and when he died in 1974 the title passed to his brother Basil who became the 11th Baron when he was 88 years old.

Basil Aylmer, the 11th Baron was married to Bessie Watson and they had a son Matthew a soldier in World War II, who was killed in Normandy in 1944. Bessie died in 1956 and Basil married again in 1960. His second wife was Helen Hogg, a widow but they had no children. Basil died in 1977.

After his death the title passed to Hugh Yates Aylmer, a grand nephew of Udolphus and a great grandson of Admiral John Aylmer. Hugh Aylmer (1907-1982) the 12th Baron, was, like his predecessors quite elderly when he inherited the title. He enjoyed his new status for a mere five years before it was claimed by a cousin, Michael Anthony Aylmer, also a great grandson of Admiral John.

Michael, the present Baron was born in 1923. He was educated by a tutor and at private schools before going to Cambridge from where he graduated in 1948 with numerous degrees including a law degree. He married an Italian Countess, Maddalena Sofia di Santa Croce, and settled in England at Dovecot House in Buckinghamshire. He was granted the title of baronet in his own right in 1948 as Sir Michael Aylmer.

Michael and the Countess have one son Julian and one daughter, Gioia Francesca, who is married to Andrew Shaw and has two daughters Elizabeth and Imogen.

Julian who was educated in Westminster and Cambridge was knighted in 1976. Married in 1990 to Belinda Parker, he has one son, Michael and one daughter Rosemary.

---

[12] Their husbands were Henry Perry- Leake and Robert Scott-Lauder. Florence had three daughters.

Barnewall of Crickstown
(Baronets)

Drimnagh Castle in Dublin was the original seat of the de Bernevals. [13] According to researches carried out by members of the Barnewall family over the course of three generations and now the subject of a book about to be published by Sir Reginald Barnewall, the first members of the family to come to Ireland were Hugo and Reginald de Berneval. They formed part of the punitive force brought to Ireland in 1215 by Prince John. As a result of that foray the de Bernevals were granted lands in Dublin in the Drimnagh, Kimmage, Ballyfermot and Terenure areas where they were settled until Cromwellian times.[14]

The family was granted other lands in Meath in the middle of the 14th century in a deed which gave the lands of Kilbrew and the advowson of Kilbrew parish to Sir Wolfram de Berneval and his wife Eva. The Manor of Kilbrew is adjacent to Crickstown. Nicholas de Berneval was the grandson of Wolfram. Nicholas was settled at Crickstown and was acknowledged as the first lord of Crickstown Castle.[15]

---

[13] Sir Reginald Barnewall.

[14] Drimnagh and its lands were granted by Cromwell to a Colonel Philip Ferneley while the other lands, along with Drimnagh Castle, were granted to a Major Elliot. -Notes by Sir Reginald Barnewall.

[15] Professor Stephen Barnwell in *The Irish Genealogist* 1959.

Nicholas's grandson, Sir Christopher Barnewall, lord of Crickstown, was the first of a long line of lawyers in the family. He was a successful career government official who held various important and well remunerated government posts including Serjeant-at-Law, Vice Treasurer for Ireland and Chief Justice of the Irish Bench. His wife was Matilda Drake, the daughter of John Drake the last lord of Drakeston and Drakesrath. They had three sons who all made their mark in Irish history – Sir Nicholas of Crickstown, Sir Robert the 1st Baron Trimlestown (see that family) and Sir Barnaby Barnewall.

What Crickstown may have looked like

Sir Barnaby, a lawyer, like his brothers, supported the winning Yorkist side in the Wars of the Roses and was rewarded for his loyalty by being appointed, in 1461, as the Second Justice in the Court of Common Pleas. Like his father he occupied lucrative government posts including his appointment as one of the Collectors of the ports of Drogheda and Dublin. The other collector at the time was Walter Delahyde. Sir Barnaby was also a member of the Company of St. George, an armed force that was raised to protect the Pale from the incursions of the Irish. Just as avaricious as his father and brothers Sir Barnaby was involved in a protracted legal case concerning the possessions of his wife Elizabeth Scurlag, the widow of John Delafield.[16] The custody of the lands had been granted by the King to

---

[16] These lands were Fieldston, Wimbledon, Swords and Bryghend.

Richard Nangle and Sir Barnaby was distrained by the Sheriff of Meath, John Plunkett of Dunsany. In the event the rightful heir, Nicholas Delafield died and the lands went to his sister Catherine Delafield who had married Richard Barnewall of Frankstown[17], a cousin of Sir Barnaby. Sir Barnaby's second wife was Margaret the daughter of Sir Thomas Plunkett of Rathmore, the Chief Justice of the King's Bench.

Sir Barnaby must have come into the possession of Stackallen as he is buried in Stackallen with his wife. There is a stone monument to Sir Barnaby and his wife Margaret above the church door in Stackallen. He was succeeded in Stackallen by his son Peter Barnewall. Peter had an only daughter who married Richard Butler, Viscount Mountgarret.[18] The Stackallen lands reverted to the Barnewall proprietors of Crickstown.

Sir Christopher of Crickstown died in 1447 and was succeeded in Crickstown by his able eldest son Sir Nicholas, an acquisitive man who added considerably to the Crickstown estates, by gaining possession of the Manor of Kilmessan and other lands. The Manor of Kilmessan was held in the family for the next two hundred years and was laid aside for the use of the heir presumptive of Crickstown until such time as he would succeed there.[19] Sir Nicholas's wife was Ismay Serjeant, an heiress. Sir Nicholas was a Chief Justice of King's Bench in Ireland by 1457 and was knighted in 1460, having been a loyal supporter of the Yorkist King. His son and successor was Christopher Barnewall of Crickstown, a lawyer, who although an extensive landowner in Meath, failed to become an important official in the government. His wife was Alice Butler the daughter of the 7th Lord Dunboyne and they had at least four sons and two daughters. The eldest son Edward was a lawyer and occupied some government posts including Chancellor of the Irish Exchequer and Sheriff of Meath. The other sons became ancestors of Barnewall families in their own right – George of Arrodstown, Co. Meath whose descendants survived there until the late 17th century, Robert of Moylagh Castle, whose family held this outpost against the Irish in the north west of Co. Meath, until dispossessed by the Cromwellians in the middle of the 17th century.

---

[17] Near Crickstown.

[18] For information on the Butler Viscounts Mountgarret see *The Landed Gentry & Aristocracy of Kilkenny* by Art Kavanagh.

[19] Professor Stephen Barnwell in *The Irish Genealogist* 1959.

By the beginning of the 16th century there were four main branches of the family in Drimnagh, Crickstown, Stackallen and Kingsland (Turvey). There were numerous sub branches holding various lands including Moylagh, Arrodstown, Robertstown and Rowestown, to mention just the Meath holdings.

The Drimnagh family became very widespread in the course of the centuries and had various holdings in Dublin, including Shankhill Castle. After the Cromwellian confiscations their holdings vanished but the lord of Shankhill Castle was still in situ there in 1673 and was able to leave something in his will to a young Henry Barnewall who lived with a cotter outside the gates of the Castle. The cotters name was Simon Barnewall.[20]

In the early part of the 16th century the lord of Crickstown was Sir Christopher Barnewall at one time Sheriff of Meath. His wife was an heiress, Catherine Fleming of Slane Castle and they had not less than 13 children, five of whom were born mute. Catherine was the heiress of both her brother the 14th Lord Slane and her grandmother, the heiress of Sir William Welles the Lord Chancellor of Ireland. Sir Christopher's son, Sir Patrick, also a Sheriff of Meath, was involved in the Nine Years War fighting against the Irish. Apart from his nickname of *'Knight of the Broad Acre'*[21] he is best remembered for having brought four archers to the hosting at Tara in 1593, though he himself was over seventy years old at the time.

One of Sir Patrick's sons became a Jesuit priest who was known to be an extremely holy man, reciting as well as his breviary the Office of the Blessed Virgin Mary on a daily basis. It was said of him that he was 'the poor man's apostle', 'most zealous and obedient' and 'omnium virtutem specimen'.

A new Crickstown Castle was built by Sir Patrick Barnewall the 1st Baronet (d.1624) of Crickstown who was granted that title in 1622. His son, Sir Richard Barnewall, the 2nd Baronet, was born in 1602 and had to endure the hardships of the Great War of 1641 and the subsequent confiscations, leading to terrible property and financial losses. He was transplanted to Connaught but managed to regain Crickstown and 2000 acres adjoining

---

[20] Ibid.
[21] He was called this because of his extensive properties – Burke's Peerage

15

after the Restoration in 1661. The castle had been destroyed by the Cromwellians.[22]

Sir Richard(1602-1664?) was married twice and it was his second wife, an Aylmer of Donadea, who provided him with an heir, Sir Patrick the 3rd Baronet. Sir Patrick (1630?-1695) inherited Crickstown and the 2000 acres and a further 1261 acres in Co. Galway in Clare barony. He was also granted a pension from the Crown of £150 per annum. He was an M.P. for Meath in 1680 and in 1689. His wife was a Butler of Kilcash and they had two sons and a number of daughters.

Sir Patrick's second son, Sir George, the 4th Baronet (d.1735), inherited but he sold or mortgaged most of his property and the remaining assets, excepting the castle, went to his sisters as his heiresses. Sir George died unmarried and the line of Crickstown proper came to an end. He was succeeded by his distant cousin, Sir George Barnewall of Crickstown the 5th baronet, who was a grandson of James of Roskeen. He died unmarried in 1750. He was succeeded by his cousin Sir Thomas Barnewall the 6th baronet (d. 1790) and he had an only daughter.

The next Barnewall of Crickstown was a descendant of Colonel James of Aughrim Co. Galway, the 5th son of the 1st baronet.

Colonel James was transplanted to Galway and in 1653 he married Mabel Barnewall, the widow of the 1st Earl of Fingall. He died c. 1661 and was buried in Lord Trimlestown's vault in Kilconnell abbey, Co. Galway. They had one son, George and two daughters, Eleanor who died unmarried and Mabel who married Col Edward Hussey of Westown, Co. Dublin.[23]

George married Mary Dillon of Huntstown, Co. Meath and they had three sons one of whom, Bartholomew, of Ballyhost, Co. Westmeath, fought in the army of King James II and was attainted for his pains. He married Jane Geoghegan of Castletown, Co. Westmeath, and they a number of children the eldest of whom, Robert of Moyrath was the ancestor of the subsequent Barons of Crickstown. Robert's brother, James, became a priest and was Vicar General of the Diocese of Meath. James lived through the Penal times and was still living in 1776.

Robert, the 8th Baronet, who was born in 1757 succeeded to the title and Crickstown in 1790. At the time he was resident in Greenanstown, Co.

---

[22] Notes by Brigid O'Brien Mullins from her Ph.D. thesis.
[23] Their grandson became the 1st Earl of Beaulieu.

Meath. He took the precaution to have the title registered with the Ulster King of Arms. He married Catherine Aylmer of Painstown, Co. Kildare. Catherine eventually became an heiress with her father, Charles. Sir Robert and Catherine had two sons, one of whom died in infancy. The surviving son was Aylmer John.

Catherine died in 1790 and Robert married again. His second wife was Margaret Palmer[24] from Dublin and they had an only daughter Mary Ann, who married Clarges Ruxton of Rahanna, Co. Louth.

When Sir Robert died in 1826 he was succeeded by his son, Sir Aylmer John (1789 – 1838), the 9th Baronet. Sir Aylmer John pursued a career in the Army and fought in the Battle of Waterloo. He was retired from the Army when he married his cousin, Esmay Barnewall from Meadstown, Co. Meath. Sir Aylmer John died suddenly in 1838 a month before the birth of his only son, Reginald Aylmer John.

Sir Reginald Aylmer John, the 10th Baronet, died in 1909 and was succeeded in the title by his 2nd cousin twice removed, John Robert Barnewall, who was born in Australia. It was John Robert's parents who were the first of the family to move to Australia in 1840[25].

Sir John Robert, the 11th Baronet, was born in 1850. He married Grace Blennerhasset in 1884 and they had two sons, Reginald John and Arthur Walter.

Sir John was succeeded in the title by his son Sir Reginald John the 12th Baronet who died in 1961.

Sir Reginald John had one son, Reginald Robert, born in 1924, who succeeded to the title as Sir Reginald Robert Barnewall, the 13th Baronet. He has lived all his life in Australia and is resident in Queensland. He was educated at Xavier College, Melbourne. He has led a very varied and interesting life and in his resume he is described as a cattle breeder, orchadist and land developer. He fought in World War II as an Officer in the Royal Australian Engineers and later served in the Allied Intelligence Bureau. He saw active service when he commanded B Squadron of the Victoria Mounted Rifles. After the war he held prestigious posts in various airlines including Southern Airlines of Melbourne, Polynesian Airlines and Eildon Aviation.

---

[24] Her father was the Governor of the Bank of Ireland – Burke's Peerage.
[25] Information from Sir Reginald the 13th and current baronet.

Sir Reginald's first wife was Elsie Frederick of Brisbane (d.1962) and they had three daughters Mary Catherine, born in 1947, Francis Patricia born in 1948 and Margaret Ann born in 1952. Sir Reginald's second wife is Maureen Daly of Victoria and they have a son Peter.

Peter is a consultant agricultural economist in Queensland and is married to Kathryn Carroll of Brisbane. They have two sons Christopher and Richard and one daughter Jessica.

Barnewall of Trimlestown
(Barons Trimlestown)

Young Barnewall with a thousand men,
High boasting at their head,
'We'll find ye here in these green glades,
At morning light', he said..

On Barnewall's bright and serried files
All burning for the fray,
A thousand valiant men they were
From Meath's broad fertile plain..

Young Barnewall was made prisoner
Fighting bravely in the van,
And all his comrades all fell slain
Around him – save one single man.

That man they sped, and away he fled
Unharmed by gallowglass
That he might tell how his comrades fell,
That morn at Tyrell's Pass.

These verses penned in 1908 by Robert Joyce Dwyer was written about an episode in the Nine Years War and occurred in 1597 when

Captain Richard Tyrell invaded Meath with about four thousand men from O'Neill's country. Young Robert was in fact held prisoner by the Earl of Tyrone for the period of about a year and following negotiations for an exchange of hostages, and the intercession of the Earl of Ormonde, he was released. He seems to have taken no further part in the Nine Years War.

Trimlestown is a townland of about 480 acres, two miles west of Trim. In the Down Survey it was stated that it contained 1 old Chapel, 2 mills, a weir and bridge and the castle of Trimlestown built in the 15th century. Sir Robert the ancestor of the Trimlestown family was knighted in 1452 or thereabouts. For his loyalty to the House of York he was created Baron of Trimlestown in 1461, by Edward IV, and made a member of the Irish Council for life. He built the beautiful castle of Trimlestown on the then most modern lines of French castles, as much family as military.[26]

Trimlestown Castle
(Courtesy IAA)

---

[26] Christopher O'Reilly, *The Barnewalls* in *Riocht na Midhe* (1957)

His other properties included Robertstown, the manor of Rathdown, lands in Naas barony, part of the manor of Athboy in the right of his wife Elizabeth daughter and heiress of Christopher Le Brune of Roebuck, Co. Dublin and also Roebuck itself an estate of 500 acres.

The first members of the family to come to Ireland were Hugo and Reginald de Berneval. They formed part of the punitive force brought to Ireland in 1215 by Prince John. As a result of that foray the de Bernevals were granted lands in Dublin in the Drimnagh, Kimmage, Ballyfermot and Terenure areas where they were settled until Cromwellian times.[27]

In the churchyard of Lusk there is a remarkable tomb to Sir Christopher Barnewall with the following inscription – 'This monument is made for the Right Worshipful Sir Christopher Barnewall of Turvey, Knight, by the Right Worshipful Sir Lucas Dillon of Moymet, Knight and Dame Marian Sharl, his wife, who married her three years after the death of her loving husband, who had issue five sons and fifteen daughters by her.'

In 1443 the Birminghams entered into a military alliance with the O'Connors against the lords of the Pale. This alliance was the cause of a lot of damage in Meath and was called the war of the 'Camnan'. This arose out of an insult given to young Birmingham by young Lord Trimlestown. It seemed they were both in the Great Court of Trim and young Barnewall hit young Birmingham 'a box on the nose', and out of that arose the war.[28] This young Barnewall was Robert the second son of Sir Christopher who received estates in the Trim area and in 1461 was created the 1st Baron Trimlestown. Lord Robert's wife was an heiress, Elizabeth de Brune and the lands of Roebuck in Dublin came into the family because of this marriage.[29]

Lord Robert's eldest son, the 2nd Baron, Sir Christopher Barnewall was incautious enough to support the claims of Lambert Simnel the pretender to the throne and though he took an oath of allegiance to the King in 1488 he was summoned to London with the other Irish conspirators where they were given a caution and made renew their oath

---

[27] Notes by Sir Reginald Barnewall.
[28] Ibid.
[29] These lands were still in the possession of the family in the early part of the 19th century when Roebuck was leased to the Corballis family (see the chapter about that family in this volume).

of allegiance to Henry VII. He did get an official posting and was made Sword of State. He fought at Knockdoe in Galway with the Earl of Kildare, who went on an expedition to curb the growing ambitions of Ulick Burke who had taken the city of Galway. 2000 men were killed in the battle of Knockdoe in 1504.

Christopher the 2nd Baron Trimlestown died a couple of years later. His eldest son, Sir John Barnewall, the 3rd Baron, succeeded him. A very able man, Sir John studied law and progressed through the judicial system to become a Second Justice of the King's Bench in Ireland. He advanced his career politically also and in 1522 was appointed Vice Treasurer of Ireland. Two years later he got the coveted post of High Treasurer and in 1534 he was made Lord Chancellor of Ireland. He was also active in the field and his military exploits included his presence at the defeat of Silken Thomas at Trim, the siege of Maynooth Castle in 1535, an expedition against the O'Briens and Fitzgerald of Desmond a year later and in 1537 a foray against the O'Connors of Offaly.

He died the following year in 1538, the same year that the Miraculous Statue of the Blessed Virgin of Trim was burned.[30] It was this Sir John Barnewall that in 1533 got grants of lands of Dunleer and other lands from Henry VIII on condition that he fortified certain houses at Kilnagross, due to the fact that a few years previously O Connor had taken Lord Delvin prisoner at the Castle of Retain belonging to Sir William D'Arcy.

John the 3rd Baron Trimlestown was married four times but apparently he had only one son and heir, Sir Patrick Barnewall, who became the 4th Baron. Like his father, Sir Patrick was very active politically and militarily. He was a member of the Irish Council and sat in the Parliament of 1541 which acknowledged Henry VIII as King of Ireland. He fought against the O'Neills of Tyrone the same year. He was very active in his own county of Meath and in 1548 he was placed in command of 120 archers, 50 horse and 60 kern 'to assemble at Trim for the defence of the Pale'.[31] He was also a Justice of the Peace and sat on many commissions one of which was to enquire into the numbers of chalices, ornaments, bells, houses and lands belonging to the churches and chapels in Meath and

---

[30] Christopher O'Reilly, *The Barnewalls* in *Riocht na Midhe* (1957)
[31] Calendar of State Papers Ireland 1509-73.

Westmeath.[32] He attended the Parliament of 1559 and was later commissioned to muster and array Meath with Sir Thomas Barnewall of Robertstown, Sir Patrick Barnewall of Crickstown, James Barnewall of Pierstown, Simon Barnewall of Kilbrew, Christopher Barnewall of Rowestown and Thomas Barnewall of Moylagh. His loyalty and service to the Crown was acknowledged by the Lord Deputy who described him as 'a ready and willing nobleman in the Queen's service'.[33]

As a reward for his services he was granted a lease of the rectory, church and parsonage of Rathregan, part of the possessions of the late Priory of St. Peter's in Trim. On the surface it would seem that Sir Patrick had embraced the new religion.

He was married twice and had two sons by his first wife. Both his sons became his heirs in succession. His eldest son, Sir Robert, the 5th Baron succeeded his father to the estates in 1563. Like his father he was very active in support of the administration and fought against Shane O'Neill for which he was knighted in 1566 at Drogheda. He was also very much involved in local administration such as executing martial law and holding musters and arrays. He was determined to study law and to this effect applied for and received permission to absent himself in England for two years. Unfortunately for him, he contracted some form of fatal illness there and died in 1573. He was succeeded by his brother Peter, the 6th Baron.

Like his father and brother, Peter, the 6th Baron (1540-1598) was in general a most willing tool of the administration but he opposed the tax on the local population for the support of the troops in the area. He was imprisoned in Dublin Castle for a short period in 1577 for this impropriety. After his release he appears to have complied and continued the family tradition of sitting on commissions. He was in Co. Down executing martial law, in Wicklow setting the limits of the new county in 1579, in Wexford in 1580, in Mayo in 1587 and on many commissions for his own county. He was knighted in 1583 in St. Patrick's Cathedral and three years later he was in command of a small army that was being readied to oppose the Burkes in Mayo. Despite his loyalty he was suspected of being in communication with Spain at the time of the Armada, as was his cousin Sir Patrick Barnewall of Crickstown. However he continued to perform active

---

[32] Fiants Philip & Mary.
[33] C.S.P.I. 1509-73

military service right up to the time of his death in 1598. His wife was a daughter of Sir Christopher Nugent the 7th Baron Delvin.

Despite his service to the Crown, Peter the 6th Baron Trimlestown appears to have remained a Catholic as in his will he left £10 to the 'poor priests and friars' and £400 to Bishop Brady. Another interesting direction in the will was his wish that '£160 be set aside as a marriage portion for my natural daughter Genet'. He was succeeded by his eldest son Robert Barnewall.

Sir Robert Barnewall the 7th Baron (1565-1639), as we have seen, was the subject of a poem written in 1908 by Robert Joyce Dwyer. Following his capture and release as outlined above he seems to have taken no further part in the Nine Years War. He appears to have been a staunch Catholic and in 1612 he signed a letter with his co religionist Peers protesting at the severity of the government against the Catholic priests. This movement was headed by his cousin Sir Patrick Barnewall of Crickstown. Sir Robert sat in the Parliament of 1615 when he was described as a 'busy and violent recusant'. Despite this he and his peers protested their loyalty to King Charles in 1625. He was a member of the Parliament of 1634. He died in 1639 on the eve of the Great War of 1641-49 that was to witness such terrible upheavals.

Sir Robert's eldest son, Christopher Barnewall predeceased his father and died as a very young man, but not before he had married and left an heir, Matthias Barnewall, and a daughter Bridget who married Christopher Cusack of Ardgragh. After Sir Robert's death in 1639 he was succeeded by his grandson, Matthias (1618-1667) who must have been a man in his twenties at the time took his seat as the 8th Baron Trimlestown in Parliament in the year his grandfather died. It was Matthias who had to endure the rigours and hardships of the Great War and the consequent Cromwellian confiscations. It is small wonder he died at the comparatively young age of 49.

Having supported the Confederates in the war, Lord Trimlestown, like his relations and peers who were Catholic, was earmarked to have his estates confiscated and in due course was ordered to remove into Connaught, where an estate would be provided for him. He was one of what were termed the 'Kilkenny submittees' a group of people who had surrendered under the terms of the articles entered into on 12th May 1652.

They were mainly gentlemen from the Pale - Nettervilles, Plunketts, Bellews and others.[34]

Under those terms the officers of the Parliamentary army engaged to mediate for them with the Parliament, 'that they might enjoy such moderate parts of their estates as should make the lives of those who chose not to go into voluntary banishment to Spain, comfortable'. It was further stipulated that 'they should in the meantime enjoy such part of their estates as had not been disposed of already'.[35]

Prendergast relates how part of Lord Trimlestown's estate had been given *in custodiam* to Mrs. Penelope Bayley, the widow of Colonel Bayley, by a special order of Lord Deputy Ireton in 1650. In May of 1652 she took a one year lease of the lands from the Government for her greater security. She then let the lands to a man called Cusack[36] who assigned them to his brother-in-law, Lord Trimlestown.[37] This little anecdote makes a few things clear. Firstly Lord Trimlestown was a very astute man and secondly the authorities did most things by the book. When the lease expired Mrs. Bayley took out a further three year lease but Lord Trimlestown refused to hand over the lands as he contended that under the articles of the 'Kilkenny submittees' he was allowed to hold them. Lord Trimlestown then bribed the surveyor, a Mr. Bryan Darley with £4 to convey this information to Mrs. Bayley. That lady was not amused and went to higher authorities. Darley was arrested and Lord Trimlestown was ejected from the lands.[38]

The order for transplantation issued in October 1653 and the 'Kilkenny submittees' were called upon to transplant. Lord Trimlestown, acting for the group argued that the articles were not adhered to as they had not enjoyed the remnants of their estates. The Commissioners replied that the Act of Parliament had more force than the articles and stated that they must remove. Lord Trimlestown appealed to the Committee of Articles at Westminster who agreed that it would be a breach of the articles if they were forced to transplant. Again the Commissoners were adamant that the Act of Parliament had precedence and ordered the

---

[34] *Cromwellian Settlement of Ireland* - Prendergast
[35] Ibid.
[36] Christopher Cusack of Ardgragh.
[37] *Cromwellian Settlement of Ireland* - Prendergast
[38] Ibid.

families involved to move to Connaught. On the 12th April they were given a concession that they could remain in their dwellings until the 1st May and the families could stay there until the 20th.[39]

Lord Trimlestown, Sir Richard Barnewall, Mr. Patrick Netterville and the others moved on to Athlone. They were not allowed to bring any of their tenants except the few who were ordered to go by the authorities. While in Athlone, attempting to ascertain where their new properties lay they were at all times restricted in their movement into and out of the town, especially if it involved movement into the Leinster side of Athlone.

In 1654 following a request from Lady Trimlestown, the authorities gave Lord Trimlestown leave to move to Leinster 'for such time as shall be thought necessary for the recovery of his health, and so continue at the said place without removal above a mile from the same, without licence from the Commander in Chief of the said precinct, where he shall reside as aforesaid; provided he return into Connaught within three months.'[40]

Unlike many of his peers, Lord Trimlestown did not live to enjoy repatriation to his beloved Co. Meath and he died in Co. Galway in 1667. His gravestone is still within the ruins of the Abbey of Kilconnell where the following epitaph can still be seen 'Here lies Mathew, twelfth Lord Baron of Trimlestown, one of the Transplanted'.[41]

He was succeeded by his eldest son, Robert the 9th Baron Trimlestown (1641?-1687).[42] Robert, who was married to a sister of the Earl of Limerick, had a number of children, as they are mentioned in a letter he wrote to his eldest son and heir Mathias, then being educated in France, about a year before his own death in 1687.

In this thoughtful letter full of earnest advice he lays out many caveats. He mentions the great difficulty he himself had in trying to build up the estate again after the Cromwellian episode. The young heir is advised not to spend any more than four hundred pounds a year and to set apart a sum for the maintenance of his brothers and sisters. He is advised not to spend any more than the estate can bring in. He should marry a Catholic girl and someone from Ireland as it is too distracting and expensive to have to travel over and back to England if he were to marry

---

[39] Ibid.
[40] *Cromwellian Settlement of Ireland* - Prendergast
[41] He was both the 12th Lord and the 8th Baron Trimlestown.
[42] Robert was the 13th Lord and the 9th Baron.

an English girl. Horse racing, hunting and hawking should be indulged in only in moderation as his ancestors who had over indulged had suffered financially by not attending to their other affairs.

Robert was evidently a devout man, for just before his death he had erected a stone asking for prayers of the people at the Holy Well of Tullaghanogue and another at the Well of Eskeroon. It seems that at that time there were large attendances at the Patron Day celebrations at both those wells.

Mathias (1666-1692) succeeded his father as 10th Baron. He, in the true family tradition of supporting Catholic monarchs, sided with King James I and after the treaty of Limerick accompanied Sarsfield to France. His estate was seized by the Williamite authorities. Mathias himself was killed in a battle in Germany and his heir was his brother John, a boy of 13 who had been sent to France for his education. To help pay for the education his relatives had got him a commission as an ensign in King James's Guards. It was proposed that he should be outlawed on this account, but the authorities, surprisingly, took the sympathetic view that he was only a child and his commission was merely a device to pay for his college fees. A marriage settlement in his favour was recognised and the estate handed back to him under the Act of Resumption.[43]

John, the 11th Baron (1679-1746), lived through the worst of the Penal Laws but would appear to have been shielded in some way from having his lands confiscated. His wife was the daughter and heir of Sir John Barnewall. They had a large family and two of his daughters married other Catholic lords – Mountgarret and Gormanston.

The 12th Baron, Robert (1730-1779), who was married twice, is the man mentioned in Robert Lovell Edgeworth's Memoirs. 'About the year 1754 Lord Trimlestown,, a Roman Catholic nobleman, who had resided for many years abroad, became famous for his skills in medicine and for his benevolent attention to persons of all ranks who applied to him'

Edgeworth's mother attended him and took up lodgings with her husband near Trim. They socialized with the Trimlestowns who were most cordial and hospitable. Lady Trimlestown[44] was described as a lady of beauty and grace, who contrary to fashion wore her hair in ringlets – at that time ladies generally had their hair powdered and rolled over a

---

[43] J.G. Simms in *Riocht na Midhe* 1962
[44] Probably Elizabeth Colt, Lord Trimlestown's second wife.

cylinder of black silk stuffed with wool, 'so as to draw the hair almost out by the roots from the forehead'.[45] Edgeworth went on to say of the noble lord 'He (Lord Trimlestown) commanded attention from his high character in the world of medical knowledge and for his philanthropy.

A remarkable tale was told of a cure effected by Lord Trimlestown. A very beautiful lady, who had begun to advance in years, sank into what was thought to be an incurable depression that exhibited itself in various nervous disorders. She began to shun appearing in public. She went to every reputable doctor in Ireland and corresponded with as many in England before turning to Lord Trimlestown as a last resort. He agreed to take her into his care on condition that she should remain three weeks at his house without any servants of her own and away from the interference of friends. She agreed to this and found 'instead of a grave and forbidding physician, a man of most agreeable manners'. The change of environment seemed to allay her complaints but within three days they returned. On the third day, without any warning, she was seized by four mutes, all dressed in white, who entered her apartment. They carried her bodily to a distant chamber hung with black and lighted with green tapers. From the ceiling, which was of considerable height, a swing was suspended in which she was placed by the mutes. One of the mutes then put the swing in motion; and as it approached one end of the room she was opposed by a grim menacing figure armed with a huge rod of birch. When she looked behind her she saw a similar figure at the other end of the room, armed in the same manner. She was frightened but not terrified and of course she stayed on the swing fearing the rods. After some time she was conveyed back to her room. After a short time a servant came to inform her that tea was being served. No mention was made of the swinging episode, but her disorders seemed to have disappeared. However the attacks recommenced a few days later. The mutes arrived again and she was given the same treatment. This continued intermittently for the space of the following two weeks and by that time she had recovered completely and continued in good health until the end of her life.[46]

Thomas, the 13th Baron (1756-1796), took the expedient step of conforming to the 'established Church' and his title, which had not been formally recognised since the attainder of his ancestor Mathias, the

---

[45] *Memoirs* – Robert Lovell Edgeworth
[46] Ibid.

Galway transplantee, was restored in 1795. Thomas didn't enjoy his triumph for long as he died the following year. He had no children so his title and estates were inherited by his first cousin, Nicholas Barnewall (1726-1813), the 14th Baron.

Nicholas was already seventy years old when he succeeded as Baron Trimlestown. His first wife was a French lady, Martha, the daughter of Joseph D'Augin, the president of the Parliament of Toulouse. They had one son, the Baron's successor, John Thomas, the 15th Baron (1773-1839). The year before his death in 1813 the very elderly Baron took the precaution to entail his estate on his only son and grandson and in case of failure of their male heirs on Richard Barnewall of Fyanstown.

Whatever intuition prompted the 14th Baron to make the entail proved to be fortuitous for the Fyanstown Barnewalls as the 16th Baron's only son died in infancy.

Thomas the 16th Baron (1796-1879), who was married to Margaret Roche of Donore, Co. Kildare, had a daughter Ann Maria whose husband was Robert Elliot of Clifton Park, Co. Roxburgh. In 2004 a friend of Richard Everard's while tramping through the Scottish Highlands with some friends came across the little church and churchyard of Linton where to their amazement they came across the graves of the 16th Lord Trimlestown, his daughter, her husband and numerous Elliots. There was a plaque on the wall below a stained glass window in the church which is worth recording here. It reads as follows:-

> This central light is sacred to the memory of the Honourable
> Anna Maria Louisa Barnewall (only child of the 16th Baron
> Trimlestown), for nearly 40 years the loving and intensely
> beloved wife of Robert Henry Elliot of Clifton. A kinder
> hearted and more utterly unselfish woman never lived.
> "Life is a leaf of paper white
> Whereon each one of us may write
> His word or two and then comes night."
> Than those inscribed by A.M.L.E. never were words more
> admirably written. How admirably can be known only to God
> and her husband.
> "Donec aspiret dies et inclinentur umbrae."

When John Thomas the 16th Baron died in 1879 he was succeeded by his distant cousin, Christopher Patrick Mary Barnewall, the 17th Baron, who was only thirty three years old at the time of his succession. Christopher didn't enjoy his honours for very long as he died in 1891. He was unmarried and so his title and estates passed to his brother, Charles who became the 18th Baron.[47]

Charles (1861- 1937) the 18th Baron, was married to an Australian lady, Margaret Stephens of Brisbane and they had two sons Reginald and Charles and four daughters Ivy, Marcella, Letitia and Geraldine[48]. After the death of his first wife in 1901, Charles married again in 1907. His second wife was Mabel Schuff of Torquay, Devon. Charles married again in 1930 and his third wife was Lady Josephine Nixon.

Reginald, the eldest son, a Captain of the Leinster Regiment was badly wounded in World War I and died from his injuries in 1918.

Charles the 19th Baron (1899-1990), the second son, who succeeded to the title in 1937 was educated at Ampleforth was a Lieutenant in the Irish Guards during World War I and survived. He married Muriel Schneider of Manchester in 1926. They had two sons, Anthony and Raymond and a daughter Diana.

The Hon. Diana married Anthony Birtwistle from Oxfordshire and they have four daughters, Caroline, Emma, Lucinda and Sophia. All four are married and have children.

Anthony the 20th Baron Trimlestown (1928-1997) succeeded to the title in 1990 on the death of his father. He was an Ampleforth student and later became a naval Architect. He joined P&O shipping and became the European Sales Executive for the company. Although married twice he had no children. His wives were Lorna Ramsay and Mary Wonderly now the Rt. Hon. The Lady Trimlestown who lives in the U.S.

After Anthony's death in 1997 the title passed to his brother Raymond, now the 21st Baron Trimlestown. Born in 1930 he lives in Surrey. He is unmarried.

---

[47] By this time the estates had dwindled away.
[48] Ivy, Marcella and Letitia all married. Their husbands were respectively, John Radcliff of Kells, Co. Meath, Major Charles Bathhurst and Lt. Col. Cuthbert Townsend from Surrey. Ivy and Letitia had families.

Bligh of Clifton Lodge
(Earls of Darnley)

Ivo Bligh the 8th Earl of Darnley, who succeeded his brother Edward (the 7th Earl), is best known as the English cricketer who was responsible for 'The Ashes'. Apparently the story goes that following an unexpected defeat of the English team by the Australians at the Oval, in 1882, a journalist wit wrote an obituary on 'the Death of English Cricket' and that all that was left was "The Ashes" The following year Ivo led a team to Australia to win back the laurels lost at the Oval. While there they stayed with the wealthy Clarke family and during their stay played a fun game against the Clarke Eleven. After the match the fun loving ladies of the Clarke household presented Ivo with an urn holding the ashes of either the ball or the bails used in the match. Ivo's eleven were very successful in Australia and they returned home as heroes of the hour, bringing with them 'The Ashes'. The 'trophy' was kept in Cobham Hall until 1929 when it was presented to the M.C.C. by Ivo's widow.

Prior to his death in 1817 William Bligh of Mutiny on the Bounty fame made a will in which he named his relative, John Bligh, the Earl of Darnley, as one of his two executors. Because of the 'bad press' he received in the novels concerning the Mutiny on his ship, the achievements of this rather remarkable man have been overshadowed.[49] Having been cast adrift

---

[49] William Bligh joined the Royal Navy in 1770 and soon rose to prominence. He was described as being an intelligent man, well-versed in science and mathematics

31

in a small boat with eighteen other officers and men, Bligh, a top class seaman, managed to get them to safety after a gruelling forty seven day trip. The descendants of the mutineers, led by Fletcher Christian, still live on Pitcairn Island to this day.

Captain William Bligh

A linen draper, John Bligh of London (1616-1666), originally from Plymouth, was employed as agent for the adventurers of the forfeited estates in post Cromwellian Co. Meath. He came to Ireland and became an adventurer himself and speculator on a large scale in confiscated lands in

---

and was also a talented writer and illustrator. At the age of 22 he became Sailing Master on the Resolution, commanded by Captain James Cook. He was appointed Captain of the sloop HMS Falcon in 1790, followed by service on HMS Medea and HMS Providence. In 1797 he commanded HMS Director at the battle of Camperdown and as Captain of HMS Glatton in 1801 took part in the battle of Copenhagen, after which he was commended for his bravery by Admiral Nelson. Also in 1801 Bligh was elected a fellow of the Royal Society, in consideration of his distinguished services in navigation and his expertise in botany and horticulture. He was appointed Governor of New South Wales in 1805 but there faced another mutiny and was imprisoned by the mutineers for two years. He returned to England after his release and in 1814 he was appointed a Rear Admiral and later Vice Admiral. He had six daughters. The Darnley's Island in the Torres Strait is called after the Bligh relatives.

Meath in the baronies of Lune and Morgallion and settled at Rathmore. He was an M.P. for Athboy and also a government official holding the post of a commissioner of Customs and Excise from 1648-1663.[50] His properties were adjacent to the confiscated lands that later became the property of King James II. John Bligh, who was married to a sister of the Bishop of Lincoln, died in 1666 and his son, Thomas, appears to have bought more land in the area at a later date bringing the family holding in the area to a healthy 25,000 acres.

Thomas (1654-1710), was an M.P. and a Peace Commissioner, but does not appear to have held any higher government post. His wife was Elizabeth Naper, the daughter of Colonel James Naper of Loughcrew and they were married in 1682. They had a number of children and the eldest son was John Bligh born in 1687.

When King James came to Ireland in 1689 the Act of Settlement was set aside and Protestants like Taylor of Kells, Peppard of Ballygarth, Bligh of Rathmore, James Nepper alias Tandy Napper of Druistown and about forty others, were outlawed and attainted unless they acknowledged James.[51] Thomas Bligh and his Protestant Meath neighbours threw in their lot with William of Orange who emerged victorious after the Battle of the Boyne and the Siege of Limerick.

It is not known but can be safely assumed that Thomas vacated his Rathmore lands during the conflict. It is most likely that he sent his wife and children to England for the period.

Thomas was succeeded in Rathmore by his son John Bligh (1687-1728). During his brief lifetime, John Bligh catapulted the Linen Draper's descendants into the ranks of the Aristocracy. His first strategic move was marrying Lady Theodosia Hyde, Baroness Clifton, the only daughter and heir of the 3rd Earl of Clarendon[52] in 1713. Eight years later he was created

---

[50] Burke's *Peerage and Baronetage*

[51] J.G. Simms in Riocht na Midhe 1962

[52] Edward Hyde, the 3rd Earl was Governor of New York and New Jersey from 1701 to 1708. He was in debtor's prison at the time of his father's death and earned himself an unsavoury reputation while in America. In the year following his daughter's marriage in 1713 he was appointed Envoy Extraordinary to Hanover. Edward had married Catherine, daughter of Henry O'Brien and his wife Catherine, in her own right Baroness Clifton of Leighton Bromswold. His wife, who on her mother's death in 1702 became Baroness Clifton of Leighton

a peer as Baron Clifton of Rathmore. The following year he was made Viscount of Darnley of Athboy, in the same year his wife died, and finally Earl of Darnley in 1725. As part of her inheritance Theodosia came into the possession of Cobham Hall and its estate, in Kent. From this time onwards Cobham Hall became the principal residence of the Earls of Darnley.

Cobham Hall

John and Theodosia had two surviving sons, Edward and John and three daughters, Mary, Ann and Theodosia. All three ladies married. Mary's husband was William Tighe of Rosanna, Co. Wicklow[53]. Ann was married twice and both her husbands were from Co. Down. Her first husband was Robert McGill and her second husband was Bernard Ward the 1st Viscount Bangor[54]. William Crosbie, the 1st Earl of Glandore, was Theodosia's husband.

Bromswold, died in New York four years later and is buried in that city - Wikipedia

[53] For further information about the Tighe family see *The Landed Gentry and Aristocracy of Wicklow* by Turtle Bunbury.

[54] They lived at Castle Ward. The mansion was commissioned by Bernard Ward, later first Viscount Bangor (1719-81), whose family first settled in the area around 1570 when they built the original Castle Ward - a tower house which stands in the farmyard close to the shore. This castle was replaced in 1710 by a house constructed a short distance north west by Bernard's father, Judge Michael Ward

After his father's death in 1728, Edward (1715-1747) became the 2nd Earl of Darnley. It is unlikely that Edward the 2nd Earl spent much time in Ireland and he seems to have been close to the court, becoming a lord in waiting to the Prince of Wales in 1742. He was also a Free Mason and was elected Grand Master, and duly installed at Fishmonger's-hall on the 28th of April 1737, 'in presence of the duke of Richmond, the earls of Crawford and Wemsys, Lord Gray, and many other respectable brethren'. During the year he was Grand Master the Prince of Wales was initiated 'at an occasional lodge convened for the purpose at the palace of Kew'. He was very active in promoting Freemasonry during his tenure of the office 'Upwards of sixty lodges were represented at every Communication during Lord Darnley's administration, and more Provincial patents were issued by him, than by any of his predecessors. Deputations were granted for Montserrat, Geneva, the Circle of Upper Saxony, the Coast of Africa, New York, and the Islands of America.'[55] Edward never married and was succeeded by his brother, John, following his premature death in 1747.

John the 3rd Earl of Darnley (1719-1781) was quite a young man when he inherited the Meath and Kent estates. In the early 19th century these estates consisted of 25,463 acres in Meath and 9,309 acres in Kent and must have been of a similar size when John inherited. He didn't rush into matrimony and was 45 years old when he married an heiress, Mary Stoyte, the daughter of a well-to-do barrister from Street, Westmeath. The 3rd Earl was an M.P. for Athboy in 1739 and an M.P. for Maidstone, Kent, for six years from 1741 until his brother's death, when he moved into the House of Lords. We must presume that, like his brother, he lived mainly at Cobham Hall and left the running of his Irish estates to agents. The family did have a residence near Athboy, called Clifton Lodge.

While there was a settlement in Athboy from very early times, in the vicinity of the ford across the Trimblestown River, the nucleus of the modern town was not built until the Normans arrived in the late 12th century. They built a small walled town which because of its security attracted the Carmelites. The monks built, in addition to their own living quarters, a church, an almshouse and a hospital. The present Protestant church was built on the site of the Carmelite church. The next major

(1683-1759) - a remarkable figure who achieved great wealth through marriage and business acumen.

[55] *History of Freemasonry* – William Preston

development did not occur until the mid to late 18th century when the modern layout of the town was designed mainly on the instructions of the 3rd Earl of Darnley.

Lord Darnley

While not neglecting his Meath properties the 3rd Earl also spent considerable sums on the Cobham mansion. The Great Hall was redesigned and decorated with ornate plasterwork under the direction of Sir William Chambers.[56] It was the 3rd Earl who left instructions to have the famous Mausoleum built in the grounds of Cobham, so that he and his

[56] He was one of the most important architects of the second half of the 18th Century, his principal work being Somerset House home of three important art galleries and of course the Witt and the Conway libraries. George the Fourth pronounced the music room at Cobham 'the finest room in England'.

descendants could be interred in style. The Mausoleum, designed by James Wyatt the famous architect, cost in the region of £9,000 to build. It consisted of a chapel with a crypt underneath and was sited deep in a wood. Prior to its construction family members were buried in Westminster.

Cobham Hall

During the public scare in both Ireland and England, following the War of Independence in America, the Volunteers were founded in Ireland in 1780. The 3rd Earl, in common with his fellow Irish landlords, formed his own corps in Meath.

The 3rd Earl and his wife, Mary, had three sons, John, Edward and William and four daughters, Mary, Theodosia, Sarah and Catherine, three of whom married. Mary's husband was Sir Lawrence Palk, while her younger sister, Theodosia married a relative, her first cousin twice removed, Thomas Cherburg Bligh, a nephew of the 1st Earl. The youngest daughter married the 3rd Marquess of Londonderry. Both younger sons entered the Army and Edward rose to the rank of General while William had to be content to become a Colonel.

John, the 4th Earl (1767-1831) succeeded his father in 1781. He was only fourteen years old when the burden of responsibility had to be undertaken. His mother, Mary, fortunately, lived until 1803, so he had a firm guiding hand at the crucial time. The restoration work to Cobham

Hall was carried on by the 4th Earl who also employed the famous Humphrey Repton to lay out the classical gardens[57]. In Ireland, when the threat came in the form of the United Irishmen, the 4th Earl was not found wanting and formed his own Yeomanry Corps of infantry in Athboy with himself as the Captain. The Corps does not appear to have been overly active as most of the disturbances in Meath were more in the Navan area.

The 4th Lord Darnley was a personal friend of the Duke of Wellington. He was a Whig. He supported the move for Catholic Emancipation and political reform. He was a great collector and a traveller. He spent huge sums on the acquisition of pictures and *objets d'art,* which adorned his stately home at Cobham. He had a London home at 46, Berkeley Square. The Darnleys were on very friendly terms with the Royal Family.[58]

Either the 4th Lord Darnley or his son was responsible for the erection of the Market House in Athboy in 1828. However this project seemed to be a failure as it had been turned into a school by 1837.

An interesting story is told about how the 4th Lord advanced money to the Duke and Duchess of Kent in 1819, when they needed to travel back from Germany to England. The Royal purse was empty and funds could not be raised for the immediate expenses but the 4th Lord was on hand to advance the necessary finance. The gratitude of the Duchess of Kent and her brother Prince Leopold (afterwards King of the Belgians) was expressed on subsequent occasions.

Lord Darnley was a keen yachtsman and spent some of the winter months shooting. His extravagant lifestyle reduced the family finances but didn't affect his social standing. Like many old families there seemed to be the odd skeleton in the cupboard. In 1825 there was a court case in London against Captain Robert Bligh, 'an elderly half-mad cousin' a nephew of the 1st Earl of Darnley, who 'for some fancied grievance had assaulted both Lord Clifton (Edward – the eldest son of the 4th Earl) and his father more than once'.

Elizabeth, the daughter of the Right Hon. William Brownlow of Lurgan, Co. Armagh, married the 4th Earl in 1791. They had two surviving

---

[57] The park at Cobham extended over an area of no less than 1,800 acres. Some of the trees were of great age and size. A chestnut tree, named the Four Sisters, was twenty five feet in girth.

[58] *The 5th Earl of Darnley* by his daughter

sons, Edward and John Duncan and three daughters. Two of the daughters married. Mary married Charles Brownlow, the 1st Lord Lurgan and Elizabeth married his brother, the Rev. John Brownlow. John Duncan, the younger son found a career in the diplomatic service and was envoy-extraordinary and minister-plenipotentiary at Hanover.

Edward the 5th Earl (1795-1835), was educated at Eton, where he went at the age of eight, and went to Oxford in 1812. He was quite a brilliant student and took a first class in the classics – apparently quite unusual for a young nobleman at the time. On the occasion of his 21st birthday over 2000 people, tenants and the poor of the district were fed at Cobham, while a serious bash was in train at the Hall where over 100 local dignitaries and friends were entertained.

A match with the daughter of the Powerscourts was explored but the Darnley family finances seemed to be at a low ebb and the Powerscourts were not sufficiently impressed with the allowance that Edward would get, so the match was sidelined.[59]

Lady de Vesci seems to have been the person who made the match between Edward, Lord Clifton and Emma Parnell. She was described as 'remarkably good looking, with laughing black eyes and still darker hair dressed in ringlets, a small straight nose, full red lips and lovely pink and white complexion'. She had received a good education, was fond of history and 'could draw fairly well'. She was also a cousin of the famous Charles Stuart Parnell.[60] In 1825 the couple were married in Abbeyleix in the old church on the de Vesci demesne.

---

[59] *The 5th Earl of Darnley* by his daughter

[60] Emma was the daughter of Henry Parnell, from Co. Laois, a cousin of the famous Charles Stuart Parnell. His father was Sir John Parnell and Henry was the second son. Henry's elder brother was a deaf mute and when he died in 1812 Henry succeeded to the title. Henry's wife was Lady Caroline Dawson the daughter of the Earl of Portarlington. There is a strange tale about Henry's marriage. It would appear he was a shy diffident young man who upon visiting the Portarlingtons met their daughters. He was very taken with the younger daughter Louisa and some time later wrote to her mother asking for her hand in marriage. Whatever mistake he made in his proposal the mother thought he wished to marry the eldest daughter Caroline and made this public. Henry didn't have the heart to dash the young lady's (and her mother's) enthusiasm and went ahead with the loveless marriage in 1801. The couple had a number of children –

Edward had made up his mind to live for at least some of the time on his Meath estate and with that in mind came to Ireland in 1826 and we get a glimpse from his letters of what conditions were like near Athboy. He spent most of his time at Clifton Lodge trying to get work done on the grounds in particular. He wrote 'In consequence of my having employed a few hands on the improvements, the gate was beset this morning by 40 or 50 wretches with spades, etc., seeking for employment which I was unable to offer them. Alas! We have much to go through in witnessing the distress of this poor country, but then the more we have to endure and the more difficult the task we propose to ourselves the more I feel assured we shall, through God's assistance, rejoice in overcoming difficulties and being of some use.' While in Meath he was kept busy attending at the Assizes and looking after road projects. He had a meeting with the tenants and the object was the employment of the poor. He noted in his letters that distress among the poorer classes was very general.

Clifton and his wife moved into Clifton Lodge in 1826. It was still in some disrepair but they set about getting it in order. They had Mrs. Eliza and Mr. Paddy Thornton as Cook and Housekeeper and Butler and Valet, Peggy was the kitchen maid, Johnny Lawless, footboy, James Eustace, coachman and groom. Then there were people who attended to the Gate and he had 50 or 60 employed on road works laying out a new approach to the house and carrying out renovations on the house itself. Work seems to have been completed on the house by 1831. Their neighbours were Martleys, Hopkins, McVeaghs and Rotherams.

In 1830 Clifton decided to stand for election in Meath against the agitator Jack Lawless and he resigned his Canterbury seat. His brother, John, also decided to stand for Meath. Clifton was elected in 1831 but his brother failed in his attempt. Clifton's father died in the same year so he had to give up his seat in the Commons and move into the House of Lords. Trouble was brewing on his Irish estates around this time, particularly on his Trim estate. 'Outrages occurred on the estate near Trim because of evictions. Houses of people who took the land were attacked and Lambert

---

boys and girls. They separated in 1813 when Lady Caroline went abroad and lived at first in Switzerland and then mainly in Paris.

Disney, the son of Lord Darnley's agent was stoned as the drove through Trim.' [61]

The 5th Earl enjoyed his new status and estates for only four years as he died in 1835 following an accident. Near the Mausoleum at Cobham while walking with his brother and Henry Parnell he saw a woodsman cutting down a tree. Lord Darnley took the axe to show his comrades the way to cut off branches. The axe slipped and nearly severed his little toe. Tetanus appeared and he died a few days later.

Edward and Emma had three sons and two daughters. Both ladies married and their husbands were brothers. Elizabeth married Sir Reginald Cust and Emma married the Rev. Arthur Cust.[62]

John Stuart (1827-1896) the eldest son became the 6th Earl upon the death of his father and the two younger sons having completed their educations at Cambridge became Vicars. John Stuart, as befitting a country gentleman, became the Lieutenant Colonel of the West Kent yeomanry militia. Like many Irish peers of his generation he had to oversee the start of the dismantling of his Meath empire. The various Land Acts of the last two decades of the 19th century conferred purchase rights on the Irish tenants and landlords had no option but to comply. John Stuart married Lady Harriet Pelham, the daughter of the 3rd Earl of Chichester. They had three sons and five daughters. Three of the ladies married, Edith, Kathleen and Constance. Their husbands were respectively, George Rasleigh, a Barrister, Major-General Brownlow and William Childe-Pemberton. The three sons were Edward, Ivo Francis and Arthur.

Edward (1851-1900) succeeded as the 7th Earl in 1896. He married Jemima Blackwood of Norton Court and they had one child, a daughter, Elizabeth, Baroness Clifton. He didn't enjoy his new status for very long as he died within four years. His successor was his brother Ivo Frances Henry already alluded to at the start of this chapter.

Ivo, the 8th Earl, an honorary Colonel in the West Kent regiment married Florence Morphy, from Australia, in 1884. They had two sons and one daughter Dorothy who married Capt. Daniel Peploe. Dorothy died in 1976 and left a family. Ivo completed the work of dismantling his Irish estates when he auctioned the town of Athboy. The Darnley estate office, now the Kirwan Arms Hotel, was finally closed in 1948.

---

[61] Riocht na Midhe 1989 – *Agrarian Violence in Meath* by Desmond Mooney.
[62] Both these gentlemen were descended from Brownlows on the maternal side.

Ivo and Florence had two sons Esme Ivo and Noel Gervase. Noel fought in both World Wars. He married Mary Frost and had two daughters Jasmine (d.1991) a TV hostess who was married to Lt. Col Sir John Johnson and Susan (d.1983) who was married to Lt. Col. Stirling of Keir. Both ladies had families.

Esme Ivo the 9thEarl (1886-1955) was at various times a Painter, Musician and flower breeder. In the early part of his life he was a Major in the RAF but later retired when he became a pacifist. In 1912 he married Daphne Mulholland the daughter of the Hon. John Mulholland. They had one son Peter and one daughter Marguerite.

Marguerite was a famous mannequin at Fortnum and Masons who modelled in advertisements for Horlicks, Ponds Cold Cream and Wills Gold Flake. Marguerite was married and divorced three times. Her husbands included a stockbroker, a Wing Commander, (Gordon Haywood by whom she had a son Gareth and a daughter Lucinda) and an hotelier. She died in 2002.

Peter the 10th Earl (1915-1980) was educated at Eton and Sandhurst. He joined the Army and rose to the rank of Major. He fought in World War II and was made a prisoner. He was released after the War. He never married.

Esme Ivo the 9th Earl divorced Daphne in 1920 and married in 1923 Nancy Kidston and they had one daughter Lady Rose who married Sir Thomas Hare. They have a family.

Esme divorced Nancy in 1936 and married again in 1940 His wife this time was Rosemary Potter from Westmoreland. They had one son Adam Ivo Stuart Bligh (b. 1941), the 11th and present Earl and two daughters Melissa and Lady Harriet who lives in Kent.

Lady Melissa married Don Manuel Torrado y de Fontcuberta from Barcelona and they had one son Manuel and two daughters Maria and Victoria. Lady Melissa divorced and married as her second husband Rev. Colin Levey. They live in Cumbria.

Adam Ivo Stuart Bligh the 11th Earl lives in Worcestershire. He was born in 1941 and was educated at Harrow and Oxford. His wife is Lady Susan Anderson and they have one son Ivo Donald and one daughter Katherine. Ivo Donald (b.1968) is married to Peta Beard from Devon and they have one son Henry Robert.

Bolton of Bective Abbey

Sir Richard Bolton, Knight (c.1570-1648), was the son of John Bolton of Great Fenton in Staffordshire, and, depending on the source, the family's origins are believed to have been in either Lancashire or Westmorland.[63] Concluding that the origins of the name are toponymic the family have claimed descent from Ughtred de Bolton whose 12th century effigy adorns the church at Bolton in Westmorland.[64] Richard Bolton commenced his career as a lawyer. However his beginnings, practising as a barrister, seem to have been marred by an encounter with the notorious, Westminster based, Court of Star Chamber. The threat of reproach from that sinister body appears to have influenced his remove to Ireland. In Dublin he first emerges as a recorder of the city in about 1606/7 and the following year he had sufficiently ingratiated himself to earn a commendation from the Lord Deputy, Sir Arthur Chichester. He soon appears as a fully devoted establishment figure when the government sponsored his election to parliament as a member for Dublin in 1613 -a

[63] The most comprehensive account of Bolton's career, from which the following is derived, appears to be the entry written by Sir John T. Gilbert for the *Dictionary of National Biography*, hereafter DNB (L. Stephen and S. Lee, eds. Vol. II, 1905, pp. 790-792).

[64] Charles Knowles Bolton, *Bolton Families in Ireland (with their English and American kindred)*. 1937.

strategy reputed to have been designed to oppose a Catholic candidate. A knighthood followed in 1618 the year in which he was made solicitor-general.

It was while serving in this post that he published, in 1621, a selection of '*The statutes of Ireland*'. He followed this in 1635 with a supplementary volume and two years later a form of handbook for Justices of the Peace, which must have had some claim to usefulness as it was reissued in 1683. By then he had been made Chief Baron of the Exchequer and within a year he was made Lord Chancellor of Ireland, replacing Sir Adam Loftus (later Viscount Ely), a nephew of one of the founding fathers of Trinity College who was alleged to have bought the position.[65]

The Chancellorship was a position of some considerable importance. As head of the Chancery he served as keeper of the Irish Great Seal which was applied to letters issued in the king's name. The Lord Chancellor was entitled to a moiety (half share) of the income derived from such writs and an annual salary of £500. Significantly his acquisition of Bective coincides with his appointment to the position, and based on his predecessors, holding the position of Chancellor seems to have been a prerequisite to obtaining the abbey property.

Located within the Pale, the twelfth century foundation at Bective was one of the first of the great Irish monastic houses to fall under the seemingly rancorous dissolution policy of Henry VIII. The Abbey and its 4,440 acres in Meath were seized and the secularisation of the religious buildings commenced under Thomas Agard, known as 'Agard of the Mint' because of his position as vice-treasurer of the Mint in the Tudor administration.[66]

Agard's possession of Bective appears to have been short, perhaps reflecting financial difficulties, and in 1544 it passed, again for a brief period, to Sir John Alen, the Lord Chancellor and head of the commission

---

[65] Connolly, op. cit., p.327.
[66] Roger Stalley, *The Cistercian Monasteries of Ireland*. 1987. p. 228; In addition to the buildings the abbot was held to have been possessed of 'two hundred and five acres of arable, seven of meadow, and thirty-three of pasture in the townland of Bective, being the demesne of the Abbey, also a water mill and fishing weir.' Amongst the chattels of the abbey which are recorded were two bells weighing 180 llbs; N.B. White (ed.), *Extents of Irish Monastic Possessions, 1540-1541*. I.M.C. 1943. p.267ff.

for the dissolution of the monasteries.[67] His efforts to highlight widespread profiteering by others through speculation and under valuation of confiscated lands redounded on him when he was himself jailed for such practices.[68] Although Alen was later reinstated as Lord Chancellor and recovered his monastic leases, by 1552 'the late house and possessions of the Bectyfe' had passed to the Treasurer of Ireland, Anthony Wyse, who paid 'the som of a thowsainde a hundredthe fourscore eight pounds aleaven pence sterling' for them.[69]

After a number of turbulent years, which saw Wyse committed to the debtor's prison and engaged in protracted legal disputes with his wife, there were a confusing series of transactions relating to the property. Following his death in 1567 Bective passed to his son-in-law, Sir Alexander Fitton, and afterwards to his son-in-law, Sir Bartholomew Dillon, a Chief Justice who resided across the Boyne at Riverstown Castle and who in 1595 had married Catherine Litton. Bective seems to have declined after this period and in 1619 the abbey was described as deserted.[70]

Sir Richard Bolton restored some stability to the ownership of the property and his descendants established a possession of the property that endured until the end of the nineteenth century. However from the late seventeenth century, the Bolton family was chiefly resident in Brazeel (Brazil), an important seventeenth century house in north County Dublin while Bective Abbey was leased to others including Sir Thomas Taylour, whose descendants, in recognition of this, became Earls of Bective.[71] A

---

[67] The exact term of Agard's possession of the property is unclear from the principal sources. Allen's association is given by Casey and Rowan (p.158) but not by Stalley (p.228, who gives Agard possession until at least 1557) or Leask who states that, according to *Fiants*, Henry VIII, No. 547, Agard was granted an extension of ten years to the original lease'; Leask op. cit. p.48.

[68] S.J. Connolly, *The Oxford Companion to Irish History*. 1998. P.12.

[69] Leask, op. cit., p.48.

[70] Hogan, op. cit., p.10.

[71] Three deeds between Thomas Taylor, 1st Earl of Bective (cr. 1766) and the Rowley family, concerning property near Kells, reveal that Lord Bective was giving his principal address as 'Bective Castle' in 1767 and in 1770; Rowley Papers, Archives Department UCD: S6/26/13-15. The Earl's father, Sir Thomas had entertained proposals for a grand building on his Kells estate before 1751. After he died in 1757 his son immediately began preparations for building –it was to be another twelve years before the scaffolding was eventually taken down and

smaller residence on the site, now incorporated in the present Bective House, appears to have provided for the Bolton family's occasional presence on their Meath estate.

Bective Abbey

Sir Richard had taken up office amid the gathering tensions of the mid-seventeenth century that spectacularly flared with the Catholic rising of 1641. Barely had he acquainted himself with the duties of office when he was subjected, with others, to impeachment proceedings for high treason. These had been initiated, it has been claimed, by Catholic members of the commons –an intrigue that has to be placed in the context of the circumstances surrounding the abiding crises of the mid-17th century.[72] Bolton's impeachment created a unique situation whereby as chairman of the House of Lords he was obliged to receive the case against himself and as a consequence temporarily stood aside to be replaced by a justice of the King's Bench. In 1642 having cleverly manoeuvred to have Catholic members of the Commons excluded from parliament through applying the

---

at least another five years before the famous Adam interiors were completed - John Harris, *Headfort House and Robert Adam*, 1973.

[72] One source states that "having assisted the Earl of Stafford in the introduction of arbitrary government into Ireland, articles of impeachment for high treason were drawn up by the House of Commons" against him. Knowles, *op. cit.*, p.3.

Oath of Supremacy, he then succeeded in his petition to have the proceedings against him dropped and was immediately reinstated to the chancellorship.[73]

The high point of his career came when he was central to the negotiations in 1643 conducted by the Earl of Ormonde, between the King and the Confederate Catholics which led to a temporary truce and military support for Charles I, in his conflict with parliament. Bolton's name also heads the signatories of the proclamation issued in 1646 announcing the terms of so-called first Ormonde Peace.

Richard Bolton was first married to Frances Walter who came from his home county of Staffordshire, suggesting perhaps that he had formed the alliance before his arrival in Ireland, and with whom he had numerous children, a least one son, Edward, and several daughters.[74] Notwithstanding the circumstances of his election to parliament in 1613 and later accusations that he was 'much opposed to concessions to Roman Catholics in Ireland' he formed an alliance with one of the most important old Catholic families of the Pale when he took Margaret Barnewall of Turvey, widow of Luke Netterville ("a lawless and ruthless rebel"), as his second wife.[75] Her father, Sir Patrick Barnewall, was the head of one branch of this impeccably Catholic family. The eldest of the eleven children of Sir Christopher Barnewall, high sheriff of Co. Dublin, he was prominent as the leading opponent of Sir Arthur Chichester (already

---

[73] D.N.B. p. 791; apparently the proceedings were 'expunged' from the records in 1661, Knowles, op. cit., p.4.

[74] LGI, 1863, p.123, states that he had two daughters and seven sons whilst DNB, p.791 simply says he left 'one son and several daughters.' That he had more than one son is confirmed in LGI, 1899, p.38. It is likely that the discrepancy reflects the confusion regarding the progeny associated from Bolton's second marriage. See n. 20 below.

[75] Luke Netterville was the second son of Nicholas, Viscount Netterville. Barnewall is a name synonymous with Meath, representing a steadfastly Catholic family whose legions of barons and knights dominate the history and politics of the region. The Turvey line, to which Bolton's wife belonged, as daughter of Sir Patrick Barnewall, was eventually raised to the peerage as Viscounts Kingsland, while the senior branch in Meath was headed by the Barons of Trimlestown. See Matthew O' Reilly, 'The Barnewalls' in *Riocht na Midhe*, Vol. I, No. 3, 1957, pp.64-8; *Burke's Dormant and Extinct Peerage*, 5 edns. 1838-1841; *Burke's Peerage and Baronetage*, (ed. C. Mosley), 106th Edition, 2 Vols., London, 1992, pp.2846-7.

encountered as Bolton's early supporter), when as Lord Deputy Chichester attempted to compel Catholic attendance at services of the established church, applying the rigours of the Castle Chamber to those who refused. Perhaps not as threatening as the Westminster court (which Richard Bolton had earlier evaded) it sought to emulate, its penalties to deviants varied from pillory and whipping to the barbarity of removing the ears of accused. Barnewall was successful in having this regime suspended. In 1646 Sir Patrick Barnewall's eldest son, Nicholas, in recognition of services during the English civil war was created Viscount Kingsland and Baron of Turvey by Charles I.[76]

There was thought to be no surviving images of Bolton who died in 1648 -'a unique portrait' was said to have existed in the residence of a descendant and later unfortunately destroyed by a fire there.[77] However, this portrait did survive and was known to exist in the hands of descendants in 1937.[78]

His eldest son, Sir Edward Bolton, who had been knighted in 1635, followed his father's career when as solicitor-general he was appointed Chief Baron of the Exchequer in 1640, but it is stated that he was later 'removed by the usurping powers.'[79] Notwithstanding this he inherited the Bective estates on his father's death in 1648 and in 1651 under the parliamentary government obtained another official post as Commissioner for the administration of justice in Ireland. He was the first of the family to be positively associated with residence at Brazeel. Otherwise very little else is known about him other than that he had married Isabella Ayloffe with whom he had two sons and a daughter.

Sir Richard Bolton's second son, Thomas, by his second wife, established a branch of the family at Tullydonnell, Co. Louth.[80] Thomas

---

[76] *Burke's Dormant, Abeyant, Forfeited and Extinct Peerages*, 1883, pp.23-4.

[77] D.N.B., p.792. It was widely accepted that it was destroyed in the destruction of Brazeel House c.1810.

[78] Knowles, op.cit., p.5.

[79] LGI 1863, p.123.

[80] LGI 1899/1904, p.38. It has not yet been established whether there is any connection between this Thomas Bolton and his namesake who was an acclaimed Silversmith in the late seventeenth and early eighteenth centuries. Robert Wyse-Jackson (*Irish Silver*, 1972, pp. 57-8) says that he was 'a clergyman's son from County Meath who became Master of the Dublin Company in 1692'. . The mace

Bolton was the father of Theophilus Bolton, who having served as Chancellor in St. Patrick's Cathedral became acquainted with Swift, who afterwards was a regular visitor to Clonfert and Cashel where Bolton at different times held the incumbency.[81] As Archbishop of Cashel he was responsible for completing the new Palace in the centre of the town, a Palladian building of the first import designed for his predecessor by Sir Edward Lovett Pearce.[82] Another of the Archbishop's legacies is his library, a precious collection of antiquarian books, considered Ireland's most important that includes thousands of items from the library of Archbishop King of Dublin (1650-1729). The library was bequeathed to the diocese of Cashel upon his death in 1729, proving that he was likely to be remembered for more than being just something of the conventional 'good bishop' whose primary achievements were to 'eat, drink, grow fat, rich and die'.[83]

After Sir Edward, who died in 1705, the Bolton family's political importance appears to have diminished considerably and at Brazeel he was succeeded by a succession of Richards, Edwards and Roberts who remain largely obscure. Early in the eighteenth century Edward Bolton of Brazeel married Letitia Molesworth, younger sister of the famous

---

of Trinity College Dublin, dated 1709, is his work and numerous other items are held in the National Museum. Thomas Bolton was later made Lord Mayor of Dublin and according to this source he died in 1736. It is possible that this is the same Thomas Bolton and that the reference to being a clergyman's son is confused with his brother, Theophilus. Significantly, his son, also Thomas, is named by Burke (LGI) as Lord Mayor of Dublin in 1716. Johnston-Liik, pp.221-1, who offers no information concerning the father reveals that this Thomas Bolton was a Physician and M.P. for Athenry (1733-41).

[81] Joseph McMinn, *Jonathan's Travels: Swift and Ireland*. 1994. p.76, 82, 84, 141-2.

[82] Edward McParland, *Public Architecture in Ireland*. 2001, p.166.

[83] The Bolton collection, having been originally housed in a purpose built building adjoining the palace, is now represented by the GPA-Bolton Library in the grounds of the Cathedral in Cashel. The quotation is derived from Bolton's own assessment and is given by Toby Barnard, *A New Anatomy of Ireland: The Irish Protestants, 1649-1770*. p.100, derived from Williams, *The Correspondence of Swift*, iv, p.330.

incarcerate, Lady Belvedere.[84] He served as an M.P. for Swords (1727-1758) and apart from serving on a number of committees held a largely undistinguished career.[85] A son, Theophilus, was for a time charged with the management of the state lottery. Throughout the eighteenth century the family continued to reside at Brazeel while Bective Abbey was occupied by Sir Thomas Taylour.

By the late eighteenth century when the Taylour Earl of Bective had moved to his newly built neo-classical mansion, Headfort, near Kells, Bective Abbey ceased to function as a residence and, once abandoned, eventually became ruinous.

The property then belonged to another Edward Bolton, an officer of the royal horse guards and it was his eldest son by his first marriage, Robert Compton Bolton, who appears to have been the last of the family to have been associated with the old house of Brazeel before its destruction by fire in about 1810. Perhaps it was because of the destruction of the old house that his eldest son, Richard, renewed the family's interest in the Bective estate when shortly before 1836 he commenced preparations to shape the present demesne. This involved removing the public road further west, away from the existing small family house located north of the abbey on the west side of the river. By 1849 the present demesne was walled in along the entire western boundary which was noted by Sir William Wilde when he conducted his journey along the Boyne.[86]

Bolton then began to develop a larger residence on the site of the old cottage placing a substantial two storey, seven-bay entrance front, facing south that was built in a sophisticated neo-classical style which is carefully expressed in the decorative restraint of architectural details and logic of the proportions. 'To promote the worship of God' Bolton also funded 'at his sole expense for his tenants and neighbours' the Church of Ireland parish church, which is located within the demesne, designed by

---

[84] This unfortunate Lady, Mary Molesworth, the wife of the 1st Earl of Belvedere was imprisoned by her husband in a room in their house for 30 years for suspected infidelity with his brother – Howard Bury Papers

[85] He inherited Brazeel form his father Richard who had inherited the estate of his brother, Sir Edward in 1705; at that time it was valued at £15,000 per annum. Johnstone-Liik, p.221.

[86] William Wilde, Beauties of the Boyne and Blackwater. 1849. p. 113.

the leading ecclesiastical architect of the mid-nineteenth century, Joseph Welland, and completed in 1854.

Richard Bolton having established himself at Bective, where he named his new house Bective Abbey in deference to the ruins that gave the family its foothold in the county, settled into local life and politics; he became a J.P. and married Frances Bomford of nearby Rahinston. [87] The Bomfords, stated to have been descended from 'a good English family,' were present in Meath by the end of the seventeenth century with the earliest recorded antecedent reputed to have died at the good age of 103.[88] Frances Bolton along with her sisters inherited the estate of her brother Robert-George Bomford when he died in 1846. Almost certainly reflecting the consequences of the Great Famine, the Rahinston estate was heavily in debt and was sold in 1852 through the Encumbered Estates' Court under the direction of Dame Annette Hesketh, Frances Bolton's older sister.[89]

It appears that the ruins of Bective Abbey and surrounding farm had, by 1862, come into the possession of the Rev. George H. Martin, Rector of Agher, who was related to the Bolton family, his father having eloped with Frances Bolton's younger sister, Susan, in 1826.[90] Martin transferred the Abbey, now a National Monument, to the Commissioners for Public Works in 1894.[91] Richard Bolton's death does not appear to have taken place until 1868 (according to monument at Bective Church) and in 1876 his widow still appears in possession of the estate, when her address is given as Bective and she is shown in possession of some 3,516 acres.[92]

---

[87] Her sister, Jemima, had married a namesake, Richard Bolton of Brooke Lodge, Waterford; however the families were unrelated. See Bolton of *Mount Bolton* in Burke's LGI 1912; Bolton of *Bective Abbey* LGI 1863.

[88] LGI, 1899, pp. 38-9; IFR, 1976, pp. 152-5.

[89] Mary Cecelia Lyons, *Illustrated Encumbered Estates Ireland, 1850-1905*. 1993, p.29

[90] Leask, op. cit. p.49; Hogan, p.9; IFR, p.152, which states that Frances Bomford's (Bolton) younger sister, Susan eloped in 1826 with Rev. Charles Rudinge Martin (d.1847), 4th son of John Martin, of Blackrock, Cork. They had four sons of whom George Henry was the youngest. See *Martin of Wiche* in LGI, 1904, p.389.

[91] Leask, op. cit., 1916, p.49.

[92] U. Hussey de Burgh, *Owners of Land of one acre and upwards*, 1876, does not list Martin as owner of any lands in Meath with Francis (Frances?) G. Bolton named as owner of 3,516 acres; John Bateman, Great Landowners of Great Britain and Ireland (1883) concur and give Bolton's address as Bective Lodge, Rahinston.

In 1885, Martin is named as the proprietor of Bective House but he is known to have left there before his death[93] and soon the Bolton family disappear entirely off radar. Some of the family emigrated to New Zealand finding a new life, while the principal branch appears to have emigrated to South Africa.

Robert the brother of Richard of Bective Abbey was married to Maria Arthur of Seafield, Co. Dublin and they had a son, who was probably the last of the Boltons of Bective. He was John Marshall Bolton who stated in 1935 that he bought Sir Richard's portrait and papers from the last of the Bective Boltons when he went off to South Africa.[94]

---

[93] Goddard H. Orpen, 'Subterranean Chambers at Clady Co. Meath in *JRSAI, 1890*, p.150. LGI, 1904, p.388, gives the year of Martin's death as 1894.
[94] This entry in the book *The Bolton Families in Ireland* does not specify who went off to South Africa but we must assume it was in fact John Marshall Bolton.

Briscoe of Bellinter

Gussie Briscoe is portrayed as something of a *Bon Vivant* and is remembered by his family as an endearing good-humoured character perhaps a little out of place in the context of the formalities that characterise the late nineteenth century in which he lived. Something of his infectious fun-loving and larger-than-life character can be gauged from his portrait, where he appears an imposing presence in the front hall of Bellinter. Stories of his exploits are legion. Among these is the one that recalls his response to a wager that he ride his horse up the servant's stairs at Bellinter. An extraordinary feat in any circumstance, the fact that the Bellinter stairs is unique as a cantilevered spiral timber staircase, offering a certain spring to the step, makes his feat in ascending it on horseback more incredible; less remarkable is that once poor creature had reached the top of the stairs it refused to descend and having stubbornly remained there for more than a week eventually had to be winched down to safety.

John Joseph Preston, 'the Squire of Bellinter' had one child, a daughter called Helen, from his marriage in 1842 to Sarah O' Meagher; however she predeceased him in 1873.[95] By then the Irish social and

---

[95] Helen Maria Agnes Preston married John Joseph Roche Kelly of Rockstown Castle, Co. Limerick in 1865; their two children, a son and a daughter, both died in infancy. LGI, 1958, p.409.

political landscape had begun to change: Gladstone's Landlord and Tenant Act, providing limited tenant's rights, had just been passed in 1870 and was soon followed by the foundation of Michael Davitt's Irish National Land League in 1879, presided over by Parnell; this was quickly followed by Gladstone's second land act (The Land Law Act) in 1881 that ensured a fairer system of rents and facilitated land purchase. It was around this time that John Joseph Preston leased Bellinter House and demesne to his friend and hunting companion, Gustavus Villiers Briscoe, the son of the rector of Kilmessan and a former chaplain to the Viceroy.

Bellinter House
(Courtesy IAA)

The first of the Briscoe family to have been established in Ireland would appear to have been Thomas Briscoe, who was granted over 500 English acres of land in south west Tipperary, in the Barony of Clanwilliam in lieu of the £100 he had adventured to the Commonwealth.[96] By the late eighteenth century they were principally resident at Tinevane, an estate on the Tipperary-Kilkenny border near Carrick-on-Suir. According to Burke's The Landed Gentry of 1879 the first of this family was Henry Briscoe, who was a J.P. for counties Tipperary,

---

[96] Prendergast's *Cromwellian Settlement of Ireland.*

Kilkenny and Waterford. The author did not appear to know anything about the antecedents of Henry Briscoe.

Henry, later a J.P., who was born in 1753, pursued a career in the military in the 1st regiment of horse in which he was enlisted in 1770. Five years later he married Margaret Sneyd and they had three sons and six daughters, four of whom married. The dowries that had to be provided with those ladies must have proved to be a drain on Henry's finances. Three of the girls married army officers and Dora married J. Wilkie the brother of Sir David Wilkie. J. Wilkie held the post of Ordnance Storekeeper.

Henry's three sons were Henry Whitby, John and Robert. The two younger sons, almost inevitably, found careers in the Army. Neither of the officers married. Henry, the eldest son succeeded his father in 1807 following that man's demise. Like his father, he was a J.P. for counties Tipperary, Kilkenny and Waterford. In the year following his succession to the estate at Tinevane he married Alicia White of Carrickbeg. Henry and Alicia had two sons and four daughters. Two of those ladies married. The elder of the two, Alicia Louisa, married, Richard Bennett, a barrister, the son of the Chief Justice of Tobago, also Richard Bennett, a Wexfordman from Blackstoops. The younger girl, Anne, married Kilkennyman, Thomas Waring.

Henry's two sons were, predictably Henry and Francis. Henry, like his father and grandfather, went on to become a J.P. for counties Tipperary, Waterford and Kilkenny. Henry was born in 1805 and he married Deborah Shaw when he was in his mid twenties. She was the daughter of Rev. Robert Shaw. They had a large family of five sons and seven daughters.

Francis was educated for the Church and obtained an M.A. degree. He was rector of Kilmessan in Co. Meath. Francis married a widow, Dorothea Long, who was the daughter of John Cornwall of Brownstown House, Co. Meath in 1854. They had two children, Gustavus and Josephine.

Gustavus V. Briscoe, or 'Gussie' as he was more widely known, had served in the Waterford militia and once established at Bellinter in 1878 and taken over Preston's pack of harriers his principal occupation appears to have been hunting. In this respect he continued the family's passion for hunting borne out by the career of his grandfather, Henry

Whitby Briscoe, who was Master of the Curraghmore Hunt and the Kilkenny Hounds and of whom it was said that 'with few exceptions he was the best gentleman huntsman of either his day or before it.'[97] When John Joseph Preston died in 1892 he controversially willed his entire estate to Gustavus including the Bellinter Harriers; this part of the bequest carried the rider that the pack name be changed and they duly became the Tara Harriers.[98]

When Gustavus Briscoe inherited the lands of Bellinter they included lands stretching from Dunshaughlin to Ardbraccan. The townlands that formed most of the estate were Ardsallagh, Old and New Balreask, Cannistown, Castletown Tara, Kilmessan, Furryhill, Hanlonstown, Knockumber, Mountwhistle, Mullaghmore, Philpotstown, Retain, Ringletown, Tullykane, Balgeeth, Mooretown, Bonfield, Balsoon, Gainstown and Drimlough.[99]

Josephine Kennedy, a niece of John Joseph Preston contested his will, which was made on four occasions, the last being the day before his death, and was successful to a degree. She was awarded an annuity of £400 in 1895.

Gustavus married Amy Smith and they had two sons and four daughters. The eldest daughter, Eileen who was born in 1883 married E.W.Hope Johnstone of Rock Lodge, Laracor.[100] The third daughter, Gladys married twice. Her first husband was a Massy from Wicklow and they had a son and a daughter. Mr. Massy died young and then Gladys married Cecil Brabazon from Westmeath. Eileen and Cecil had a son Aubrey, a famous jockey, and a daughter Lelia. Muriel the fourth daughter married Hugh Malcomson from Portlaw in Waterford and they had a son and two daughters. Hugh was killed in action in World War I and later

---

[97] 'The Late Henry W. Briscoe, Esq., D.L., M.F.H.' (c.1895) from an unidentified publication received by Kevin Mulligan from Mr. George Briscoe.

[98] J.J.Preston had apparently made four wills; the final one in which everything was left to his friend was made just the day before his death. A niece contested part of the will and was eventually granted an annuity of £400 in 1895. Noel French, *Bellinter House*, 1993, pp. 13-4; Slevin, op.cit., p.144.

[99] *Bellinter* by Noel French

[100] His family lived at Raehills, a magnificent property in Dumfrieshire. His son Percy succeeded in getting the family title back and he is now the present Lord Annandale. Eileen died giving birth to Percy. – George Briscoe.

Muriel married Major Bert Scott, who for many years was the Irish Racing Starter. Muriel and the Major had one son.

John Joseph Preston Briscoe was the elder of the two sons and he died in 1913 at a comparatively young age, and unmarried. Because of his ill health it was his brother Cecil Henry who succeeded to the Bellinter estate in 1908 following the death of Gustavus.

Gussie Briscoe unwittingly found himself at the centre of a national controversy in 1902 when he and his tenants facilitated a team of treasure hunters associated with the British Israelites who wished to excavate the Hill of Tara, ostensibly to find the tomb of Princess Tea Tephi and ultimately the Ark of Covenant. The event was summarised some years later by Padraic Colum which appears to make Briscoe the villain of the piece: 'A man who had some property rights on the Hill of Tara let his land to the British-Israelite Association. That curious association was about to begin digging operations [in search of the Ark of the Covenant]. In Ireland at the time there was no public body that could take action to prevent such vandalism. A few writers determined that they would challenge the right of any man to deal destructively with an ancient monument: W.B. Yeats, George Moore, Douglas Hyde and Arthur Griffith, went up to Tara. The owner of the land...sat on a ditch, grim and glowering, a gun across his knees, and challenged any of the gentlemen from Dublin to walk across his field. He would shoot the first one who would set foot on his property. Arthur Griffith stepped out and walked across the field. Not a shot was fired.[101]'

In reality Gussie seemed more concerned with the protection of his property rights in a period when landlords generally were having their rights questioned, and through legislation, increasingly undermined. He had been misled by the Board of Works and later received an apology; the lack of seriousness with which he treated the efforts of the British-Israelites[102] and his attitude to their efforts was characteristic –he appreciated the entertainment value and he repeatedly buried objects, such as boxes and coins, to observe their reactions.

It fell to the lot of Gustavus to preside over the dissolution of most of the estate. In 1903, following the Wyndham Land Act, the tenants were

---

[101] Padraig Colum, *The Road Around Ireland*. 1930.

[102] It was apparently stated in the Bible that anyone who touched the Ark of the Covenant would drop dead.

given the right to buy out their leases. The Briscoes retained the demesne which was substantial, consisting of almost 1000 acres. Gustavus's record as a landlord was exemplary. He was reported to have said on many occasions that 'no tenant should ever be evicted'.[103]

Economics and the Land Commission finally caught up with Bellinter demesne itself by the end of the 1920's. Then owned by Gustavus's younger son, Cecil Henry, most of the estate lands of Bellinter had already been sold to tenants, including the Hill of Tara, under the terms of the Wyndham Act. When Cecil Henry reached the age of 21, in 1907, he had inherited lands and houses from the Briscoes of Tipperary[104]. These included Tinevane, a house in Fairview in Dublin and the ground occupied by the police station in Dalkey.[105] During World War 1 Cecil Henry leased Bellinter and only returned when the War was over. He and his wife, Phyllis Heard, moved into a smaller house on the estate when they returned, as the cost of the upkeep was becoming a burden.

Cecil Henry and Phyllis had one son George and two daughters Constance and Stella. Constance was first married to Major Peter Moor and they had one son Michael. Her second husband was Major Morrogh-Ryan and they had a daughter Nicola who is married to John Maxwell. Stella married Lancelot Smith[106] from Donabate and they have one son and one daughter.

During the Civil War in Ireland, many large houses were burnt for various reasons; some out of vindictiveness and begrudery and others to prevent their being used as fortified places by the opposition. Bellinter was marked out as a target but the tenants and the local people intervened and saved the property. It was reported that the tenants pointed out the excellent record of Gustavus Briscoe as far as his tenants were concerned. Henry Cecil, however, took no chances and moved out as much of his valuables and furniture as was possible and maintained an overnight vigil in the house.

---

[103] *Bellinter* by Noel French

[104] George Briscoe states that he was always led to believe that Gustavus inherited the ground rents of the town of Carrick-on-Suir.

[105] Ibid.

[106] Lancelot Smith was very well known in the hunting world having been Master of the Fingal Harriers, East Galway Foxhounds, Galway Blazers, Island and finally the Meath Hunt. – George Briscoe.

The Meath Hunt Ball in Bellinter House in 1937

Seated: Captain Fowler M.F.H., Mrs. Connell M.F.H., Mrs Winter, The Countess of Fingall, Lady Dunsany. Standing: Captain Winter, Mr.& Mrs. Briscoe and Captain E. Fanshawe. (Courtesy George Briscoe)

In 1924 he considered selling the house and demesne, writing in August to Dublin based estate agents: 'As I hear there are some people looking for places round here I think it would be as well to have this place on Dockrell's list for sale.'[107] However, the estate was given a short reprieve when in 1931 Cecil Henry came into an inheritance and spent a considerable amount renovating Bellinter. Prior to this time the house was lit by oil lamps but as part of the renovations Cecil Henry installed a lighting and heating system that was highly efficient.[108] This was accomplished by the use of a huge diesel engine which charged a huge number of batteries every month. The batteries were able to keep the

---

[107] Cecil Henry Briscoe to Thomas Dockrell and Sons, August 1924, National Archives?

[108] This system was just as efficient as the power from the E.S.B. with one difference – this system operated on 110 volts as compared to the ESB's 220 volts. – George Briscoe.

house lit until they 'ran down'. He also installed running water by pumping a supply from the Boyne to a huge tank in an attic room which provided water for the bathrooms upstairs and downstairs and for the kitchen.[109]

Cecil & Phyllis Briscoe 1947
(Courtesy George Briscoe)

The passage of time did nothing to help the inevitable decline of the building and the maintenance of the house was becoming very

---

[109] George Briscoe.

burdensome. The roof was leaking and on one occasion Cecil Henry's son George and the butler had to clear off snow from the roof in the middle of the night, as the channels that took the water from the roof were blocked resulting in internal flooding from melting snow. On another occasion a local farmer pointed out to George that a large section of the back roof had been blown off in a storm in the previous days. The family hadn't noticed.

George Briscoe & Lancelot H. Smith
Tara Harriers Opening Meet at Bellinter 1950
(Courtesy George Briscoe)

George tried to farm the demesne lands by going into the dairy business, in the 1950s but when a Mr. Holdsworth made a very substantial offer for the house and lands in 1955 it was too good to refuse. The Holdsworth family lived in the house for a time and they too farmed the land, but later sold the land to the Land Commission. The Land Commission divided up the land which was sold to local farmers.

61

George Briscoe and his wife Louisa were invited to take over a wing of Bective House following the sale to the Holdworths, while Cecil Henry and his wife continued on in their house on the Bellinter property. The owner of Bective, Mr. Bird, invited George to bring his famous Tara Harriers (a pack of hounds) with him. Mr. Bird was Master of the Meath Hunt for a number of years in the mid 1950s and George Briscoe was the Master of the Tara Harriers. George's first cousin, George Malcolmson was Master of the Ward Union Hunt during the same period. Much of George's time was spent organising the hectic hunting schedules and social diary that went with it. George has had a remarkable record in hunting. He was Master of the Tara Harriers for 62 seasons, hunted hounds for 50 and was Chairman of the Meaths Foxhounds for 17. Although he no longer rides to hounds he seldom misses a hunt.[110]

George with his sisters Constance (on left) and Stella in 2001

---

[110] *The Irish Field* March 6 2004

Cecil Henry died in 1963 and his wife died three years later. They were buried in Kilmessan. George and his wife Louise built a house at Assey and later moved to a property in Craystown where they now live.

George and Louise were married in 1947 and they have one daughter, Lorraine, who is married to John McDowell (of The Happy Ring House under the Clock in O'Connell Street, Dublin). Lorraine and John have two daughters. Louise died in 2001 and George married again. His second wife is Jean Wilson the widow of James Wilson of Boltown House, Kells. Jean is a member of the well-known Craigie family.

Writing about Bellinter, one commentator stated that 'it is miraculous that the house has survived -especially as country houses bought by the Land Commission after 1923 tended to be demolished.[111]' That it has is due to its rescue in 1966 by the Sisters of Sion who, until its sale in 2003, had operated a conference and retreat centre at Bellinter. It is now proposed that it shall become a 'boutique' hotel.

---

[111] Mary Cecelia Lyons, *Illustrated Encumbered Estates: Ireland, 1850-1905*, 1993, p.XXII.

Conyngham of Slane
(Marquesses Conyngham)

Few Irish towns have quite such a beautiful lead in as the estate village of Slane, now one of the most "driven-thru" towns on the main Dublin – Navan Road. As you round the corner from the Dublin Road, Slane rises up in front of you on the opposite banks of the River Boyne. It is said that the road from Dublin to Slane was built for the visit of King George IV to Slane in the early 1820s.

Because of the huge 'rock' concerts Slane has become a household word in Ireland and further afield as has the name of Lord Henry Mount Charles, the eldest son of the present Conyngham owner of the Castle and estate the 7th Marquess Conyngham.

David Bowie in 1987, U2 in 2001, and Madonna in 2004 are just a sample of the superstars that have appeared at the venue. Huge crowds of young and not so young have descended on the otherwise quiet village to listen to and view their idols.

The centre of Slane features four handsome identikit granite houses which stand opposite one another and bear testament to the occasion when King George IV visited the Conynghams.

William Burton Conyngham, who lived in the 18th century, was perhaps the outstanding member of the family in times past. Co. Meath and Ireland are indebted to him because his interest in recording the antiquities of the county Meath led to his employing the best antiquarian draughtsmen of the time including Gabriel Beranger, Angelo Bigari, Austin Cooper and John Barralet to record the condition of the antiquities. These records were later used by people such as O'Donovan and Archdall.[112]

Slane Castle
Photograph of engraving by George Petrie in *Excursions through Ireland* 1820 (Courtesy IAA).

William was one of the founder members of the Royal Irish Academy of which he was a Vice President and treasurer. He travelled extensively and had a keen interest in the antiquities of Portugal and Spain. Arising from this he sent James Murphy, a promising young architect from Cork, to Portugal to continue the work and paid all his expenses. Murphy stayed in Portugal for many years and was quite successful. He wrote a book about Portuguese antiquities in which he acknowledged William Burton as his patron. Another young man who benefited from the patronage of the great man was Gilbert Stuart an American artist and portrait painter who did two identical portraits of

---

[112] C.E.Trench in *Riocht na Midhe* 1987

William Burton, one of which is in Slane Castle and the other in the National Gallery.[113]

In Donegal William was responsible for the building of roads and a town called Rutland on an island now known as Rutland Island (Inis Mhic an Duirn). It was served by a ferry from a jetty built by him in the Rosses and now known as Burtonport. The road from Mount Charles to Glenties and on to Burton's Port cost in the region of £50,000 to build and William paid almost £30,000 of this out of his own resources. He also built a huge grain store there. The grain was given to him by the tenants in lieu of rent.[114] About the same time a 'hostelry' was built there which is now Burtonport House.[115] While William was careful with his Donegal estate he did not neglect Slane as we can see from the comments of Arthur Young who toured Ireland in the late 1770s.

> 'Taking the road to Slane the country was very pleasant all the way; much of it on the banks of the Boyne, variegated with some woods, planted hedge-rows and gentle hills: the cabins continue much the same, the same plenty of poultry, pigs and cows. I had the pleasure of meeting Colonel Burton at the Castle, in whom I was so fortunate as to find, on repeated occasions, the utmost assiduity to procure me every species of information, entering into the spirit of my design with the most liberal ideas. Every farmer has a little flax, from a rood to an acre and all the cottages a spot, if they have any land, they go through the whole process themselves and spin and weave it. From hence to Drogheda there is a considerable manufacture of course cloth, which is exported to Liverpool, about 1s. a yard. At Navan there is a fabrick of sacking for home consumption; the weavers earn 1s. a day at these works.'

William was particularly concerned to improve the entrance to Dublin city from the west and contributed to the cost of the road building. In 1772 he was a member of the newly appointed Dublin's Wide Streets Commission and was one of its most active members up to the time of his

---

[113] Ibid.
[114] Padraig Ua Cnaimhsi, in the *Rosses Annual* 1995
[115] Ibid.

death. The new road from Island Bridge to Park Gate was named Conyngham Road in recognition of all that he had done for the city.

At a time when many landlords were lavishing their money on self aggrandisement, William, with his farsightedness and generosity of spirit employed his wealth and gave of his time mainly for the benefit of his countrymen. His contribution to the development of modern Ireland should not be forgotten.

Slane Castle after the fire in 1991
(Courtesy IAA)

The Castle was built by William. It was begun in the1780s under the direction of James Wyatt and also to the design of Francis Johnston who was responsible for the Gothic entrance gates and the great entrance hall.[116] The Castle itself is a huge pile and is a very early Gothic Revival castle, this type of architecture being in vogue at the time with the aristocracy. The ballroom was designed by Thomas Hopper a favourite at the court of King George IV.

---

[116] James Wyatt was of course involved in all these designs also.

In 1991 there was a serious fire at the castle and extensive damage resulted. The east wing was almost totally destroyed. Lord Henry Mount Charles applied for state funding at the time to assist in the restoration of this priceless part of Irish Heritage but to no avail. With the determination that characterises his fundraising activities Lord Henry succeeded in restoring the castle from his private finances. In the course of restoration many hidden defects were discovered and these too were put to rights.

Slane Castle from a painting
(Courtesy IAA)

The first member of this family to come to Ireland was Alexander Conyngham, a Scots Protestant minister who took up an appointment in Co. Donegal, in the parishes of Enver and Killynard in 1611. He was probably prompted to go to Ireland by John Murray, the Earl of Annandale, a substantial Scots landowner who owned large properties in the Raphoe area of Donegal.[117] When his superior, Dean Adair, was consecrated the Bishop of Killaloe in 1630, Alexander was chosen to fill that man's post as Dean of Adair. In the intervening period between 1611

___

[117] These were granted to him after the Flight of the Earls during the Plantation of Ulster.

and 1630 he got a lease of the property known as Mount Charles. Alexander's wife was Marian, a daughter of George Murray of Broughton and a grand niece of the Earl of Annandale.[118] They had a huge brood of children totalling twenty seven in all, but of these only four sons and five daughters survived into adulthood. Dean Alexander died in 1660. His eldest son, Albert, was appointed lieutenant general of the ordnance in Ireland the same year his father died and was granted a knighthood for his services. He was married to Margaret Leslie the daughter of the Bishop of Meath and they had an only son Henry.

Sir Albert was Muster Master General during the Williamite Wars[119] and fought at the Battle of the Boyne (1690 A.D.) and at Limerick, during the siege there. He was killed shortly afterwards by remnants of the Jacobite rebels at Coloney, near Sligo. His son Henry was also in the service of King William during the conflict.

It is in connection with the sales of the forfeited estates in 1703 that the name of Conyngham first appears with reference to Slane, formerly in the possession of the old Fleming family[120]. Like most of the purchasers of these estates, the Conynghams as we have seen were already established in Ireland before the time of the Cromwellian confiscations and before the forfeitures of 1688.

Sir Albert's son, Henry, was the first of the family to acquire property in Meath, namely in the baronies of Slane, Upper and Lower.

---

[118] Lodge

[119] *A New Anatomy of Ireland* – Toby Barnard.

[120] The Flemings came to Ireland with the Normans, as the name implies. They remained steadfastly Anglo Irish and one of the chief supporters of the English government in the Pale, until 1641 when the time came to choose between supporting their fellow Catholics in the confederacy and siding with the Puritans under Cromwell. Lord Slane died in the same year and his title passed to his son Charles who was also party to the rebellion. Charles was exempted from pardon by the victorious Cromwellians and went abroad to fight in the service of King Louis XIV. He was killed in Italy in 1661. His brother Randal inherited and was restored to the estates in 1663 by King Charles II. Randal's son, Christopher supported King James II and fought at the Battle of the Boyne. After that war he fled to France and the estates were confiscated once more. Christopher (d. 1726) managed to have his titles reinstated in 1708 but not his lands. He had no son. When his daughter died unmarried that seemed to end the Fleming connection with Slane.

Henry was born about 1670 and he married an heiress, Mary, the daughter of Sir John Williams of Minster Court, Kent in 1796. He was a career Army officer and had attained the rank of Brigadier by the time of his marriage. He, too, had seen active service during the Williamite War. It is significant too, that his sister, Katherine, married the up and coming young lawyer, William Connolly, later of Castletown, a commissioner over the Revenue Board while his other sister married James Bonnell the Accountant General and secretary to the commissioners overseeing the latest confiscation of rebels' estates.[121] In addition Henry was the agent for the Annandale estate in Donegal. In this capacity he was noted as a champion of the impoverished tenants on the Donegal estate, when he 'lectured the Murrays of Broughton about policy (towards the tenants)'.[122]

Brigadier Henry and Mary had at least two sons and one daughter, Mary, who married Francis Burton, a substantial landowner from Co. Clare. The two sons were William and Henry.

On 10th April 1703 Brigadier Henry Conyngham purchased 806 profitable acres in the townlands of Rochestown (220 acres) Roestown (128 acres, with the tucking mill and the corn mill thereon) Stackallan (198 acres), Abelstown (113 acres), Barnwelltown (40 acres), Corballis (107 acres) and all other lands in the tenure of John Blackley as tenant to the trustees.[123] For these 806 acres Conyngham paid £1766 and a rent of £160. This lot came out of the estate of James II, the previous proprietors having been Richard Fleming, James Fleming, Robert Barnewall and Richard Barnewall.[124]

Less than a week later the Brigadier bought a further 1,422 acres which included the village and Castle of Slane. It is most likely that the

---

[121] *A New Anatomy of Ireland* – Toby Barnard.

[122] Ibid.

[123] General Ginkell was granted the entire Slane estates by the grateful King William of Orange, in addition to other lands, including over 1000 acres that formerly belonged to King James II in Co. Meath. He sold the lands to various purchasers prior to the year 1700. Following the Act of Resumption in 1700 the purchasers had to hand back the lands but received one third of what they had paid in compensation. The lands were sold at auction by the Government in 1703 and most of the buyers were in fact those who had already purchased from Ginkell.

[124] T.Trench The Flemings and Conynghams of Slane in *Riocht na Midhe* 1987

Castle was in very bad repair and it is almost definite that Mary never saw her husband's Meath property though work was commenced on the building of the Slane mansion shortly after the purchase of the lands.[125] The Brigadier pursued his career in the Army and rose to the rank of Major General. He was posted to Spain where he took part in the War of the Spanish Succession. One of his companions there was Dudley Cosby of Stradbally, Co. Laois. Both men blamed the vindictiveness of the Duke of Ormonde for their despatch to Spain.[126] Despite the inconvenience of having to campaign abroad, Henry travelled in style and brought with him, during the campaign, 'a heavy weight of silver consecrated to conviviality'.[127] Henry was killed at St. Estevans in Spain in 1706. His widow married again but died in 1710 leaving a young family. The two boys and their sister were probably reared in her family home at Minster Court in Kent.

The eldest son, William, was either delicate or in some way incapacitated as he never make any significant mark in life.[128] His brother, Henry, on the other hand was spectacularly successful. He succeeded in 1738.

Born about 1700 Henry was an M.P. at the age of twenty five and was a career Army Officer who rose to the rank of Colonel. He continued in Parliament until 1753 when he was created a peer as Baron Conyngham of Mount Charles, Co. Donegal. He was a man who was eager for advancement and when denied the Mastership of the Ordnance he applied for the position of Alnager.[129] His importunity also led to his being given the Viscountcy in 1756.[130] In 1781 further honours were bestowed on him when he was created an Earl. Henry married an heiress in 1744 but they had no family. He was a noted internationally accredited antiquarian.[131] The couples childless state was very much to the benefit of Henry's nephews, Francis Pierpoint Burton, from Co. Clare, and his brother

---

125 *A New Anatomy of Ireland* – Toby Barnard.
126 *A New Anatomy of Ireland* – Toby Barnard.
127 Ibid.
128 He was described as 'a wastrel heir' by Toby Barnard.
129 An Alnager was a paid official who had responsibility for the quality of cloth imported into the country.
130 *A New Anatomy of Ireland* – Toby Barnard.
131 C.E.Trench in *Riocht na Midhe* 1987

William both of whom inherited the possessions (the title of Baron Conyngham going to Francis) when Henry died in 1781 shortly after his latest receipt of honours. The Baron in his will divided the estates giving his nephew Francis the estates in Clare and Limerick and England and the title while his nephew William got the Donegal and Slane estates. When William died in 1796, a confirmed bachelor, the estates were reunited again when they were inherited by Francis Pierpoint's son Henry.

Young Henry, now the 3rd Baron Conyngham (1766-1832), had a portfolio of estates including Slane, Minster Court, Donegal, Limerick and Clare. By the middle of the next century these estates, which had been added to in the intervening period by successive Barons were by any standards huge. John Bateman, in his book, *Great Landowners of Great Britain and Ireland* gave the estate acreages as follows: - Meath 7060, Kent 9737, Donegal 122,300 and Limerick and Clare 27613. This amounted to a staggering 166,710 acres. The rent roll from this land must have been colossal.

Of the two nephews of the 2nd Baron, Francis and William, the latter was the much more interesting. While Francis travelled on his 'grand tour' taking in Turkey, Egypt, Greece and Italy it is not known whether William did a similar tour. William has already been alluded to but his stature was such that further information about this remarkable man is warranted.

William was commissioned in the Army as a captain at the age of twenty six. He was promoted to the rank of Colonel four years later in the 12th Dragoons. He resigned from the army in 1775 and took up the post of Comptroller and Commissioner of the Barrack Board. While his uncle the 1st Baron was still alive and living mainly in Paris, William looked after Slane. He spent some of his time living in Dublin at a few addresses – Sackville Street, Lower Merrion Street and finally Harcourt Place.[132]

He had entrepreneurial flare and in 1763 he set up the largest flour mill in the then British Isles, at Slane, in partnership with a man called Townley Balfour of Townley Hall. He was involved in setting up the Boyne Navigation and in setting up a cotton factory in Slane headed up by a Robert Colello.[133]

---

[132] C.E.Trench in *Riocht na Midhe* 1987
[133] Ibid.

After his uncle's death he took the name Conyngham in addition to Burton. He set his plans for the restoration and modernisation of the Castle in motion and consulted James Wyatt and James Gandon the famous architects of their time. Gandon who designed the Custom House was introduced to William Burton and noted that he 'had very large possessions in different parts of Ireland and had a princely residence at Slane and he was also a great patron of the Fine Arts'. Burton seems to have had some falling out with Gandon and thoroughly disapproved of Gandon's design for the Four Courts. Wyatt was the architect who looked after the alterations at Slane.[134]

The interior of the castle was completed by Francis Johnston for William's nephew - who inherited William's lands in 1796 and became the 1st Marquess Conyngham - and his wife Elizabeth, who became the last favourite of George IV - though in her fifties at the time. Elizabeth was once described unkindly by Princess Lieven[135] as 'having not an idea in her head, not a word to say for herself: nothing but a hand to accept pearls and diamonds with and an enormous balcony to wear them on'.[136]

The 1st Marquess (1766-1832) was the eldest son of Francis Pierpoint the 2nd Baron and nephew of the remarkable William. His mother was Elizabeth the daughter of the Rt. Hon. Nathaniel Clements. He had a twin brother, Francis Nathaniel and three sisters two of whom married.[137] Francis Nathaniel, a Colonel in the Clare Militia, married Valentia the daughter of Lord Cloncurry and set up home in Carrigaholt Castle. They had one son, Henry who in turn had three boys, two of whom appear to have been Army officers, J.P.s and Sheriffs in Co. Clare at various times. None of them had any families and Francis Nathaniel's descendants died out in the male line. One of his granddaughters, Lucy Ann, who was married to Captain Ormsby Rose, had a family.

Henry, the 1st Marquess had numerous honours bestowed on him. An Army officer, he was created Viscount Mount Charles and Earl

---

[134] Ibid.

[135] Princess Lieven was the wife of the Russian ambassador to London. When her husband was recalled she decided to stay in Paris and had a famous salon. She was on very friendly terms with some of the most powerful men of her time, Wellington, Metternich and Guizot.

[136] *The Hidden Houses of Ireland* by Marianne Heron

[137] Catherine married Rev. J.S. Fermor and Ellena's husband was Stewart Weldon.

Conyngham in 1797 and Viscount Slane, Earl of Mount Charles and Marquess Conyngham in 1816. He was also made a peer in England with the title of Baron Minster of Minster Abbey, Kent. In 1801 he was made a Knight of the Order of St. Patrick[138]. His wife was Elizabeth Dennison and they had three sons and two daughters. Both ladies married and the younger of the two Harriet Maria had an only daughter who became the Countess of Charlemont and died in 1882.

In the years leading up to the 1798 rebellion Yeomanry Corps were formed in many areas of Co. Meath with a view to protecting their lands from the very real threat of French invasion. Landowners, with the permission of the authorities were encouraged to form and arm their own Corps. In the Slane area Captain Viscount Conyngham was in command of the Corps drawn largely from amongst his own tenants. While the French invasions fizzled out in storms off the south-west coast of Ireland the new threat of a mass insurrection by the United Irishmen jangled the nerves of every law abiding citizen in the country. The Yeomanry Corps in Meath were put on red alert. In the event the insurrection in Meath proved to be half-hearted, brief and easily quenchable as the rebels found to their cost on the Hill of Tara. The rebels were defeated by a force of regular troops augmented by local Yeomanry Corps. This combined group was commanded by the Catholic Lord Fingall and most of the troops and Yeomen were of the same persuasion.

The 1st Marquess was very much involved in making improvements to his estates and at Slane he built houses. In 1818 he had over 70,000 trees planted on his Fennor lands.[139]

The successor to the 1st Marquess, who died in 1832, was his second son Francis Nathaniel (1797-1876), the 2nd Marquess Conyngham, an able man who rose to the rank of General in the Army. He was also Lord Lieutenant of Co. Meath and a vice admiral of Ulster. He was Postmaster General in England for two years, 1834 and 1835. He filled the office of

---

[138] The Order of St. Patrick was instituted by King George III in 1783, for the purpose of establishing in Ireland a fraternity of knights as a counterpart to the Order of the Garter in England and the Order of the Thistle in Scotland.
[139] Eileen McCracken – Tree planting in Co. Meath – in *Riocht na Midhe* 1988

Lord Chamberlain[140] from 1835-1839. His wife was Lady Jane Paget the daughter of the 1st Marquess of Anglesey.

They had a number of children, two sons and four daughters. The eldest of the sons was George Henry, who succeeded as the 3rd Marquess Conyngham in 1876. The younger son, Francis Nathaniel, was a Navy officer and an M.P. for Clare. Although married he had no family. The fours daughters all married very well. The eldest, Jane, who was a lady of the bedchamber to Queen Victoria, married the 2nd Lord Churchill[141]. Gustavus Lambart of Beau Parc, Co. Meath married Francis.[142] Elizabeth the 3rd daughter's husband was George Leopold Bryan of Jenkinstown, Co. Kilkenny[143] and the youngest daughter, Cecilia, married Theodore Brinckman, the 2nd Baronet of Monk Bretton[144].

Lord Conyngham got a very bad press from a Mr. William Forster[145], a Quaker, who took it upon himself to tour Ireland in 1846 to see at first hand the effects of the famine on the poor. In Donegal he spoke of 'the miserable and neglected tenantry of the Marquis of Conyngham, an absentee proprietor who holds an immense tract of land here'[146]

Perhaps because of the stinging report the 2nd Marquess took active measures to help alleviate the hardships of the poor. In Donegal he made the grain store in Burtonport available to the authorities as a food store and his agent there Robert Russell, who had his residence at nearby Lackbeg House, was probably most instrumental in setting up a soup-kitchen in the village. 'As the soup-kitchen was but a stone's throw away from Lackbeg House, we can assume that Robert Russell and his bailiffs

---

[140] The Lord Chamberlain was the chief functionary of the court, and was responsible for organizing all court functions. Until recently, the Lord Chamberlain also had the role of licenser of plays in the city of London, Westminster and certain other areas.

[141] Lord Churchill's elder brother was the ancestor of the famous Sir Winston Churchill, the P.M. of England during the mid 20th century.

[142] When the last of that family died out in the late 20th century Beau Parc reverted to Lord Henry Mount Charles.

[143] For information on that family see *The Landed Gentry & Aristocracy of Kilkenny* by Art Kavanagh.

[144] Burke's Peerage & Baronetage

[145] He was the father of the infamous 'Buckshot Forster' Irish Chief Secretary in the later decades of the century.

[146] *The Great Hunger* by Cecil Woodham Smith

would have taken an active part in the preparation and distribution of the food'.[147]

The second Marquess died in 1876 and was succeeded by his eldest son, George Henry the 3rd Marquess Conyngham (1825-1882). George was a career Army officer and attained the rank of Lieutenant General. He was also Lieutenant Colonel of the Royal East Kent Yeomanry. As an equerry to Queen Victoria he spent a period in London. He was married to Lady Jane Stanhope, the daughter and heir of the 4th Earl of Harrington. They had two sons and five daughters, four of whom married, putting a slight dint in the family chest. Interestingly two of the daughters, Constance and Jane married brothers named Combe from Surrey.

George Henry was fifty one years old when he succeeded to the Conyngham fortunes and only lived another six years to enjoy them. His eldest son, Henry Francis had to cut short his Army career when he became the 4th Marquess Conyngham at the age of twenty five. Henry Francis had one brother Charles Arthur who, although married twice, had no children.

The 4th Marquess (1857-1897), a Vice Admiral of Ulster and a Lieutenant in the Scots Guards had the unenviable task of dismantling the Irish part of the Conyngham empire, because of the Land Acts of the last two decades of the 19th century. His wife was Frances de Molyens, the daughter of the 4th Lord Ventry, who rejoiced in the Christian name of Dayrolles. They had two sons Victor and Frederick and five daughters.[148] The elder of the two sons, Victor George Henry (1883- 1918), an Army officer, became the 5th Marquess in 1897 after the death of his father.

Frederick (1890-1974), an Army Officer, became the 6th Marquess after his brother's death in 1918. He was married three times. His first wife was Bessie Tobin and they had no family. He divorced Bessie after a marriage that lasted seven years. He married his second wife, Antoinette Custance of Somerset in 1922 and that marriage lasted until her death in 1966. Frederick then married a widow, Stella Thompson. Frederick and

---

[147] Padraig Ua Cnaimhsi, in the *Rosses Annual* 1995

[148] Three of the daughters married. The eldest, Blanche, married a descendant of the 1st Marquess of Hertford. He was Edward Seymour, an Army Officer who served in North and South Africa (Boer War). The 3rd daughter, Hersey, married William a son of Sir David Baird while her younger sister, Edena married Thomas Ainsworth. All three ladies had families and their descendants are living today.

Antoinette his second wife had two sons, Frederick William Henry, the 7th Marquess and John Victor (died without having had a family in 1963).

The 7th Marquess, an Eton old boy, became an officer in the Army rising to the rank of Captain before retiring to look after the family properties. He has been married on four occasions. His first wife was Eileen Newsam from Beau Parc Co. Meath and they have three sons, Henry Vivian, Simon Charles and Patrick. He divorced his wife in 1970 and the following year he married Elizabeth Hughes from Hantshire. His third wife was Daphne Armour who passed away in 1986. Some time later his Lordship married Lady Annabelle Agnew from Bournemouth.[149]

His eldest son and heir, Henry Vivian, the Earl of Mount Charles, born in 1951, was educated at Harrow and Harvard. In 1971 Henry Vivian married Juliet Kitson from Cornwall and they have a son Alexander and a daughter Henrietta. Henry Vivian and Juliet were divorced in 1985 and afterward he married his second wife Lady Iona Grimston.

Simon Charles a Harrovian, now living in Scotland, was married to Emma Breeze and they have a daughter Chloe. Following his divorce Simon married a Co. Meath lady, Carole le Poer Power from Beau Parc. They have a daughter Frances.

Patrick's wife is Siobhan Ramos. They live in Co. Louth.

---

[149] Burkes Peerage & Baronetage

Corballis of Ratoath Manor

The Corballis family was remarkable for a number of different reasons: they were substantial Catholic landowners prior to the period of the Williamite Wars; their entire property was forfeited after the defeat of the Jacobites and during the period of the worst of the Penal Laws; within a century they had managed to claw their way back financially and socially, while still retaining the religion of their forefathers.

The ancestor of the Corballis family appears to have been a Thomas Corbally from Dunshaughlin who married Ann Woodtown of Nuttstown in 1571.[150] It would seem that his wife brought a dowry of several farms of land in Jordanstown, Nuttstown and Palmerstown. These farms were given to three sons Simon[151], Robert and Philip.

In 1690 Robert Corballis of Nuttstown, a Catholic, sided with King James II and fought at the Battle of the Boyne and was present at the capture of Trim. He was executed in 1694. He had two children who were made wards of the Preston family of Gormanston.

---

[150] Fiants of Edward VI   1550 John de la Hyde got a grant of lands in the Dunshauglin area some of which were occupied by Thomas Corbally.

[151] Simon's descendants became Protestant and prospered. They bought Rathbeale House in Swords and were instrumental in founding the committee that started the Fairyhouse Races. Members of this family married into such families as the Nettervilles, Gormanstons and that of Lord Mowbaly – Danny Parkinson in *The Corballis Family of Nuttstown*

John Corballis of York Street and New Street in Dublin appears to have been the son of a Robert Corballis who had lands in Saggart. According to researches carried out by a family member, Dom Placid, a Benedictine monk, the Saggart estate consisted of lands in Saggart, Tussagard, Saggart Village, Johnville, Kingswood, Jobstown, Crooksling and Rathcoole. Under the Penal Laws the family lost their Saggart lands. The Corballis lands were granted to various government grantees including the Berwicks and Robertsons.[152]

John's wife was Jane McManus. They had a number of children, the oldest of whom, John (1735-1805), married Elizabeth Mooney.[153] John junior seems to have been well educated and his son Richard attested to this. John senior was actively involved in promoting the education of Catholic children and in his will he made bequests to more than ten schools and churches.

John Corballis, his son John and his grandsons were timber importers. They were the first Catholic timber importers in Dublin.[154] Their growing wealth meant they could acquire properties and Richard, one of John's heirs, obtained the lease of Rosemount in Clonskeagh in 1780 while James his younger brother got that of Roebuck House nearby in 1787.[155] The two sons Richard and James Anthony were well educated and moved in high social circles. The family has a firearms certificate issued to Richard Corballis in 1803 permitting him to be the owner of 'a blunderbuss, one fowling piece and four pistols'.

Richard was given control of the family business some time before his father died. John who died in 1805 had been in bad health for a period. After his death the assets were divided evenly between the two sons

[152] There is no reference to a Corballis (except a village of the name in Dublin) in either the Meath or Dublin Books of the Down Survey. It is possible that the Corballis mentioned by Dom Placid may have been a tenant of some of the large landholders in the area but I have been unable to find any reference to the family during that period. – A.K.

[153] Another son, James, was the father of Ann Corballis who helped Ann Mullaly found George's Hill Presentation convent. Ann lived in the convent and is buried under the altar in the convent chapel.

[154] Danny Parkinson *The Corballis Family of Nuttstown*

[155] The lands in the area were owned by Lord Trimlestown, a Catholic – Corballis notes

Richard and James Anthony (1770-1842) and his four daughters were provided for in John's will. James Anthony, the second son of John Corballis (d.1805) was living in Roebuck House until he bought Ratoath Manor and part of Dunboyne in 1813. He was already married at the time and had a young family. His wife was Anne Kenny, whose father owned properties in counties Meath and Dublin. James and Anne were married some time prior to 1802 and their children were reared in Roebuck House until they moved to Ratoath, in 1813. They had two sons and two daughters. One of the sons and one of the daughters died unmarried. The other daughter married a Knaresborough from Co. Kilkenny and the eldest son James Joseph succeeded his father in Ratoath when James Anthony died in 1842.

James Anthony Corballis of Ratoath Manor
(photo courtesy Corballis Family)

James Joseph (1802- 1840), who was educated at Clongowes settled into the life of a country squire and was made a J.P. His wife was Mary

Netterville Barron from Co. Waterford.[156] James Joseph and Mary had two sons, who survived and two daughters - Emily who died unmarried in 1927 and Elizabeth who died in infancy. The second son, William became a Captain in the 17th Foot and died at a comparatively young age in 1880.[157] About the year 1822 James and his wife commissioned the erection of the High Altar in St. Mary's Pro Cathedral in Dublin in memory of John Corballis and his wife Mary McManus. The sculptor was Sir Peter Turnerelli. Inscriptions were carved on the rear of the tabernacle and on the inside.[158]

The eldest son James Henry (1835-1903) married Constance Jerningham, an English lady of gentle birth in 1863.[159] They were married in Brussels where the Jerninghams were living and honeymooned in Paris. They returned to Ratoath where they were met in the usual fashion by the estate tenants who unharnessed the horses at Moulden Bridge and dragged the carriage to the hall door of the Manor House. James Henry moved out of Ireland in 1869 and lived in various residences in Scotland. These included Reelig House, Knockrobbie, Moniack Castle, Nairn and Inverness.

James Henry and Constance had five sons and five daughters. Two of the daughters became nuns in English nunneries[160] and three of them

---

[156] The Barrons are a very distinguished and ancient family whose primal ancestor was one of the Fitzgeralds of Leinster.

[157] William had property in Dublin and was in receipt of one quarter of the Dunboyne Estate rents during the life of Amelia Corballis, his aunt. He was a well known sportsman who was fond of hunting and fishing and was a great friend of Captain the Hon. Edward Preston of Gormanston. William died at Gormanston and was buried in the family vault in the Pro Cathedral- Seamus Corballis *Notes*

[158] The two Corballis vaults beneath the High Altar contain the remains of many family members.

[159] From Cossey Hall Norfolk. She was said to have been descended from William the Conqueror and to have had three martyrs numbered amongst her antecedents. They were Blessed Margaret Plantagenet the Countess of Salisbury, The Venerable Philip Howard (Earl of Arundel) and Venerable William Howard (Viscount Stafford). This marriage also meant the Corballis family were now connected to the 13th Viscount Gormanston who was married to Lucretia Jerningham.

[160] Emily, the second daughter had a very adventurous life, though a nun. She entered the order of St. Vincent de Paul and was sent to France to the hospital of St. Joseph. She was then sent to Monaco where she spent twelve years in the

married. All three married Englishmen and one, Laura, married Lt. General Sir Walter Leslie from Banffshire.

Cossey Hall (Norfolk)
(Photo courtesy Corballis Family)

All three ladies were married in the first decade of the 20th century and these weddings must have proved to be a financial drain[161] on the family finances as it was around this time that James Frederick, who succeeded to Ratoath in 1903, began his correspondence with his wealthy cousin Richard John, with a view to getting some help to overcome his problems. James Henry was very interested in sport and wrote a book

---

Prince of Monaco's hospital. When the war broke out in 1914 she took charge of the field hospital at Roubaix, France. She was captured by the Germans at Rastatt and sent to Cologne for interrogation as they thought she was a spy. She wrote to the Kaiser to complain and was promptly released. She returned to France where she resumed her work with the wounded. She was awarded the Croix de Guerre in 1917. In 1927 she was awarded the Cross of the Chevalier of the Legion of Honour. She died at Pau Hospital, where she was the Superior, in 1940.
[161] Nuns too had to be provided with a dowry when they entered an order at this time.

entitled *Forty Five Years of Sport*.[162] He died in 1903 and his wife died in 1914. Both are buried in Kensal Green, London.

James Henry's sons were James Frederick, Charles (Dom Placid O.S.B., mentioned above, a monk in Fort Augustus[163] died in 1949), Frederick Francis, Herbert Joseph and Myles who died unmarried in South Africa in 1901.[164] Frederick Francis, a devout Catholic, was honoured with the position of Privy Chamberlain to the Pope and was Chairman of the Belgian Refugee Committee in Newcastle in World War I. A partner in a firm of Stockbrokers (Messrs Wise Spoke & Co.) much of his life was spent in the service of others. He was appointed Chief Scout Commissioner of Roman Catholic Scouts by Sir Robert Baden Powell, the Chief Scout. His work with the St. Vincent de Paul led to his being elected President of the Westminster Central Council of the Society. He was awarded the Bene Merenti Medal in 1927 and died unmarried seven years later. The fourth son, Herbert Joseph emigrated to Canada and his children, two sons who died unmarried, and his two daughters resided there for their lives.[165]

James Frederick (1865 –1945), the eldest son, another great sportsman, was educated at St. Benedict's College, Fort Augustus and later at College de la Paix at Namur in Belgium. He pursued an Army Career and was a Captain in the Boer War. He served in two regiments – the Cameron Highlanders and the Royal Irish and later lectured on military matters. He worked for a time as assistant general manager of South African Breweries. His father died in 1903 and James Frederick and his family returned to Ireland the following year. The family lived for a time in Macmine Castle, in Co. Wexford where some of the children received

---

[162] Corballis *Notes* published 1891.

[163] Fort Augustus was a Benedictine Monastery near Lough Ness in Scotland. It opened as a boarding school in 1878 and closed in 1993. Dom Placid wrote a history of the Dominican Order – *Corballis Notes*

[164] Myles had secured a position with the King Williams Town Brewery in East London in South Africa. He had just arrived there in company with his friend Pierce Loftus of Mount Loftus Co. Kilkenny when he fell ill. His brother James Frederick rushed to his bedside but the young man died a short time later. He was a noted sportsman who loved shooting and fishing.

[165] The three ladies married and have children and grandchildren. Etheldreda's husband was Arthur Latham, Brigit was married to Ernest Petrie and Evelyn's spouse was A. Henshaw.

their education from the Benedictine Monks from Maredsous in Belgium who had settled at Edermine House for the duration of the war. James Frederick had to manage the downgrading of the estate following the Wyndham Acts. During World War I he acted as a recruiting Officer and later got employment for a couple of years in the Ministry of Labour.

James Frederick Corballis
(Courtesy Corballis Family)

James Frederick seriously considered selling up his Ratoath properties and emigrating to South Africa as he indicated in correspondence to his wealthy cousin Richard John in Dublin. However some solution was found to overcome his financial problems, when Richard John promised to leave him and his family substantial monies in his will.[166] The family moved back to Ratoath in 1919. Prior to all these

---

[166] Danny Parkinson in his book *The Corballis Family of Nuttstown*

irritating annoyances James Frederick found a wife and was married in 1889. His bride was Sybil Beadon from Somerset. They had five sons and three daughters. Two of the daughters found husbands in England and one died young. Barbara the eldest married Brigadier Sutton from Suffolk and they have descendants.[167] Patricia's husband was a surgeon, Patrick McKenna, whose family were from Dublin[168].

James Frederick's sons were James Cecil, Richard, Basil, Anthony and Philip. The three eldest sons who were all born in the 1890s were old enough to have to become army personnel during the First World War. The eldest son, James Cecil, an Oxford student, became a Captain in the 5th Battalion of the Leinster Regiment and came through the war unscathed. He became a lecturer at the National University of Ireland. Richard was not so lucky and he died in 1921 from the effects of wounds received in the war[169]. Basil came through World War I and continued his Army career rising to the rank of Lieutenant Colonel, in which capacity he served in World War II. He retired from the Army in 1946 and lived until 1966 when he died aged 70. He was awarded the Military Cross for his conspicuous gallantry on the first day of the Battle of the Somme – 1st July 1916.[170]

The two younger sons, Anthony and Philip, who were both just boys during the First World War, having completed their degrees, emigrated to New Zealand where, perhaps hankering after the forsaken Ratoath lands they became farmers, got married and had families.Anthony was married to Barbara Cameron whose family had acquired a farm called Marangai, near Wanganui. They had two sons, Myles[171] and Neil. Neil, now a retired farmer is married to Gillian Higgs and they have one son Antony and two daughters Catherine and Anna. Philip (Mike) married Betty Harris from New Zealand and they farmed near Marton. They have four sons. Michael, the eldest is an academic and an expert in particular fields of psychology. He married Barbara Wheeler from New Zealand and they have two sons Paul and Timothy both born in the late 1960s. Jonathan is a retired lawyer and lives near Brighton with his second wife Karen. By his first

---

[167] They had two sons and a daughter.
[168] Dr. Ryan late Archbishop of Dublin has a McKenna ancestor – *Corballis Notes*
[169] He served in France and Mesopotamia during the war and was severely wounded at Hill 60. He died in Penzance and is buried there. – *Corballis Notes*
[170] Ibid.
[171] Myles was killed tragically in an accident when he was just four years old.

marriage to Judith Mintoff they have a son Toby born in 1965. David, Jonathan's twin, now retired was the headmaster of Otago Boys High School. He married Patricia Stickney and they have one son Michael and one daughter Anna both born in the 1970s. Richard (Dick) is a former head of the English faculties at two New Zealand Universities, Canterbury University and Massey. He married Penny Dawson and they have three children all born in the 1970s – James (who died tragically as a young man), Patrick and Antonia.

James Cecil Corballis, known in the family as Tommy, benefited from his cousin's will and received a substantial part of the estate after Richard John's death in 1931[172]. A decision was made to move to Co. Wicklow where the family lived at Rossanagh. Ratoath Manor remained the property of Patricia McKenna, Tommy's sister. She sold the property in 1951 to the Augustinian nuns who converted the house into a nursing home.[173] James Cecil married Ada Flynn[174] from Dublin just after the end of World War I and they had two sons, James Jerningham and Richard and one daughter Jennifer. Jennifer's husband was Raymond O'Neill S.C. from Dublin and they have two sons Peter and Shane, both born in the late 1960s and early 70s.

Richard born in 1926 and educated at Glenstal Priory became a director in Hamilton & Hamilton. He married Barbara McGuire[175] from Dublin and they have three sons and one daughter, Alanna. The three sons, Simon, Basil and Philip all educated in Ireland, were born in the 1950s and 60s.

The eldest son, James Jerningham (1919-1986) of Gorteen, Delgany was educated at Ampleforth and Kings Inns Dublin. He was a Governor of the Rotunda and a member of the Executive Committee of Stewart's Hospital. His wife is Mary Emmet[176] and they have four children all born

---

[172] This man was Richard John Corballis of Rosemount. See later in this chapter for information about the Rosemount family.

[173] Ratoath Manor has been extended and modernised in recent times and continues as a nursing home.

[174] She was a cousin of the poet William Allingham.

[175] A daughter of Senator E.A. McGuire, former owner of Brown Thomas.

[176] Mary is a descendant of Thomas Addis Emmet, the brother of Robert Emmet who was executed in Dublin in 1803 after the rebellion of that year.

in the 1950s –Seamus, Timothy, Belinda and Sarah Jane. All are married and live in Ireland.

The Corballis family of Rosemount, Dublin, as we have seen descended from Richard Corballis ((1769-1847). Richard's wife was a Taylor from Nonsuch House in Castlepollard, Co. Westmeath. The Taylors were a well to do Catholic family and owned Castlepollard Castle and Frean's Castle near Athboy. Richard and Deborah Taylor were married in 1791. They had four sons and four daughters. They lived at Rosemount at the time. The girls were educated in their early years by a tutor and Archbishop Murray was a regular visitor to the household and became their confessor. He recommended that they should be sent to St. Mary's Convent in York for their further education. This was done. The eldest girl, Margaret came home from York and became the first postulant in the Loreto Convent in Rathfarnham, which had been newly established by Sister Frances Ball[177]. Two of her younger sisters followed and gave their lives in the service of God and their fellow man. Anna Maria, the youngest was responsible for establishing the Presentation Convent Girls School in Mount Mellick. This was made possible by the £1000 her father left her in his will and the £400 paid to her annually.

Richard Corballis established the first girls National School in Donnybrook and bestowed on it an annual income to maintain the school and provide a teacher. He specified in his will that this was to continue. His son, John Richard built the boys National School in Donnybrook and presented the three stained glass windows that still adorn the area above the High Altar in the Sacred Heart Church in Donnybrook.

According to Burke's Irish Family Record, Richard's eldest son, Bartholomew was noted as being 'Chairman of the Catholic Association of Ireland from 1827-1832 and Champion of Catholic Emancipation.' Bartholomew went to live abroad and spent some time in Bordeaux, Berwick on Tweed and finally Edinburgh. He seems to have received financial support from his brother Robert and from his father, who interestingly enough disinherited him. He married a Joan Tindall in Scotland and had seven children, four of whom were still living in 1877. The eldest of these, Richard, who was born in 1836, eventually ended up in South Africa and nothing more was heard of him. Bartholomew's children

---

[177] Her family is best remembered for giving the name to Ballsbridge.

were not forgotten by the Dublin Corballis family and a trust was set up for the purpose of looking after them. One of Bartholomew's daughters, Margaret, joined an order of nuns in Le Changquets Convent, Whitebourne. Two of his other daughters were Anna Maria and Catherine. Anna Maria went on to marry a Protestant minister, Rev. Achilles Daunt and Catherine joined an order of nuns, the Ursulines in Swansea and eventually became Mother Superior of the order.

Bartholomew was superceded by his younger brother John Richard, who became a lawyer. This extraordinary man was the first Catholic in Ireland, since the Reformation, to be awarded the Gold Medal for academic excellence in Trinity College.[178] A few years after he was awarded the Gold Medal he received a Papal knighthood. He was employed by the state in a legal capacity, while carrying on a lucrative private practice and was a Bencher of the King's Inns, Commissioner of Charitable Bequests, Crown Prosecutor on the Home Circuit and Law Adviser to the Crown in Ireland (1853-64). He inherited Rosemount and other properties from his father. He married Jane Eleanor Martyn[179] from Tulira Castle, Co. Galway the daughter of Edward Martyn of literary fame. His son, Richard John (1831-1931), a bachelor, was the last of the male line of this branch of the family to live in Ireland. Richard John had three brothers and three sisters, Mary who married the Rt. Hon. Stephen Woulfe Flanagan, Jane, and Frances who became a nun. The brothers were John Bartholomew, Edward and James Anthony. All three were Army officers and both John Bartholomew and James Anthony were married and had families. James Anthony's descendant today is Edward Anthony Beals Corballis of Connecticut who is married to Catherine Wood.

Richard John was quite eccentric and became a recluse in later life. He had some correspondence with James Frederick Corballis of Ratoath prior to 1910. As early as 1904 Richard John wrote that he was thinking of selling out all his Irish properties and removing to Bath in England. Later it would seem that the Ratoath family were in serious financial difficulty. James wrote to Richard John asking him to guarantee a promissory note.

---

[178] The medal, which is still in the possession of the family, was awarded in 1816 for academic achievement in science.

[179] Jane was the aunt of the famous Edward Martyn of literary fame, first President of Sinn Fein and friend of Lady Gregory and W.B.Yeats. The Martyns were a noted Catholic gentry family and one of the tribes of Galway.

Initially Richard John agreed to do this but later changed his mind. The desperate James Frederick threatened that he would emigrate to South Africa, but the matter appeared to have been ironed out as follows. Richard John was most anxious that the Corballis name would continue in Ireland and in his will he indicated that all his properties and money would be left to James Frederick's family. This move probably satisfied the creditors for a time. However because Richard John lived for such a long time it would seem that it became necessary for him to advance money to James Frederick. In his final will he left the bulk of his £436,000 estate in trust 'to pay the income thereof to James Cecil Corballis, whom I helped to educate at Oxford, for his life and after death for his children as he shall appoint....it is my object in so leaving the residue of my estate that the name of the family shall be maintained in Ireland where they have always lived'. In this year, 2005 there are over twenty descendants of James Anthony Corballis or Ratoath Manor (1770-1842) living in Ireland, many of whom bear the surname Corballis.

Other bequests in Richard John's will saw Rosemount going to Stephen Woulfe Flanagan, his cousin, with some money in trust and £5000 to each of his sons and £1000 to each of his daughters. He left some money to his nephew Rev. John Corballis and to his other nephew Edward and his children.

Everard of Randlestown

The most well-known, if not the most famous of all the family may well have been Sir Nugent Talbot Everard who was a Senator of the Irish Free State. In 1929 the passing of Sir Nugent Everard was noted by the members of the Senate, a number of whom in proposing a vote of regret at his passing spoke about his excellent qualities. Sir Grattan T. Esmonde, a Wexford Senator, in his seconding of the proposal stated 'He was one for whom I had the greatest respect—I might almost say affection. He was one of the original members of the Seanad and I am very glad, for the Seanad's own credit, that they re-elected him a member recently. I need not dilate upon his services to the country. He was a leading agriculturist and was the founder of the Irish tobacco industry. He was a member of a great many committees and associations, including the Agricultural Co-Operative Association, which is endeavoring to do so much for this country. We have lost a very distinguished man and a very noble patriot in Senator Sir Nugent Everard.'

The earliest records of the family occur in vague terms within the Dundalk region of county Louth and it was much later that they rose to prominence, and simultaneously, in Counties Tipperary and Meath. Extensive family research has now revealed the family descends from a number of that name who were settled in and around Dundalk by the fourteenth century; for example Matthew Everard of Mandevilstown, Co. Louth is mentioned in the Plea Rolls in 1318.[180] It was in fact not until the fifteenth century that the family association with Randlestown developed, the circumstances of this outlined as a result of an Act of Parliament in 1475 which confirmed Richard Everard in possession of the property, with the explanation that his grandfather, John Everard, had gained possession through his marriage to Joan Cardy; she was a daughter and co-heiress of 'Olive Rendill' the daughter and heiress of 'Owen Randil of Randillstown.'[181]

It is reasonable to accept the family claims that Richard Everard was in possession of Randlestown before his death in 1575 when he contended with Michael Cusack of Rathaldron for lands at Randlestown and Simonstown. As revealed by this source a picture of the family at this time is largely constructed through official state papers, mostly of a legal nature and generally concerning mundane land disputes –except as in the instance when in August 1555 Patrick Everard of Clongill, located near Randlestown, was pardoned for the accidental killing of a tailor, Donoghe M'Markes.[182] Another official document, an inquisition held in Navan in 1578, offers an early picture of the Everard's possessions in Randlestown which comprised a castle, five houses and 100 acres.[183]

Sir John Everard was at the centre of a power struggle between Protestants and Catholics that occurred in Ireland during the early years of the reign of King James I (1566-1625).[184] James had become King of England after the death of Queen Elizabeth in 1603. The same power

---

[180] Richard H.A.J. Everard, 'The Family of Everard: Part I' in *The Irish Genealogist*, 1988. There is evidence that the family continued to hold an interest in properties in County Louth down to the sixteenth century at least, when James Everard of Randlestown was shown at his death in 1564 to be possessed of 10 acres in the town of Dundalk as well as other lands including 60 acres at Kardiffstown, near Ardee; Everard, 1993.

[181] Ibid.

[182] Ibid. This may also be the same Patrick who was pardoned for 'alienation' in 1551 – Fiants of Edward VI No. 743

[183] National Archives: Ms RC 9/8

[184] James was the son of Mary Queen of Scots, an almost fanatical Catholic. James, himself, appears to have accepted his role as the Head of the Church of England, when he became monarch of England in 1603.

struggle had occurred in England prior to and during the time of what is known as the Gunpowder Plot when Guy Fawkes (ex.1606) made the abortive attempt to blow up the house of Parliament. The King, understandably, was less than sympathetic to the Irish Catholic point of view.

King James I

In 1613 when the Irish Catholic Lords of the Pale proposed him as Speaker of the Irish House of Commons, following his dismissal as a judge because he refused to take the Oath of Supremacy, Sir John Everard was projected into the limelight. The House had been 'packed' with Scots and English lords who the Irish Lords maintained were not entitled to attend the House, much less vote. They fully realized that they were in the minority and could not win the vote, so when a recess was called and supporters of Sir John Davies, the other candidate, retired to assess their situation, the Irish Lords voted and elected Sir John Everard as Speaker. When the others returned they removed Sir John Everard by force and elected Davies in his place.

This Sir John was, according to Burke's Landed Gentry, a son of Redmond Everard who had settled in Tipperary. Redmond was a brother of Richard of Randlestown.

By the middle of the seventeenth century Randlestown was presided over by John Everard; his eldest son, Richard, lived in the district of Kilberry at Rathcoon where the family had earlier established a 'manor house or castle.'[185] In 1641 both father and son were implicated in events associated with the rising of that year. This opportunist, and ultimately unsuccessful, rising, which commenced in Ulster, had evolved from deepening displeasure in the aftermath of the Ulster Plantation. It will be remembered that the Ulster Plantation had been implemented in the wake of the Flight of the Earls in 1607. The consequence of the Plantation, as one commentator noted, meant that there was 'not a more discontented people in Europe.' This disenchantment was joined by the growing unease and suspicion of the Old English, that comprised families such as the Everards, who were increasingly undermined by a distinctly puritanical administration in Dublin (until 1639 led by 'Black Tom Tyrant'-Thomas Wentworth) that found its counterpart in a virulently anti-Catholic English parliament. The leader of the rising, Sir Phelim O'Neill, had garnered wide support that included the old English. Forged documents claiming a Royal imprimatur for the resurgence were used. In effect the rising was presented as 'a defence of the Roman Catholic faith in the guise of a fight for the King.'

Initially the Old English were understandably distrustful of their king, who had reneged on 'the Graces' –the long promised concessions that had been granted to them in 1628 in return for the financial support they had given to Charles I in the War against Spain. However, recognising that the general goodwill of the King was better than the animosity of the English Parliament, they joined with the Gaelic Irish under O'Neill's bogus claims to form the 'Catholic Army'. The immediate consequence of this long feared coalescence of the Old English and the Gaelic Irish, agreed early in December, was to spread the revolt further south and into the heart of the Pale.[186] From Ulster, where the insurgents had encountered only limited local resistance, they turned south to Dundalk, which they captured on 31 October. In Meath, under the leadership of Rory O' More, they had their first engagement with a

---

[185] Everard, 1993, op. cit., p.582.
[186] Brendan Fitzpatrick, The Seventeenth Century: The War of Religions, 1988, pp.171-2

government force (en route to Drogheda) which they defeated at Julianstown Bridge on November 29.

It was perhaps in this shared belief that they were defending their King and their religion, that John Everard and his son involved themselves in the rising and participated in some of the earliest associated activities in the region. No doubt responsibility to the family motto, *virtue in actione consistit*, also played its part. On or about the 25 November 1641 the Parish Clerk of Navan, William Robinson, claimed that he and the minister, Roger Puttock were robbed by insurgents of all their goods and chattels, valued at £10. It was claimed that the participants comprised a number of the local gentry, and both John and Richard Everard were named.

As a consequence of their alleged actions they joined the long list of 'Irish Papists' whose lands were confiscated following Cromwell's successful campaign. In 1656 Richard Everard found himself facing the dilemma of travelling to a fiery underworld or the boggy west when he was listed for transplantation with the offer of obscure lands in Galway. The 724 acres that comprised Randlestown were settled on a Cromwellian adventurer, John Downes, while the 1425 acres that comprised Rathcoon, Kilberry and Demailestown were divided amongst adventurers and soldiers Thomas Pittcock, Captain Arthur Squibbs, Ralph Marsh and Edward Barry.

Fortunately prudence had guided the Everards to show repentance through abiding by the first Ormond Peace of 1643, resolving thereafter to live 'quietly and inoffensively at home.' This was recognised in 1663 when under the Act of Settlement a Decree of Innocence was issued in their favour, stating that 'John and Richard behaved themselves civillie and never acted anything against his late Majestie or his Majestie that now is.'[187] By this time John Everard was deceased and his son was to live a further three years. Thomas Everard, Richard's eldest son, was the principal beneficiary of the Decree of Innocence as he 'never did nor could act anything prejudicial to his Majestie being but the age of seaven years in the beginning of the rebellion' and on 20 August 1663 the Sheriff of County Meath was ordered 'without delay…[to] give and deliver or cause

[187] Everard, 1993, op. cit., pp.582-3.

the possession of the premises with the appurtenances to be given and delivered unto Thomas Everard.'[188]

After twenty years of quiet and inconspicuous occupation of Randlestown, Thomas Everard died in 1681. His funeral expenses note the not insubstantial sum of £11 spent on 'shoes, hat and stockings' for Mathias Everard, the thirteen year old heir to Randlestown -perhaps an early demonstration of his keen interest in promoting the dignity of his family.

Coinciding with Mathias Everard's succession to Randlestown in 1688 at the age of 21, was the overthrow of James II and his replacement by his daughter, Mary and her husband King William III, prince of Orange. When the deposed King arrived in Ireland the following year, the young Everard, was presented with the opportunity to follow the family tradition and motto. No doubt carried by the militant mood of the country he showed his support for the King by joining the Jacobite army, then under the leadership of 'lying Dick Talbot', the Earl of Tyrconnell, who was actively purging it of Protestant officers.[189]

Like many of his peers, Mathias Everard was outlawed following the Battle of the Boyne in 1690 and risked the forfeiture of his landed estate. In the face of such a prospect he withdrew with the remainder of the defeated army west of the Shannon. It is possible that he travelled to Limerick as part of the attempt to hold the country that remained in Jacobite possession as he reappears as a Lieutenant Colonel of the city's garrison in August 1691. It is not known if he was present in the preceding August to hear the spectacular culmination some ten miles away of Sarsfield's celebrated interception of William's siege train or to witness, days later, the withdrawal of the king's demoralised army from the walls of the city.

However, despite these momentous events, within a year the War was all but won under William's brilliant commander, Baron Van Ginkel. Everard would have been close to the negotiations[190] that resulted in the

---

[188] Ibid., p.585.

[189] Tyrconnell's older brother, Sir Robert Talbott, possessed Liscartan Castle, an important mediaeval property close to Randlestown. R.C. Simmington, *The Civil Survey of County Meath, 1654-1656.* 1940.

[190] One of the negotiators was Matthias Barnewall, 10th Baron Trimblestown. Everard and Barnewall shared a common ancestor in the 1st Viscount Netterville,

cessation of the war and which produced the Treaty of Limerick. Having an estate already secured under the Act of settlement Everard was well appraised of the benefit of 'surrender on terms.' The Gaelic Irish who had little hope of recovering lost estates and nothing to lose in fighting on in France, consequently followed Sarsfield to France and represented the first of the celebrated Wild Geese who spread a 'grey wing on every tide'. As one of the so called 'articlemen,' Matthias was permitted by observing 'their Majestie's obedience' to return to his estate and could hope to enjoy religious freedom in so far 'as was consistent with the laws of Ireland or as they did enjoy in the reign of King Charles II.'[191]

On the 8th of August Ginkell signed a decree of safe passage to Everard requiring:

> ' ...all officers Military and Civill and all others whome itt may concern to permit the said Mathyas Everard to pass with his family, servants, tenants and followers to his dwelling house or houses or any part of this Kingdome with their goods, Cattle, horses and Armes without any Lott Hindrance or Molestation.[192]'

It was probably a very relieved Matthias Everard who returned to his house and estate at Randlestown. His cousin Patrick, an M.P. for Kells in the parliament of James II wasn't as lucky and lost his estates in Navan and Roscommon. In the early 1700s Matthias demolished the old tower house at Randlestown and built a more modern dwelling.[193] Matthias was unmarried and when he died in 1714 he was succeeded in his estates by his brother Christopher who was married twice.

Christopher's first wife was Teresa Baggott from Kildare and by her he had two daughters. His second wife was Teresa Plunkett of Tulrath a niece of the 10th Lord Dunsany and they had three sons. Christopher was

---

while Mathias Everard's mother, Anne Barnewall, represented another branch of the family as a daughter of Thomas Barnewall of Robertstown, Co. Meath; at least three other Everard ancestors had married a member of the Barnewall family and there is evidence for a close business relationship between the families. Burke's Peerage and Baronetage, 1992 ; Everard, 1993.

[191] Everard, 1993; Charles Chenevix Trench, Grace's Card: Irish Catholic Landlords 1690-1800.

[192] Everard, 1993.

[193] Richard Everard in Sir Nugent Everard and his efforts to revive Randlestown in *Riocht na Midhe* 2000

succeeded after his death in 1732 by his son, John. His other sons, Thomas and Francis went to the Continent where they found employment as soldiers. Thomas, a Captain in a Cavalry regiment was killed in Bohemia in 1757. His brother, Francis, rose to the rank of Colonel in the King of Naples regiment of Foot Guards.

Randlestown House

John Everard (1722-1764) took the expedient step of turning Protestant. He married Margaret, a daughter of Hugh O'Reilly of Ballinlough Castle, Co. Westmeath. His wife may well have pre deceased him as he appointed Lord Bellew and Sir William Baggott as guardians of his only son, Thomas, who was reared at Ballinlough[194]. This gentleman was High Sheriff of Meath in 1795 and a year later he was Captain of the Navan Yeoman Cavalry. He founded his own corps in 1798 known as the Kilberry Cavalry. He was married to his cousin Barbara O'Reilly of Ballinlough Castle and they had seven sons and three daughters. Two of those ladies married. Their husbands were brothers. Margaret married

---

[194] Richard Everard in Sir Nugent Everard and his efforts to revive Randlestown in *Riocht na Midhe* 2000

Joseph Barnewall of Bloomsbury, Co. Meath and Barbara married Patrick Barnewall who lived at Causestown.

Remarkably six of the seven sons pursued careers in the Army and Navy. The odd one out was George who became rector of the family parish of Donaghpatrick. Three of the six died from yellow fever in the West Indies. According as the older brothers died the estate was passed on to the next until finally it came to the youngest, Richard, in 1863. The eldest of the brothers, John kept up the family tradition of marrying cousins, by choosing as his wife another Barbara O'Reilly from Ballinlough, but they had no family.

The third of the brothers, Matthias, had an extraordinary Army career, fought in many engagements and was highly decorated. He rose to the rank of Major General and was awarded the Order of the Bath. He died in 1862. He was very fond of his horse because in his will he expressly desired that 'my horse to be sent with care to my family estates in Ireland, to be kept there for the rest of his life'.[195]

During the 40 or 50 year period between the death of Thomas and his wife Barbara and the return of Richard's eldest son Nugent Talbot, already mentioned at the start of this chapter, the estate, house and demesne were rented out to tenants and the affairs were handled by an agent. The house and demesne were let to the Meredyth family[196].

The 7th and youngest son, Richard inherited in 1862 and was in his 63rd year at the time. Like his brothers he had found a career in the Army and served in Australia and in India. His wife was Arabella Mathilde d'Amboise, daughter of Le Marquis d'Amboise and they had three sons and six daughters. He didn't enjoy his inheritance for long as he died seven weeks later. His eldest son, Nugent Talbot Everard succeeded to the Randlestown estates. Nugent's younger brother Arundell became a clergyman in England while the youngest son James emigrated to New Zealand where there are numerous Everards to this day. James's eldest son, Reginald Talbot visited Ireland and Randlestown in the 1950s and Reginald's grandson Michael and his wife Cheryle visited in the recent past.[197]

---

[195] Ibid.

[196] Ibid.

[197] Richard Everard in Sir Nugent Everard and his efforts to revive Randlestown in *Riocht na Midhe* 2000

Nugent Talbot Everard was born in Torquay and his two first names were given to him in deference to the two great families with whom the Everards were connected – the Nugent/O'Reillys of Ballinlough and the Talbots of Malahide who were also connected with the O'Reillys via Margaret O'Reilly. Margaret was the elder sister of Barbara O'Reilly who had married Thomas Everard.

Nugent was only thirteen when he inherited and was already at Harrow. From there he proceeded to Cambridge and prior to completing his time there he came to live at Randlestown in 1870. John Nevin, the farm manager, and the son of the previous farm manager, William Nevin, had this to say when he wrote in 1940 of his lifelong service to the Everard family:-'Nugent was the first of the Everard family to make his home in Randlestown for upward of 60 years, previous the house & estate were rented continually. And a great many changes and repair had to take place. The house and yards had to be renovated. Nugent Everard commenced to make his home modern and to live up to a country gentleman's life, in hunting and sporting. And the Meath Militia he joined as Lieutenant.'

Nugent was promoted in the Militia – Captain in 1881, Major in 1898 and Colonel in 1902. He married Sylvia Humphreys of Ballyhaise House, Co. Cavan in 1873.

The estate contained 2,311 acres in Randlestown, Clarkstown, Ballyhist, Kilberry, Damailstown, Rathcoon, Rathpark and Tuiterath. Between 1876 and 1907 he raised several loans from the Commissioners of Public Works in order to improve his demesne lands for agricultural use.

They kept a full staff of servants in the house – 'as many as 13' Nevin said. In his early years Nugent spent a lot of time hunting and shooting and as late as 1908 he hosted the Meath hunt at Randlestown with Lord and Lady Fingall as guests of honour. He also turned his attentions to farming. 'He commenced a herd of Hereford cattle breeding, which afterwards became famous for prizes and sales at good prices. He brought from England the best herd he could procure'[198]

He is probably best remembered for his attempt to revive the tobacco industry in Ireland. With government permission he cultivated about 20 acres on his own demesne and erected curing sheds. His son,

---

[198] John Nevin in his Memoirs

Richard was sent to the U.S. to gain experience in that area of expertise. This experiment gave valuable employment to many local people. As time progressed Nugent involved many other growers including Lord Dunraven at Adare. The advent of the war of 1916-18 severely curtailed the tobacco experiment as the need was for food production. It fizzled out entirely after 1922.

Sir Nugent Everard
(Courtesy Meath Co. Library)

Perhaps influenced by Horace Plunkett, Nugent became deeply involved in the Co-Operative Movement and was President of the Society in 1905. In 1902 Colonel Nugent Everard was one of the three landlord representatives (with the Earl of Mayo and Colonel Hutchinson-Poë) at the Land Conference in Dublin which produced a report that recommended a massive scheme of land purchase by the government - the purchased land to be offered for sale to the tenants. These recommendations were incorporated into the Wyndham Act of 1903.

Mr. John Browne – Estate Worker

Nugent was High Sheriff of Meath in 1883 and a few years later he was the Lieutenant of the County. He was a member of the Grand Jury until the time of its abolition and then he was a County Councillor from 1900 –1920. He was a magistrate and a J.P. from 1873 until 1923.

In recognition of his contribution to public life, Nugent was created a Baronet in 1911. To mark the event, Sir Nugent installed a huge stained glass window in the staircase of Randlestown which incorporated the Everard Coat of Arms. Because of his work on behalf of Irish tenant farmers he was appointed as a Senator of the Irish Free State by President Cosgrave. When his six years were up he contested a by election and was re-elected shortly before his death in 1929.

Some time before 1916 the Meath Militia was renamed the 5th Battalion Prince of Wales' Leinster Regiment and Sir Nugent, as their Colonel, went with his men to the front in Belgium. His son, Major Richard, also fought in World War I in the Duke of Wellington Regiment.

Richard was a J.P. from 1919 –1923. He died in 1929. His wife was Louise Metge of Athlumney, Navan. They lived at Woodview in Randlestown. They had two sons Nugent Henry and Matthias Richard both born in 1905 and 1906. Nugent Henry joined the Army in 1926. He married in England and had a family. He gradually sold off his Meath assets. In 1931 Woodview was sold to John Nicholson. Hannays was sold in 1934, Damailstown in 1936 (to the Irish Land Commission), and half of Randlestown in 1938. Finally in 1943 Sir Nugent sold Randlestown House and 412 acres to Gerald Williamson for £12,500. The Williamsons lived and farmed there until the 1960s when Tara Mines bought the house and lands as they needed the land for a tailing pond for the mine water. The house was later demolished.

The poignancy of the passing of such a property and its once proud family was captured by John Nevin when he said – 'Randlestown of old is now more like a wilderness, since house and places are closed down. And the lands as in former days return to the eleven months system. For one who has seen Randlestown's past, during the life of Sir Nugent and Lady Everard, what a dark cloud shrouds over it, when all is still and lonely and the old folks dropping away'

Fowler of Rahinston

When the Empress 'Sisi' of Austria stayed for a month at Summerhill, in Co. Meath, in order to enjoy the 'best hunting in Europe' she socialized with the local aristocracy and gentry. One such family was the Fowler family of Rahinston. During her stay, the Empress, who had her own string of hunting horses on holiday with her, took a fancy to a horse belonging to Louisa, a young daughter of Robert Fowler, her neighbour. When told of the Empress's wish to buy the animal Robert Fowler was heard to say 'I'm not going to have any damned Empress buying my daughter's horse!'[199]

Robert's son, Bob Fowler, an Etonian in 1910, became something of a celebrity when he showed his bowling prowess by taking eight wickets for nine runs in the annual match against Harrow. The game has gone down in history as 'Fowler's Match'. These annual matches were played at Lord's and attracted huge crowds, sometimes in excess of 20,000. Newspapers devoted two and three pages to the previews and analyses of the sides. On the day in question, Harrow, who were firm favourites to win, were nearly out of sight until Bob Fowler began to bowl. By that stage nearly half the 20,000 spectators had gone home but those who stayed

---

[199] Mark Bence Jones – *The Twilight of the Ascendancy*

witnessed a spectacle that as cricket enthusiasts they never forgot. It was said that the cheering could be heard as far away as Euston Station. These annual matches began in 1805 and this year marks the 200th anniversary of the fixture.

According to family tradition Sir Robert Fowler, a Crusader, was knighted by King Richard I following the siege of Acre in 1191. The progenitor of this family and the first to come to Ireland was Robert Fowler who was born in England in Co. Lincolnshire the eldest son of George Fowler and Mary Hurst. After finishing in Cambridge, Robert received a prestigious appointment as one of the Chaplains to King George II. He was consecrated Bishop of Killaloe and Killfenora in 1773 and two years later was appointed Archbishop of Dublin. A seat on the Privy Council followed and in 1783 the Archbishop was made the first Chancellor of the newly established Order of St. Patrick.

Archbishop Robert Fowler
(Courtesy Mr. John Fowler)

His wife was Mildred Dealtry, an heiress from Lincolnshire. They had one son, Robert, and two daughters. The daughters were Mildred and Frances both of whom married. The elder of the two married Edmund Butler, Earl of Kilkenny and Frances's husband was Hon. Rev. Richard Bourke who was later to become the Bishop of Waterford and whose grandson became the Earl of Mayo.

Robert II (1767 – 1841), later Bishop of Ferns & Ossory, was sent to school in England where he attended Westminster School and afterwards Christ Church Oxford. He graduated as a Cleric and was appointed Dean of St. Patrick's in Dublin. He married Hon. Louisa Gardiner the daughter of Luke Gardiner, Viscount Mountjoy,[200] in 1796. That family is still remembered today by the Dublin streets named in honour of Luke Gardiner – Gardiner Place, Gardiner Lane, Gardiner Row, Gardiner Street Upper and Gardiner Street Lower. The Rev. Dean Robert was promoted to the post of Archdeacon of Dublin and later was given the appointment of Bishop of Ossory and Ferns.

Bishop Robert Fowler (1767-1841)
(Courtesy Mr. John Fowler)

---

[200] Luke Gardiner, Lord Mountjoy, was the unfortunate man who, while in command of the Dublin Militia, was piked to death at the Battle of New Ross. Mountjoy had ridden out from the defences of New Ross in an attempt to persuade the Wexford rebel group commanded by Kelly (the Boy from Killane) to give up the attack. He was immediately surrounded by some of the rebels and killed instantly. Luke Gardiner was a liberal who had successfully proposed the first Catholic Relief Act in 1793. – See *Ireland 1798 The Battles* by Art Kavanagh.

The family appears to have acquired Rahinston at some time during the early 1800s and at the same time the Bishop leased a house in Merrion Square, Dublin for which he paid £105 annually. The Bishop kept meticulous accounts that are quite revealing. According to the accounts for 1831-32 his son Robert Fowler was given an annuity of almost £1400 per annum – a huge sum of money in those days – out of a total income of £8,553.11s.7d. Robert of course may have been paying a mortgage on Rahinston which would account for the rather large annuity[201].

Hon. Louisa Gardiner (from a portrait)
(Courtesy John Fowler)

While people in modern times constantly gripe about the local taxes they have to pay the Bishop's accounts reveal an alarming number of taxes, unheard of today. For example there were six separate taxes paid annually on his leased property in Merrion Square – the Grand Jury and

---

[201] Fowler Papers Ms. 624 in NLI

Wide Street Tax of £5.6s.2 ½d., Tax for watering in Merrion Sq. 15s., Cleaning tax for Merrion Square 19s, Paving tax for Merrion Square £9.5s.2d., Grand Jury Cess on Merrion Square £5.2s.3 ½d. and a Watch Tax of £1.15s.1d.

In addition to the annuity to his eldest son, Robert Fowler, he paid a smaller annuity to his second son, the Rev. Luke Fowler. This amounted annually to £276.18s.4d.but was paid quarterly. In addition he had to pay numerous servants including S Cox, R. Harman and E. Mooney who appear to have been influential people in the Bishop's entourage. His annual payment to the Royal Exchange for insurance on his Lordship's life came to a whopping £106.8s.6d while his house insurance amounted to £7.1s.3d. Various large sums were deposited in the Bishop's London bank from time to time.[202]

His Lordship's total expenditure for the year came to £8,876.7s.7 ¾d. Rentals for the period came from various sources – the Moylough estate £4524. 6s. 10 ½d., See of Ossory £966.11s.2d. and Michael Cox for the lands of Grovine £1600. Others who paid the bishop were John Flood, Samuel Davis, Coldhurst, Lord Ashbrooke, J. Power, Mrs. Humphrey and Tighe. There were other smaller payments bringing the total to £8,553.11s.7d. This of course meant that there was a shortfall in the accounts but in true accountancy fashion the balance was carried forward to the following year.[203]

Accounts for 1832-33 followed a similar pattern but the expenses only amounted to £5650 while the rental had fallen to £5228.8s.11 ½d. In 1834 the totals again showed a shortfall. Expenditure was £7753 and income only £6068. In 1835 the expenses rose again to a record £9924.15s.0d.while the rentals and other incomes amounted to only £7857.12s.11d. It would appear that the shortfalls were caused mainly by arrears of rents.

In the actual rental accounts themselves the names of the tenants included Brady, Fagan, Handbury, Magee, Smith, Farrell, Holton, Gaughran, Fitzsimons, Garry, Rooney, Hughes, Ryan, Larkin, Ford, Dean, Mealey, Kerr, Cusack, Gorey, Walsh, Monaghan, Jones, Keeffe, Watson, Allen, Lawless, Murray, Ennis, Halligan, Tracey, Dempsey, Flynn, Cooke,

---

[202] Ibid.
[203] Ibid.

Fox, Reynolds, Anderson and Pigott. As we might expect the same names appeared from one year to the next.

The Bishop died in 1841 and Robert Fowler of Rahinston was his main beneficiary. Robert continued the practice of keeping accounts though less detailed that those that existed during the Bishop's time. It is very interesting to note that in the accounts for 1845 expenses were £6119.5s. while Rentals for the year were £7283.14s.5d. Obviously the effects of the famine hadn't impacted on the tenant farmers of Co. Meath in that year. However by 1847 there was a sizeable reduction in the amounts of both expenses and rentals. The expenses were £5181.0s.5d. while income was just short of that at £4939.19s.7d.

The Fowler fortunes appeared to have dwindled somewhat further by 1854 when the expenses for the year came to just £4308.15s.8d. The Fowler family themselves were farming their immediate land and in 1854 they bought sheep and cattle at Ballinasloe for £391.4s.0d. and they paid £89.4s.8d. for drainage. A man called Richardson and a Mrs. Griffith were paid regularly. Before, during and after the famine years, Robert III gained a reputation for husbandry. He introduced the idea of conserving animal fodder and lectured widely on the subject.[204]

Robert Fowler III (1797-1868), the Bishop's eldest son, appears to have been educated in Ireland. He is described in Burke's Landed Gentry as being of Rahinston and Rathmoylan. He was married twice. His first wife was Jane the daughter of the Hon. John Crichton, whose son was the third Lord Erne.[205] Robert was given appointments to local offices and was at various times a Justice of the Peace (J.P.) and a Deputy Lieutenant (D.L.).

He was married in 1820 and his wife only lived for a further eight years, dying in 1828. Robert and Jane had two sons, Robert and John Richard and two daughters, Jane Margaret and Louisa Catherine[206]. Jane probably died after the birth of her youngest daughter, Louisa Catherine, who was born in 1828.

Robert III, now a young widower, married again in 1831. His 2nd wife was Lady Harriet Wandesforde Butler, the eldest daughter of the 2nd

---

[204] Mr. John Fowler.

[205] The Crichtons are a Fermanagh family seated at Crom Castle.

[206] Both of these daughters married. Jane Margaret's husband was Gartside Tipping of Crumsall Hall, Co. Lancaster and Louisa Catherine was married to James Sclater of Newick Park, Sussex. Both ladies had families.

Marquess of Ormonde. They had a number of children most of whom seem to have died in infancy. One daughter, Anne Mildred, survived to adulthood and married.[207]

Robert Fowler III grandson of Archbishop
(Courtesy Mr. John Fowler)

The eldest son, Robert Fowler IV (1824-1897), was a highly educated man, who obtained an M.A. degree and later attended King's Inns and qualified as a Barrister. He succeeded his father in Rahinston and Rathmoylan in 1863. He received appointments as High Sheriff in 1871, and was a J.P. and a D.L. His wife was Laetitia Coddington of Oldbridge, Co. Meath. They had four sons, Robert, John Sharman, George Hurst and Francis and three daughters, including Louisa[208] (whose horse was coveted

---

[207] Her husband was James Dashwood, the son of Admiral Dashwood.
[208] Louisa's son, Sir Alexander Godley, was Commander-in-Chief of the Anzacs in the Dardenelles in World War I. He survived that debacle and

by the Empress Sisi). The youngest of the sons, Francis, died while still in his early teens.

Robert IV had occasion to write to the Times in 1840 when the *Dublin Pilot* appended his name to "The Leinster and Charlemont Address to the people of Great Britain". He stated 'I have seen in a supplement to the *Dublin Pilot*, my name affixed to "The Leinster and Charlemont Address to the people of Great Britain." Connected by property in England as well as in Ireland I shall feel obliged by your stating to the public that : I did not sign that address nor did I authorize anyone to sign it for me. Consequently my name to it is a forgery.'

Captain Robert Fowler (from a painting)
(Courtesy Mr. John Fowler)

The eldest son, Robert V, was born in 1857 and lived for almost a hundred years dying at Rahinston in 1957. He bought a commission in the Army and attained the rank of Captain before retiring to Rahinston on the death of his father in 1897. The Captain occupied the usual posts of J.P.

---

lived to publish his memoirs *Life of an Irish Soldier, Reminiscences of General Sir Alexander Godley* in 1939.

and D.L. and was High Sheriff for the county in 1899. His wife was Mabel Glyn an heiress and a relative of the Wolvertons.[209] They had two sons, Robert St.Leger and George Glyn both of whom were Army officers and both of whom died young and unmarried. George died from wounds received at the Battle of Loos in 1915 and Robert St. Leger died in 1925.

The second son of Robert IV, Sir John Sharman Fowler, who was born in 1864 and was knighted in 1926. He was a career Army officer rising to the rank of Lieutenant General. He fought in various battles including Chitral[210] (where he was mentioned in despatches). He was part of the Tirah Expeditionary Force[211] (from where he got similar accolades). He fought in South Africa and in World War I. He married Mary Brooke from Dublin the daughter of John Monck Brooke a relative of the Brookes of Summerton[212]. They had two daughters Letitia and Mary Mabel. Neither of these ladies married. John Sharman died just as the Second World War was about to break out in 1939.

George Hurst (1866-1920) was the third son of Robert IV. He received his education at Cheltenham and at the Royal Agricultural College at Cirencester. He appears to have come back to Ireland to practice his theories and was domiciled at Eureka, near Kells, Co. Meath and was agent for the Headfort Estate. He was also a J.P. His wife was Mabel a member of the well known Blakiston-Houston family from Co. Down. George and Mabel had two sons, Frank and Bryan John and one daughter Jane who married Michael Villiers-Stuart from Co. Antrim.

Frank, who was educated at Repton and Cambridge, was an RAF officer who served with distinction in World Wars I and II. He received

---

[209] The Glyns (Barons Wolverton) had a number of seats in Buckinghamshire.

[210] It was at this battle in Pakistan that the machine gun was used for the first time by the British Army. In the late 19th century the British established a garrison in Chitral, as at that time it was thought that there existed easy passage from Russia to British India.

[211] This was a sizeable army by any standards. It was composed of some 33,000 men with a backup of 20,000 camp followers – cooks, hospital staff etc. Sir Winston Churchill was part of this force also, which sought to close off the north of India from Afghanistan by controlling the passes such as the Khyber and Bolan passes.

[212] The Brookes, baronets, had seats at Coolgreaney in Co. Wexford and also in Gardiners Row in Dublin.

numerous decorations including a DSC[213], AFC[214] and the Croix de Guerre. He seems to have lived most of his life in Strangford, Co. Down, where he was a J.P. and a D.L. He never married.

Bryan John attended Cheltenham and Woolwich and as a career Army officer attained the rank of Brigadier. Like his brother Frank he served in both World Wars. He too was highly decorated and was awarded an MC[215] in 1918 and a DSO[216] in 1945. Despite the war he managed to find time to marry in 1944. His wife was Mary Patteson Nickalls the daughter of Lt. Col. Cecil Patteson Nickalls and widow of Lt. Col. Hugh Carr Walford. Their children are John Robert Henry Fowler and Jessica Jane. The family lived in Rathmoylan until 1957 when the Captain died and Bryan John succeeded.

Rahinston from a Lithograph
(Courtesy Mr. John Fowler)

---

[213] Distinguished Service Cross.
[214] Air Force Cross.
[215] Military Cross.
[216] Companion of the Distinguished Service Order.

John Fowler of Rahinston the very well known horse trainer of international repute and his equally famous sister Jessica Harrington have trained and bred horses that have become household names today. John's proudest sporting occasions were when his horses Maid of Money and Opera Hat won the Irish Grand National (1989) and the Melling Chase (1997) respectively.

John, an Eton old boy and a graduate of McGill University, is married to the Hon. Jennifer Chichester daughter of the Marquess of Donegal. He represented Ireland in the equestrian events in the Mexico Olympics of 1968.

Jessica, who married David Lloyd in 1968, has one son, James William and one daughter Tara Jane. Jessica is one of Ireland's finest horsewomen, as apart from being one of the country's leading trainers, she has represented Ireland in three-day eventing at the Olympics, World Championships and European Championships. Having first started training over 10 years ago, Jessie has become best known for the exploits of Moscow Flyer, winner of the Arkle and the Queen Mother Champion Chase at successive Cheltenham Festivals, but she has also trained many other fine National Hunt horses, including Space Trucker, Spirit Leader, and Mac's Joy.[217]

---

[217] *Favourite Racing* on the net.

Hamilton of Hamwood

A rather romantic family tradition has it that the Hamiltons were party to a plan to rescue Mary Queen of Scots, who was about to be kidnapped by Bothwell, so that he could force her into marriage and thereby help secure the throne of England for Elizabeth I. The Hamiltons along with the Gordons were defeated in a skirmish and fled from Scotland in two ships, one of which ended up in Ireland, carrying the Hamiltons. There may be some truth in the story as James Hepburn the 4th Earl of Bothwell did in fact kidnap Mary Queen of Scots and became her third husband in 1567. It is also a fact that Bothwell was responsible for the murder of the Earl of Darnley the Queen's second husband. The Scots nobles rose against Bothwell and he was forced to flee to Denmark where he died insane. It is also a fact that James Hamilton, the Earl of Arran, an enemy of Bothwell did in fact help prevent the abduction of Mary at an earlier time.

Be that as it may the first of this family in Ireland was Hugh Hamilton who was made a denizen of Ireland in 1616. He settled at Lisbane near Bangor in Co. Down. His father was Sir James Hamilton of Fynnart. Hugh was the 4th son. Hugh was married but his wife's name is not on record. He had three sons – John the ancestor of the Co. Down Hamiltons of Ballymenoch and Ballyvernon, Alexander the ancestor of the Co. Laois and Co. Meath Hamiltons, and Robert who had no son.[218]

---

[218] He had a daughter Ursula, who married John Blackwood and from whom descended the Barons Dufferin.

Hugh lived through the turbulent times of the Cromwellian Wars and came out smelling of roses with estates intact including one at Killyleagh where both Alexander and Robert were settled.

Alexander married another Hamilton, Jean, the daughter of John Hamilton of Belfast and they had one son Hugh II and one daughter, Jane. Jane married William Sloane, a brother of Sir Hans Sloane, but her descendants died out. Alexander died in 1676.

Hugh II married Mary Ross of Portavo, Co. Down and they resided at Ballybrenagh. Mary was a granddaughter of a Hamilton, Captain Hans Hamilton. They had two sons, Alexander II and George and a daughter Jane. George of Tyrella was married but his son George died unmarried.

Alexander Hamilton of Knock.
d 1768

(Courtesy Mrs. Anne Hamilton)

Alexander II of Knock, Dublin and Newtown Hamilton[219], Co Armagh was the ancestor of a very large number of Hamiltons many of whom have spread all over the world where they continue to this day. According to family sources he was a land agent who amassed lands

---

[219] This place, which is situated on the roads leading respectively from Dundalk (Co. Louth) to Armagh, and from Newry to Castle-Blayney and Monaghan, in the midst of the Fews mountains, owes its origin and importance to the late Mr. Hamilton, who laid the foundation of the present town about the year 1770, previously to which time, the whole district was a dreary, wild, and uninhabited waste. – Lewis Topographical Dictionary of Ireland.

worth over £50,000 - a huge sum of money at the time. He had five sons who were educated at Finglas in Co. Dublin. A quaint story relates how the father had the heads of all five shaved and then made to wear wigs so that their hair could not be pulled when they were in school.[220]

The fourth son, Charles (1740?-1818), having finished his schooling decided to try his hand at wine importing. In those days quite a lot of claret was drunk and there was an ever increasing demand for quality wine. At about the same time that Charles embarked on his wine importing career another member of a gentry family was doing the same. He was Hugh Barton who gave his name to the Wine Company still known today as Barton & Guestier. Charles however was not cut out for the trade being 'a very sober, moral and industrious man'[221] and so he reluctantly decided to leave the business. He went to live at Mount Venus near Marlay Park in Dublin.

Charles Hamilton of Hamwood,
d 1818

(Courtesy Mrs. Anne Hamilton)

---

[220] A more likely reason might have been that he wanted to prevent their getting lice.
[221] From the diaries of his daughter-in-law, Caroline Hamilton.

Shortly afterwards Charles met his future wife, Miss Elizabeth Chetwood,[222] who was on a visit from England, where she lived with her grandparents and within a short time they were married. He was at that time the land agent for the Archbishop of Dublin and for Lord Lansdowne. He decided to settle in Co. Meath and he built a house there for the not inconsiderable sum of £2,500.[223] This house, the name of which was devised from the word Hamilton and Chetwood was used mainly as a summer retreat and the family maintained a house in Dublin at 40 Dominick Street. Charles had business interests in Dublin and was the owner of land in Ringsend which was leased to a James Hill for £30. 12s. 11d per annum. He was also involved with Viscount Harberton (later of Carbery Co.Kildare), who appeared to be his partner, in some land dealings in the Fitzwilliam Square area of Dublin.

Caroline Hamilton, Charles's daughter-in-law, wrote about the family journeys to and from Hamwood 'with cartloads of silver, plate and chattels and a cow bringing up the rear. Fresh fruit and vegetables were brought to Dublin from Hamwood twice a week.'

Land agents were not paid a salary but were paid between four and five per cent of the amount of the rentals they collected. On some estates with large rentals this could amount to quite a substantial sum. In addition many agents became middlemen themselves and so made even more profits.

Charles had a narrow escape from death in the Rebellion of 1798 when he was captured by the rebels and taken to Dunboyne. His life was spared by the intervention of a blacksmith named O'Reilly who knew him. He was subsequently released without harm. As a mark of his gratitude Charles employed O'Reilly from that time onwards whenever his horses needed shoeing or whenever implements needed mending. O'Reilly's descendants in the same line of business continued to receive employment from the Hamiltons of Hamwood down to the middle of the last century when the horse made its exit from the land.[224]

---

[222] Her father was Crewe Chetwood from Woodbrook in Co. Laois.
[223] Marianne Heron in *The Hidden Houses of Ireland*
[224] Ibid.

The Duke of Leinster's land agent was killed in the rebellion of 1798 and Charles Hamilton applied for the vacant post. He was successful and from then onwards his star was in the ascendant.

Charles and Elizabeth had five sons and one daughter, Henrietta, who married Major General Prevost.[225] The five sons were Charles, Robert, George, William and John. Both Robert and John sought their fortunes in Liverpool where they became successful merchants. In Liverpool, only John married and he had one daughter, Anne who died in 1854. Robert died unmarried in 1822.

William although married twice left no male descendants and his female descendants appear to have died out also. His first wife was the daughter of Brigadier Beauchamp Colclough[226] of Canada but formerly from Kildavin, Co. Carlow. It was probably William who accompanied George to Canada.

We will deal with the descendants of Charles of Hamwood, the eldest son later.

The most prolific man of the family was George, the third son, who established a Hamilton family in Canada where they are well represented to this day. George (d.1839) settled first in Quebec and later at Hawkesbury near Ontario where he became involved in the lumber business.

It is recorded that in 1808 the Hamilton brothers[227] bought islands and wharves and developed sawmills. The Hawkesbury sawmills contributed to the development of the wharves on Chenail Island which became the site of the village of Hawkesbury Mills. According to some authorities a dam was built with earth and concrete slabs[228], and five

---

[225] Major General Prevost was the commander of the English forces in East Florida during the American War of Independence. He was accompanied by his wife and family during the campaign. He is best remembered for his very successful defence of Savannah where he was besieged by a combined force of Americans and French in 1779.

[226] This man was descended from Thomas Colclough of Tintern Abbey, Co. Wexford, an Elizabethan family that survived into the last century when the last of the line died. (See Wexford Gentry Vol. I for notices of that family).

[227] This would imply that one or other of his brothers went to Canada with George.

[228] Mary Higgins Clément (1983)

sawmills were powered by a hydraulic dam linking the two major islands. In the 1870s the Hamilton Island was further developed with the arrival of the Atlantic railroad in Hawkesbury. Trains brought lumber to the mills[229] and wood was shipped on barges pulled by tugboats to various markets.[230]

George's wife was Susannah Craigie from Perthshire and they had five sons and two daughters neither of whom married. The five sons were Robert, George, John, Charles and Francis who died young.

The descendants of **Robert Hamilton** have all died out except the children and grandchildren of his daughters Isabella and Susan who married Lt. Col. Thomas Irwin of Carnagh Co. Armagh and Hon. Sir Walter Cassells , a Canadian Judge, respectively.

George Hamilton's descendants are quite numerous. His second son, Charles Chetwode, a parson, was the father of a father and son duo, who were very distinguished soldiers in the Boer War and in World Wars I and II. They lived mainly in England. They were Francis Alexander Chetwode Hamilton (1879-1956) and his son Thomas Francis Chetwode Hamilton (1911- ??) who both rose to the rank of Lt. Colonel.

Rev. Crew Chetwode Hamilton (1886-1967) was the brother of Lt. Col. Thomas Francis and his son Guy Tancred Hamilton is the father of Simon, Thomas, Julia and Sarah. Guy Tancred and his family live in Surrey.

Charles Chetwode had two other sons, Sir George Rostrevor Hamilton and Eric Knightly Chetwode Hamilton who both have a large number of descendants. Sir George, in addition to being a very important Civil Servant was a poet and a writer and was Vice President of the Royal Society of Literature.[231] His son, Patrick, fought in World War II and has two sons and a daughter.

Rt. Rev. Eric Knightly Chetwode (1890-1962) was Chaplain to King George VI and to HM the Queen until his death in 1962. One of his sons, a World War II veteran was also a very successful government official and was at one time the UK representative to the UN General Assembly. His eldest son is married to Audrey Naper from Loughcrew and they have a

---

[229] Thomas (1896)

[230] Mary Higgins Clément (1983)

[231] He was quite prolific and was either the writer or the editor of over thirty publications. His best known poem was A *Cross in Flanders*. Sir George was a friend and mentor of the poet Walter de la Mare.

family of three girls. His second son, John, was killed in action in Italy in 1943. Rt. Rev. Eric Hamilton's two daughters Mary and Susan are both married and have families.

John Hamilton the third son of George of Quebec stayed on at Hawkesbury Mills and one of his sons Edmund Charles of Somerford Manor in Wiltshire has descendants.

Charles Hamilton (1834-1919), effectively the last of the sons of George of Quebec, after attending Oxford became a pastor and in due course, because of his intelligence and talents was appointed Bishop of Ottawa. In 1862 he married Frances Thompson, the daughter of the Deputy Commissary General of Canada. They had four sons Charles Robert, Hubert, Harold and George and four daughters who survived to adulthood, Lilian, Mabel, Ethel and Mary Agnes. Charles Robert (1867-1970), a barrister, is represented today in Canada by the children and grand children of his daughters Edith (married Louis Bigger) and Violet (married Hugh Bostock in 1930). Hubert (1873-1905) was killed accidentally when he dived into a half filled swimming pool. His wife was Mabel Caulfield (of the Earl of Charlemont's family). They had no children. Harold (1876-1919) an Anglican scholar and a pastor was unmarried. Two of the four daughters of Bishop Charles married and had families – Lilian who married Rev. Lennox Smith and Mabel who married Edward Martin, a barrister.

We now revert back to the main branch of the family. The eldest son Charles (1772-1857) after his initial schooling went to Trinity College in Dublin. After his studies there were completed he was called to the Bar. It is probable that he practiced, at least until the time his father died in 1818. His wife, whom he married in 1801, was Caroline Tighe of Rossanagh, Co. Wicklow the diarist of the family. In addition to being a very devoted mother Caroline found time to display her artistic talents. She painted numerous very worthy artistic works but her enduring legacy must surely be her humorous sketches which look satirically at the lives of the gentry as she perceived them. They had three sons, Charles William, William Tighe and Frederick John and three daughters, Sarah, Mary and Caroline Elizabeth. Two of those ladies married, Sarah the eldest and Caroline Elizabeth the youngest. Their husbands were Rev. Hon. Francis Howard (2nd son of the Earl of Wicklow) and Captain Trevor Stannans respectively. Sarah and the Rev. Hon. Francis had a family.

Charles Hamilton, of Hamwood.
d 1857

(Courtesy Mrs. Anne Hamilton)

William Tighe (1807-1863)[232] was married to one of the Ponsonbys (Lords Bessborough) and they had one son Frederick Fitz Roy who appears to have died young. Frederick John (1816-1893) was married to Frances Gethin (granddaughter of Sir Richard Gethin of Sligo) and they have descendants.

The eldest son, Charles William (1802-1880), became a J.P. for Co. Meath. His wife was Letitia Armstrong from Mount Heaton, Co. Offaly. They had three sons, Charles Robert, Edward Chetwood (1847-1937) and Arthur (1848-1941). All three were married but the family of Edward Chetwood seems to have died out in late 1800s. Of Arthur's sons only Edward Richard Monck had children. Edward emigrated to Canada where

---

[232] There is a portrait of William Tighe when he was a child in Hamwood. In the portrait he is dressed as a girl – seemingly a 19th century superstitious practice. Little boys were dressed in this manner to prevent fairies from stealing them away to become changelings - Marianne Heron in *The Hidden Houses of Ireland*

his descendants live. Another of Arthur's sons, Geoffrey was killed at Gallipoli in World War I.

Charles W. Hamilton of Hamwood.

(Courtesy Mrs. Anne Hamilton)

Charles Robert (1846-1913), a J.P. of counties Meath and Dublin had the task of dismantling the estate under the Land Acts of the three decades prior to his death. His wife was Louisa Brooke of Summerton, Co. Dublin and Coolgreany, Co. Wexford. They had two sons, Gerald Francis and Frederick Arthur, who survived to adulthood and six daughters only one of whom married. She was Lilian, the youngest and her husband was Major John Bonham, from Newcastle, Co. Down. Two of the daughters, Eva Henrietta and Letitia Marion were very highly reputable artists. Eva specialised in portrait painting while her sister Letitia, RHA, was an important landscape painter. They both died in the 1960s.

Frederick Arthur (1880-1962) was educated at Sandhurst and got a commission in the Army rising to the rank of Lt. Col. He served in the Boer War, in World War I and in the Afghan War. He received an OBE in 1919. He married Phyllis Williams the daughter of Major General Sir Godfrey Williams. They lived in Great Obsession in England where Lt. Col. Hamilton was a J.P. They had two sons, Godfrey John (1912- ?) and Hopton Fownes (1913-?). Both sons got commissions in the Army and Godfrey John rose to the rank of General while Hopton became a Lt. Colonel. Both men were married and they have numerous children and grandchildren.

Charles R Hamilton

(Courtesy Mrs. Anne Hamilton)

The eldest surviving son and heir of Charles Robert was his 2nd son Gerald Francis (1877-1961). Gerald Francis was educated at Haileybury and later at Downton Agricultural College. His first wife was Violet Travers, a cousin from Canada, and they had one son Charles and two daughters Esme and Elizabeth.

Charles (1918-2005) was educated at Stowe and Sandhurst. He served in World War II and rose to the rank of Major. He married Anne Spicer of Carnew Castle, Co. Wicklow. Anne's sister, the artist Philippa Dacres-Dixon has a daughter Emily who is married to the Hon. William Bunbury, heir apparent to the present Lord Rathdonnell.

Charles and Anne have one son Charles Ralph and one daughter Annabel Honour.

Charles Ralph is married to Francesca Edwards and they have one son Frederick Charles who was born in 2001.

Langford of Summerhill
(Barons Langford)

Dean Swift[233]   wrote of some of his parishioners in the parish of Laracor -

> Mr. Percival is Ditching, Mrs Percival in her Kitchen,
> Mr. Wesley Switching, Mrs. Wesley Stitching,[234]
> Sir Arthur Langford, Riching.

Langford was a thorn in the Dean's side owing to his support for a Presbyterian minister at his private chapel. Because he refused to close the Presbyterian Meeting House at Summerhill he felt the lash of Swift's tongue 'I have always looked upon you as an honest gentleman of great charity and piety in your way, and I hope you will remember at the same time, that it becomes you to be a legal man, and that you will not promote or encourage, much less give a beginning to a thing directly contrary to the law. You know the dissenters in Ireland are suffered to have their

---

[233] At Laracor, a mile or two from Trim, and twenty miles from Dublin, Swift ministered to a congregation of about fifteen persons, and had abundant leisure for cultivating his garden, making a canal (after the Dutch fashion of Moor Park), planting willows, and rebuilding the vicarage. He was there in 1700.

[234] These were the grandparents of the famous Duke of Wellington, Arthur Wellesley who changed his name back from Wesley in 1798 when he served in India. In the 16th century the family name was in fact Wellesley.

conventicles only by connivance and that only in places where they formerly used to meet'

The Rowleys settled in Ireland in the early part of the 17th century. Three brothers, John, Nathaniel and William were the first of that family to arrive on this island. It is most likely they came to Ireland with Chichester the Lord Deputy. They probably benefited from the distribution of lands in the Plantation of Ulster. They appear to have been granted some lands in Derry and Edward, John's son was based at Castle Roe near Londonderry where he was elected an M.P.

John made a very good match with the daughter of an up and coming landlord, Sir Hugh Clotworthy[235], from neighbouring Co. Antrim. Sir John Rowley was John's son and heir.

The Rowley connection with Meath began in 1671 when Sir John Rowley, M.P. married Mary the only child and heir of Sir Hercules Langford of Summerhill and his wife Mary Upton. Sir John Rowley and Mary Langford had only one son and one daughter. The daughter was Letitia and her husband was Arthur Loftus, the 3rd Viscount Loftus of Ely. Letitia was widowed in the mid 1700s and she married again. Her second husband was Nicholas Loftus a cousin of her husband and she was his second wife.

The only son, Hercules Rowley, married his cousin Frances Upton of Castle Upton, Co. Antrim, in 1705. It must have been he who inherited from Sir Hercules Langford as that man's will was proved in 1683. Hercules and Frances had one son who was later entitled The Hon. Hercules Langford Rowley.

The Hon. Hercules was born about 1714 at Summerhill. He was High Sheriff of Co. Meath in 1738 and was M.P. for Londonderry. Sir John Blaquiere wrote of him that he was a man "of very great property - courts popularity and has almost constantly been adverse to government" Rev John R. Scott said of him that "His language unadorned by any curious solutions or accurate polish is plain strong and clear ... his manner is warm and spirited and even vehement ... His matter the product of extensive information long thought and old experience, is entitled to and receives reverent regard." At the time of his death in 1794 his estate was considerable and was worth £18,000 p.a. The Langfords owned almost

---

[235] Sir Hugh's son, John was created the Earl of Massareene by King Charles II.

10,000 acres in three different counties, 2,231 in Meath, 3,855 in Limerick and 3,659 in Dublin.[236]

Summerhill
(Courtesy IAA)

In October of 1732 the Hon. Hercules married his cousin, the Hon. Elizabeth Ormsby Upton the daughter and heir of Clotworthy Upton who died in the same year. Elizabeth also inherited the Ormsby lands in Limerick. In 1766 Elizabeth was created Baroness Summerhill and Viscountess Langford of Langford Lodge, Antrim[237] with remainder to her male heirs. Hercules and Elizabeth had three sons, Hercules, Clotworthy and Arthur and two daughters Jane and Catherine. Jane married Thomas Taylour the Earl of Bective in 1754 and their third son became the 3rd Baron Langford. Catherine married Edward Pakenham, Lord Longford, in 1768.[238]

---

[236] *Great Landowners of Great Britain and Ireland* – John Bateman
[237] Langford Lodge, near Belfast, later passed to the Pakenhams and is now an Aviation Museum.
[238] Lady Longford appears to have become wealthy in her own right as in her will made in 1813 she left some hefty bequests e.g. £1000 each to her daughters and

Arthur the 3rd son died unmarried and Clotworthy the 2nd son became a career Army officer rising to the rank of Major in the 5th Dragoons. Clotworthy married Elizabeth Crosbie a granddaughter of the Earl of Mornington.[239] Clotworthy died in 1781.They had an only daughter Frances.

After the death of Elizabeth the Baroness in 1791, her eldest son, Hercules succeeded to become the 2nd Viscount. Her husband, the Hon. Hercules survived three years longer and died in 1794 at the age of eighty.

Hercules (1737-1796), Elizabeth's son, was an M.P. for Co. Antrim until he took his seat in the House of Lords in 1791, the year his mother died. In the year prior to this in 1790 the Langfords got a licence to hold an annual fair at Summerhill[240] Arthur Young in his travels in Ireland visited Summerhill. He had this to say – 'The country is cheerful and rich; and if the Irish cabins continue like what I have hitherto seen, I shall not hesitate to pronounce their inhabitants as well off as most English cottagers. They are built of mud wall 18 inches or 2 feet thick and well thatched, which are far warmer than the thin clay walls in England. Here are few cottars without a cow and sometimes two. A belly full invariably of potatoes and generally turf for fuel from a bog. It is true they have not always chimneys to their cabins, the door serving for that and window too. Every cottage swarms with poultry and most of them have pigs. The plantation and ornamented grounds at Summerhill are extensive and form a fine environ, spreading over the hills and having a noble appearance from the high lands above the bog. The house is large and handsome with an elegant hall, a cube of 30 feet, and many very good and convenient apartments

Hercules never married and after his death in 1796 he was succeeded by his niece Frances. In the same year that her grandfather died (1794) Frances married her cousin, the Hon. Clotworthy Taylour. Born in 1763 Clotworthy was the 4th son of Lord Headfort[241]. He was an M.P. for Trim and also for Meath during the later decades of the century until his elevation to the peerage as Baron Langford in 1800. He was High Sheriff of

---

granddaughter and sums of £200 to many other family members and smaller sums to various servants and acquaintances.

[239] Morningtons had the surname Wellesley from which family the famous Duke of Wellington descended.

[240] Danny Cusack in *Riocht na Midhe* 1998

[241] See that family in this volume.

Meath in 1796. After his marriage to Frances in 1794 Clotworthy assumed the name and arms of Rowley. The Baron and his wife had two sons and two daughters both of whom married, Elizabeth to Admiral Ferguson and Harriet to Chevalier Antoine de Satgé.

Bodyrhyddan Hall

The second son Richard Thomas was a career Army officer rising to the rank of Colonel. He settled at Flint in Wales where he married an English lady, Charlotte Shipley the niece of a baronet.[242] The newly-weds decided to honeymoon travelling in Egypt and the Sudan in 1835-36. From diaries and sketches recording their experiences an article *A Honeymoon in Egypt and the Sudan* was written by Peter Rowley-Conwy c.2002 A.D. They were accompanied on the trip by Charlotte's brother William Shipley-Conwy. They travelled to Petra, the ancient Jordanian city and left their

---

[242] Charlotte died in 1871 and the Colonel married again the following year to Alice Berners from Flint. Charlotte was the last of the Conwys from Flint, a very distinguished family who could trace their lineage back to Hugh Conwy who lived in the early 12th century.

signatures behind engraved on the walls of the Khazneh, an archaic tomb in that place. Charlotte was thought to have been the first European woman ever to have visited Petra.

Khazneh in Jordan

Richard was an M.P. for Harwich from 1860 to 1865. The Colonel and Charlotte had one son and two daughters. It was the Colonel's son who introduced the name Conwy into the family when he inherited Bodrhyddan Estate. While he was christened Conwy Greville he changed his surname to Rowley-Conwy.

Conwy's third son Geoffrey survived to adulthood and was an officer in the Army. He fought in the First World War and was killed in action at Gallipoli in 1915. Geoffrey was married to Bertha Cochran and they had three children – a son Geoffrey and a daughter Rose Marian.[243] Geoffrey later succeeded as the 9th Baron Langford.

The eldest son (of the 1st Baron) Hercules Langford the 2nd Baron (1795-1839), a D.L. for counties Meath and Dublin was married in 1818 to Louisa Rhodes. He was a noted sportsman and in 1828 he bought two

---

[243] Rose Marian married Ralph Becher Skinner and they had one son David and two daughters Meriel and Rosalind.

famous horses – a mare called Peri and a stallion called Sir Hercules. This stallion stood at Summerhill, in Ireland, and later in England where he ranked among the top sires. He was noted for the silver hairs on his flanks and quarters and at the root of his tail, which he often passed on to his descendants.

Sir Hercules

The 2nd Baron and Louisa had three sons, Clotworthy, Hercules and Hugh. Hugh, predictably found a commission in the Army and settled in England. Although married twice, Hugh had no children.

Hercules the second son (1828-1904) settled on the Dublin property of Marlay Park, which thankfully has not entirely disappeared. He was a part time Army officer, a J.P. and a D.L. for Co. Meath and honorary Colonel in the 5th Battalion of the Leinster Regiment. Like many wealthy men of his time he had a pad in London and was a member of the Kildare Club on St. Stephen's Green in Dublin and the Carlton in London. His wife was Louisa, a sister of Baron Blythswood.[244]

Louisa and Hercules of Marlay Park had two sons and three daughters. Two of those ladies married and one of them, Gladys, married Claude Guinness. The two sons were Hercules Douglas and Arthur. Both

---

[244] Descended from the Scots family of Campbell.

men had commissions in the Army and Hercules Douglas of Marlay Park was a J.P. and a D.L. for Co. Dublin.[245]

Clotworthy Rowley (3rd Baron Langford)

---

[245] Arthur became a diplomat and was consul in Tahiti from 1908 until 1912 and from there he moved as consul to Bordeaux. His wife was a Chilean, Margarita the daughter of Hugh Jamieson. Hercules Douglas married Mary Allen from Wiltshire and they had two daughters Ivy and Monica who married respectively Reginald Boulter from Surrey and Edward Huskinson from Nottinghamshire.

Clotworthy (1825-1854), the eldest son of the 2nd Baron, succeeded his father in 1839 when that man died at the comparatively young age of forty four. Clotworthy was only fourteen at the time. In 1846 when he was just 21 years old, Clotworthy now the 3rd Baron Langford married Louisa Connolly from Castletown, the daughter of Colonel Michael Edward Connolly who was an M.P. for Kildare. They had three sons, Hercules Edward, William Chambré and Randolph Thomas. The youngest boy was just one year old when tragedy struck the family. Louisa was drowned in a tragic accident. Randolph Thomas became a Navy officer after his early education and married Rosetta Fletcher of Addison Lodge, Dublin and Kati Kati New Zealand. They had a son Clotworthy Wellington who became in due course the 7th Baron Langford.

Hercules Edward (1848-1919) succeeded as the 4th Baron in 1854 when he was just six years old. Having been educated at Eton he got a commission in the Army and rose to the rank of Lt. Colonel. He also occupied various official posts and was State Steward to the Lord Lieutenant of Ireland from 1862 to 1892 and Comptroller from 1895 to 1902. It was during his tenure as Baron that the most glamorous and exciting young woman to have ever graced the steps of Summerhill in the person of the Empress 'Sisi' of Austria arrived. She came there for a month in the spring of 1879, having been alerted to the fact that the best hunting in the British Isles was to be had in Co. Meath. She rented Summerhill from the young Lord Langford who stayed there as a member of her party for that month and for the month the Empress stayed in 1880. She was reputed to have been an excellent horsewoman 'taking the banks and ditches more recklessly than the most daredevil Irish'.[246] Her bravery and beauty captured the hearts of the men folk, though it is probable that the gentle ladies felt many a flutter of jealousy and envy.

Hercules Edward had to oversee the dismantling of the Langford empire in Ireland following the various Land Acts of the late 19th and early 20th centuries. Although, on paper at least, the family seemed to be very wealthy, the fact that they were compelled to rent the house meant that their annual outgoings were extremely high. It is probable that the repayment of borrowings was the biggest drain on the family finances. These troublesome annoyances were just that and did not prevent the

---

[246] *Twilight of the Ascendancy* – Mark Bence Jones

family members from participating to the full in the social scene. In the late 1890s Lord Langford was given permission to hold a dinner party in the Strangers Room, in the Kildare Club. The dinner party was in honour of the Viceroy. The committee were at pains to point out to his lordship that people living within a twenty mile radius of Dublin could not be brought in as guests.[247] A couple of years later, in 1901, tragedy struck the household when Lord Langford's wife, Georgina, died. She was the daughter of Sir Richard Sutton of Norwood Park, Nottingham.

They had been married since 1889 and they had three sons John Hercules, George Cecil and Noel Maud. The Baron remarried in 1915. His 2nd wife was Margaret Mitchell-Carruthers. The First World War took a heavy toll on the families of the gentry and aristocracy. Lord Langford lost his son, which was all the more poignant since his other son was mentally unstable.[248] He now had no immediate heir as his brother was old and had no family, but he had a nephew in New Zealand, Clotworthy Wellington. His brother Colonel William Chambré looked after the estate during the last years of the 4th Baron's life.

However tragedy struck this family once again when in 1921 Summerhill was burned by the I.R.A. The following is an account of the incident from the Langford Papers.

'On the night of 4 February, when Colonel and Mrs Rowley were away, the five servants who lived in the house were sitting together in the kitchen and heard a knock on the back door. The English butler, without opening the door, asked who it was; a voice answered: 'a friend.' The butler was taking no chances and left the door shut, hoping the intruder would go away, but a whistle blew and a few minutes later he and the other servants heard the back door being battered in. They escaped through a door in the basement and went out into the darkness; they could hear windows being smashed and they saw two men heading in the direction of the garage, where the petrol was stored. As the servants walked down the avenue on their way to the farm they came in sight of the house and saw the kitchen wing ablaze and flames coming also from the

---

247 *Twilight of the Ascendancy* – Mark Bence Jones
248 Ibid.

drawing room. Later, from further away, they could see that the house was on fire in several different places.'[249]

The 4th Baron did not have to endure the early death of his eldest son John Hercules as he was already deceased then the 5th Baron died in 1922 aged only 28. The 5th Baron was succeeded by his uncle, William Chambré Rowley, the 2nd son of the 3rd Baron. William Chambré was 73 years old when he became the 6th Baron Langford of Summerhill. A career Army officer, William Chambré, rose to the rank of Lt. Colonel. He fought in the Afghan Wars in 1879-1880 and received the Croix de Guerre in World War One, when he was quite elderly.

In due course Colonel Rowley, the 6th Baron, following the death of his nephew in 1922, sought compensation from the Free State Government for Summerhill and its contents. After three years of wrangling with the Compensation Board it was finally agreed that a sum of £43,500 would be paid. This was less than one third of the estimated value of the house and contents but represented the final offer of settlement. Colonel Rowley accepted the money which was paid in 1924. He invested the money in gilt-edged stocks.[250] Colonel Rowley and his wife moved to Middlesex and continued living there until their deaths. During the period after the burning and the date of settlement, the Colonel had consulted his New Zealand relatives about the possibility of rebuilding the house and maintaining a family presence there but none of them were overly anxious to live in Ireland. Arthur Rowley, the British Consul General in Barcelona wrote that he had 'no wish to live in that unfortunate country'. His sister, Mrs. Milner, who lived in England, stated that 'nothing would induce me to live in Ireland....a country of murderers'. [251]

Although married to Lady Mabel Newton, who lived to the ripe old age of 102, he had no children. He died in 1931 and Lady Mabel lived until 1966.

The next in line for the title was Clotworthy Wellington, mentioned above who became 7th Baron in 1931, when his uncle William Chambré died. Clotworthy was 46 at the time. Clotworthy appears to have spent some time in New Zealand as he joined the Army there and fought in the

---

[249] The Langford Papers as quoted in *Twilight of the Ascendancy*
[250] Ibid.
[251] Ibid

uniform of that country in World War I. His wife was Eileen Shiel from Ballsbridge, Dublin and they had two children but both died young. The 7th Baron lived until 1952 and on his death the title passed to Arthur Rowley, mentioned above, a grandson of the first Baron.

Sir Arthur (knighted in 1932) was in the diplomatic corps and in addition to his consular posts mentioned above was appointed Consul General in Barcelona (1918-1923). This was followed by postings to Antwerp (1923-1930) and then to Paris (1930-1932). As already mentioned he was married to Margarita Jamieson who died in 1928. Sir Arthur married again in 1929. His wife was Maud Alice Lelacheur from Guernsey. He had no children by either of his wives.

Ruins of Summerhill 1960
(Courtesy IAA)

Arthur the 8th Baron Langford only lived a further year to enjoy his title, dying in 1953. The title then passed to Geoffrey Alexander Rowley-Conwy mentioned above, the 9th Baron.

Geoffrey (1912- ?) an Army officer with the rank of Colonel was decorated for his gallantry and bravery during the 2nd World War. He was captured in Singapore and made a prisoner of war but managed to escape. He was made a freeman of the City of London in 1977. Married in 1939 he divorced his wife, Ruth St. John Murphy from Little Island, Cork, in 1956. Geoffrey remarried in 1957 and his second wife was Grete von Freiesleben from Copenhagen. Geoffrey and Grete have three sons, Peter Alexander and John Seymour, born prior to the marriage and a third son Owain Grenville, the heir. Geoffrey married for a third time in 1975 and he and his wife, Susan Denham have two children, Christopher Geoffrey and Charlotte Susan.

Three of his four sons are married and have children. Peter Alexander, a very famous archaeologist and lecturer in Durham University married Deborah Stevens and they have two daughters Gabrielle and Eleanor. John Seymour, a scientist, married Emma Brown and they have two sons William and Huw and a daughter Katherine. Owain Grenville married Joanna Featherstone and they have a son Thomas and a daughter Madeleine.

Plunkett of Dunsany
(Barons of Dunsany)

Perhaps the most famous of all the Plunkett Barons of Dunsany was Edward John Moreton Drax Plunkett, the 18th Baron, 1878–1957, a most prolific and talented author.

He was reputed to have said of Yeats that he was 'a rebel, a mystic and an ass but really a genius in a queer way'.[252]He befriended and encouraged the poet Francis Ledwidge, a labourer, tragically killed in World War I, whose poetry has proved to be enduring. [253]

Often dealing with the fantastic and the supernatural, Dunsany's works are frequently set in wholly imaginary worlds and involve myths and legends of his own making. His prose works include *A Dreamer's Tales* (1910), *The Book of Wonder* (1912), *My Talks with Dean Spanley* (1936), *The Story of Mona Sheehy* (1937), and *A Glimpse from a Watch Tower* (1946). Lord Dunsany's plays include *The Glittering Gate* (1909), *The Gods of the Mountain* (1911), and *The Golden Doom* (1912). These books were reportedly mostly written with a quill pen. His works were most popular in the early years of the century, but as Ireland and Europe moved relentlessly into post World

---

[252] *Biography of Lord Dunsany* by Mark Amory

[253] Edward, the present Lord Dunsany is adamant that his grandfather was totally opposed to Ledwidge joining the Army. He stated publicly at the time that 'a law should be passed prohibiting poets from joining armies.'

War II modernism, interest in his works declined, but interest in his writings is burgeoning once again especially in Eastern European countries.

Horace Plunkett (1854 – 1932), Edward's uncle, might be seen by some people as a more significant figure not alone on the family stage but because he was a man of international importance due to his passionate involvement with the Co-Operative movement. The Plunkett Foundation which is today a vibrant force promoting the philosophy of co-operation said of him:-

'Horace Plunkett was a truly extraordinary figure: a combination of the idealist with a man of business; a poor public speaker and yet a great publicist; a man of strong family affections who never married; a man who drove his subordinates hard yet inspired in many a life-long devotion; an aristocrat of great charm and exquisite manners who drew his metaphors from the cowboys on the Wyoming cattle range. But beneath these superficial contradictions were attributes of courage, strength of character and a desire to serve. In the words of his friend Lady Fingall, "Ireland had laid her burden on him" an appropriate comment because his was indeed a dedicated life.'[254]

Having graduated from Oxford, Horace Plunkett decided to try his hand at ranching in America. He went to Wyoming where he bought a ranch on the Powder River. He returned occasionally from America, mainly to try to help out his sister Mary, who had married Chambre Ponsonby of Kilcooley.[255] Chambre had gone to visit Horace at his ranch with a view to possibly moving there but died tragically on his way home in 1884. Horace came back to Ireland eventually some time after his father's death in 1889.

A deep thinking man, he was much concerned with the plight of the Irish farmers. He decided to set up a co-operative in the dairy sector and his first experiment was in south west Ireland. The historian who wrote the copy for the Plunkett Foundation takes up the story:-

'Farmers were at first suspicious of a landlord and a Protestant, and the early years were a constant struggle against commercial opposition and inherent fatalism. But the idea was sound. Irish farmers soon appreciated the benefits of controlling the production and marketing of their staple commodity, and in 1894

---

[254] From a biography of Horace Plunkett on the Plunkett Foundation website
[255] See *The Tipperary Gentry* by Art Kavanagh and Wm. Hayes

Plunkett founded the Irish Agricultural Organisation Society with 33 affiliated dairy co-operative societies or "creameries", as they were popularly known.'[256]

Within four years there were more than 200 societies affiliated to the IAOS. Horace now turned his attention to the lack of administration in the agricultural sector and began a campaign in the House of Commons where he was an M.P. for South Dublin. His relentless pressure led to the setting up of the Department of Agriculture and Technical Instruction, a body of which he was vice president.

When King Edward VII and Queen Alexandra came to Ireland in 1903 on their coronation visit they brought with them a motor car which they used for touring the poorer areas of the West known as the Congested Districts. In Connemara it broke down, but was got going again by the chauffeur of Horace Plunkett, who was the proud owner of a De Dion Bouton. At the end of the tour the King made Plunkett a KCVO[257] which his friends thought hardly adequate in view of all that he had done for Irish agriculture.[258]

Horace was elected Chairman of the Irish Convention which was held in the aftermath of the 1916 rebellion. The purpose of this Convention was to try to get agreement from all shades of Unionism, north and south, on their approach to Home Rule. As ever the Northern Unionists were intractable and the Convention achieved nothing.

Because of his independent way of thinking he became a persona non grata politically. He was denounced by Edward Carson as a traitor to unionism in 1919 and in 1923 his fine mansion, Kilteragh[259], in Foxrock,

---

[256] From a biography of Horace Plunkett on the Plunkett Foundation website
[257] Knight Commander of the Royal Victorian Order.
[258] Mark Bence Jones – *The Twilight of the Ascendancy*
[259] Kilteragh a large villa at Foxrock, between the Dublin Mountains and the sea was built by Horace Plunkett to the design of a Swedish architect. It was fan shaped to catch the sun. Plunkett's own bedroom was on the roof and open to the elements. It could be turned to face whichever way he fancied by means of a handle reached from his bed. The house was always full of guests. People would come out from Dublin for luncheon or dinner; people came from other parts of the country; 'everyone interesting or interested who visited Ireland' came here. The talk was nearly always about Ireland and the way in which the country should in future be governed. His dream was that the new Irish constitution should be signed on the stoep or porch outside his windows, which he had copied from the

near Dublin city, was almost destroyed by the nationalists in the Civil War. He left Ireland after that and lived out the rest of his life in London. He died in 1932. Inscribed on his headstone in the churchyard of St Mary's at Byfleet are the words, "Behold the sower went forth to sow".

Down through the later centuries the Dunsanys had often lived abroad and often married foreigners. Their values and their friends came largely from the English upper classes. The family, as such, had never been interested in money, nor in the efficiency which leads to money. They had been soldiers, politicians and country gentlemen.[260]

The origins of the family reach so far back into antiquity that no one is quite sure where the family originated. Lady Fingall's account of the origins of the family is as good as any 'the first of the family in Ireland came here with white jennets from which the family were called Blanc jenet and in time Planc jenet and so Plunkett.'

They definitely 'arrived' in Co. Meath when Sir Christopher Plunkett, the primal ancestor of the family married the daughter and heir of Sir Lucas Cusack, of Killeen in the early 15th century. They had two sons John and Christopher. John became the ancestor of the Killeen branch and Christopher the ancestor of the Dunsany family. Christopher's wife was the daughter and heir of a younger son of the 3rd Earl of Kildare and he was settled at Dunsany which relatively adjacent to Killeen.

Tradition has it that the boundary between the Killeen and Dunsany lands was settled by the then wives of the Lords of Killeen and Dunsany having a race. Each woman started walking from her own castle and the boundary was put up at the meeting place. The Lady of Killeen gained a few yards for her husband. Lady Dunsany it appeared held a grudge because of this and refused to attend Killeen church in the future. She went on to persuade her husband to build an identical church at Dunsany except it was to be a foot bigger in all its dimensions.

Dunsany Castle was built probably by Hugh de Lacy in the early 13th century. The castle consisted of two huge tower blocks later joined by a hall in the late 18th century. The 13th Lord carried out substantial improvements including the replacement of the windows and refurbishment of the library. The work in the library 'combines gothic

---

one at Groote Schuur, Cecil Rhodes's house near Cape Town- Mark Bence Jones – *The Twilight of the Ascendancy*
[260] Ibid.

book-cases and graining effect simulating wood plus a remarkable groined ceiling to engender a quite magical atmosphere'[261] The works were supervised by James Shiel. The plasterwork in the drawing room on the first floor is by Michael Stapleton.

Dunsany Castle

The earlier Dunsanys always managed to marry well and the 4th Baron was no exception. His wife was the daughter and heir of Philip Birmingham. However his good fortune was short lived as he was killed by the O'Connors of Offaly in 1521.

Patrick the 7th Baron received an enamelled cup from Queen Elizabeth the First, which is still in Dunsany. The same man said 'We were always fighting on the wrong side. We fought for Perkin Warbeck and for Lambert Simnel'.[262] The 8th Baron is remembered only because during his tenure of Dunsany, Oldcastle (where they had lands) was given a licence for a fair.[263]

---

[261] *Burkes Peerage and Baronetage*
[262] These men were pretenders to the throne
[263] Danny Cusack in *Riocht na Midhe* 1998

The 7th Baron's grandson, Patrick Plunkett, the 9th Lord Dunsany fought for Charles I against Cromwell and was imprisoned. His lands were declared forfeit. While her husband was languishing in jail, Lady Dunsany defended her castle and 'was torn weeping from the scene of her former happiness and was exiled to Connaught' as Lecky said. This is what Prendergast had to say about the episode 'Other adventurers whose lots had fallen in the barony of Skreen, in the county of Meath, were anxious to plant and commence the improvement of that neighbourhood. In their lot lay the castle and lands late the estate of Lord Dunsany. In 1655 they had sent their agents over to Ireland, and on the 13th July in that year proceeded to the castle of Dunsany, accompanied by the high constable and sheriff of the county bearing the order of the Council, and demanded entrance and possession of the place for the adventurers. But the Lord Dunsany's lady denied the possession unless she was forcibly carried thence. There was a pause; probably the sheriff was friendly, and advised a delay - a report to the principals, perhaps, in London or Bristol. Next year they came themselves, Hans Graham and others; and on the 4th July, 1656, the high constable with his force was ordered peremptorily to put the adventurers into the quiet possession of the castle; and Major Stanley, justice of the peace, was ordered to keep the peace there, whilst poor Lady Dunsany should be removed by main force from her home by the high constable and his men.'[264]

Although the Lord was restored to his titles and castle by Charles II he only recovered part of his estates. He was succeeded in his title and estates by his grandson, Christopher, who upon his death relinquished them to his brother Randal.[265]

Randal Plunkett (d. 1735), a staunch Catholic, fought for James II against the Protestant King William III and he too suffered by being attainted.[266] His lands were further depleted but were rescued in the early

---

[264] *Cromwellian Settlement of Ireland* - Prendergast

[265] The Christian name, Randal, was brought to the family when Randal's mother married the 10th Baron. She was the daughter of Randal, the 1st Earl of Antrim.

[266] Many of the Catholic Lords of Co. Meath all fought in the Williamite Wars and Lord Slane lost his life at the Battle of the Boyne. Lady Slane with her children fled to Dublin and threw herself on the mercy of William of Orange who gave her safe conduct to France on condition that she renounced all claim to the lands and properties of Slane. Fortunately the Slanes had a French estate and also a French

decades of the 18th century when his son Edward, later the 12th Baron of Dunsany turned Protestant.

Relations between the Plunketts of Killeen and the Plunketts of Dunsany were always very close and it was Randal, the 13th Baron who shielded his Killeen relatives during the worst period of the Penal Laws. He did this by pretending ownership of the Killeen Castle and lands. According to the law, as a Protestant, he was entitled to the ownership of estates belonging to his Catholic relatives. This arrangement worked extremely well and the Plunketts of Killeen were left undisturbed in their occupancy of the Castle and lands.

Randal Plunkett the 13th Baron Dunsany
(Courtesy Lord & Lady Dunsany)

---

title. A Fleming family in France today continues to use the title Lords of Slane and it is thought that one of their members was buried secretly in the Fleming vault during the last century.

Lady Fingall saw a letter from a later Lord Dunsany written to his cousin at Killeen 'My dear Fingall, I am an old man now and shall soon have to meet my Maker. I do not want to go to Him with a lie upon my soul. Could you not get someone else to swear that the land and property are theirs?'[267]

According to a letter written to Lady Fingall by Lord Dunsany he noted that one of his ancestors had 'neglected to avail himself of the Treaty of Limerick by signing something by a certain date, so he went on the run and died on the run and lost everything. The estates were only restored to his grandson in 1732' He went on to say he had just then consulted documents which were in the room where he wrote his letter.

Edward the 12th Baron was always in financial difficulties. His fortunes were at such a low ebb in the mid 1700s that his son, Randal (1738-1821) was unable to attend school and was unable to write his name at the age of sixteen. However he had cousins at the court of Spain and he went there where he received an education.[268] When he returned as 13th Baron Dunsany the castle was in such disrepair that he said he would abandon it if the roof was faulty. The roof, upon inspection, proved to be rainproof and he moved into the castle and began to make improvements. He managed to get the attainder on the family reversed and took his seat in the House of Lords[269]. As part of his improvements to the castle and grounds and in order to obtain more privacy he succeeded in having a road that ran close to the castle closed by Act of Parliament. People still insisted on using the old road but Randal, the 13th Baron, a large man, is said to have stood guard at the bridge and threw trespassers bodily into the waters below if they tried to cross.

Randal's wife was a Mandeville from Tipperary and they had two sons and four daughters, two of whom married, Margaret to the 11th Earl of Louth[270] and the youngest, Anna Maria, to Philip Roche of Donore, Co. Kildare.

In 1798, following a council of war among the Plunketts a decision was made to defend Killeen (from the rebels) rather than both castles and

---

[267] *Seventy Years Young* by Lady Fingall
[268] *Biography of Lord Dunsany* by Mark Amory
[269] Ibid.
[270] The Louths were also Plunketts and were related to the families of Killeen and Dunsany but only very distantly.

so Dunsany was abandoned for a short period. During the rebellion Dunsany castle was taken over by the rebels and might have been destroyed entirely had it not been for the local brewer who prevented them from sacking the cellars. He is reported to have said 'Boys, if you enter the Lord's cellar, it shall be over my dead body!' In order to return the favour the Dunsany family 'drank no other beer than that supplied by the brewer and his descendants, though it was not good, and so it was a relief when the firm eventually failed, as had the rebellion'.[271] In the years after the rebellion there was still unrest among the people that caused some unease even in the castles. In 1805 Lord Dunsany was much alarmed by reports of meetings taking place near his Castle, and reported that many assaults were connected with these meetings and that the meetings were simply moving from parish to parish without anyone trying to suppress them.[272]

The 13th Baron spent some of his time abroad and on the night he died in Brussels it is said that his ghost appeared in an archway at Dunsany.

Randal's eldest son, Edward (1773 – 1848), later the 14th Baron pursued an Army Career and became a Colonel in the Coldstream Guards. He spent a lot of time abroad fighting in America in the War of 1812 and in Europe against Napoleon. He also lived for several years in Italy. He was married in 1803 to Charlotte, a daughter of Lord Cloncurry. Following his father's death in 1821 he retired to Dunsany with his wife and family. There were two sons and a daughter Emily.[273] The two sons were predictably Randal and Edward. Life at Dunsany was generally pleasant and serene but during the period of the Tithe and agrarian unrest extra precautions had to be taken. For example in 1831 labour unrest reached such a level that special constables were sworn in at Dunshaughlin and Lord Dunsany sent his ladies to Dublin and also swore in special constables.[274]

Edward, the 14th Baron, had the unpleasant experience of opening his paper one morning only to see the Reversion of the Family Estates

---

[271] *Biography of Lord Dunsany* by Mark Amory
[272] *Riocht na Midhe 1987* - Desmond Mooney – The origins of Agrarian Violence in Meath
[273] Emily married George Price, went to Jamaica with him and died there in 1864.
[274] *Riocht na Midhe 1989* – Desmond Mooney 's article *Agrarian Violence in Meath*

offered for sale.[275] His heir Randal (1804 – 1852), later the 15th Baron, was the culprit. He was a 'ne'er do well' and during his time the family fortunes sank once more.

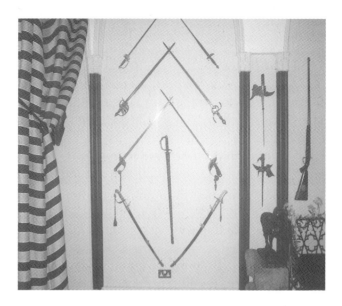

Entrance Hall, Dunsany
(Courtesy Lord & Lady Dunsany)

The 16th Baron, the prudent younger son restored the situation to something bordering the status quo as he managed to buy back some of the lands and acquired coalmines which later became valuable. He was an officer in the Navy and rose to the rank of Admiral. He was also a D.L. for County Meath when in residence there. His wife, whom he married in 1846, was the daughter of Lord Shelburne. They had four sons and two daughters who married.[276]

The sons were Randall, John William, Horace and Edward who died in childhood. Randall (1848-1883) also died at a comparatively young age, six years before his father. He was an M.P. for Gloucester from 1874-80. Horace has already been alluded to earlier in this chapter and John William was the father of Edward the writer. When the 16th Baron died in

---

[275] *Biography of Lord Dunsany* by Mark Amory
[276] Mary married Chambre Brabazon Ponsonby of Kilcooley, Co.

1884 he left everything except the castle (and title) directly to his grandson Edward, much to the chagrin of the boy's father.

Detail from Entrance Hall, Dunsany
(Courtesy Lord & Lady Dunsany)

John William, the 17th Baron (1853-1899) was neither prudent nor thrifty and was overly fond of the bottle. He also dabbled in drugs for medicinal purposes, because of his delicate state of health and experimented with Roentgen rays. One could have been X-rayed in Dunsany in 1900 but not in hospital before 1905. A Cambridge graduate, John William represented Gloucester in the House of Commons from 1886 to 1892. He married Ernle Grosvenor in 1877. Edward John Moreton Drax and his brother Reggie were born in London and shortly afterwards the family moved to Kent, to Ernle's house, Dunstall Priory near Shoreham. John William the 17th Baron and his wife separated and the children had to shuttle from Kent to Dunsany and back again. He died in 1899 aged 48. Edward was 21. The 17th Baron left many debts which were later paid by his son Edward. Edward's brother Reggie was left an income of £500 per annum.

Uncle Horace seemed to take charge of family affairs and Reggie went off to join the Navy. He fought in World War I and was present at the Battle of Jutland where over 6,000 English sailors lost their lives. After that battle he was recommended for promotion. Admiral Sir David Beatty who made the recommendation said 'he was most valuable in observing the effect of our fire thereby enabling me to take advantage of the enemy's discomfiture'.[277] Reggie was promoted to Rear Admiral in 1928 and was commander in chief of the British Navy forces of the America – West Indies station.

Edward (1878-1957) received his early education at the hands of a governess and when he was nine he was sent to a local boarding school, which he thoroughly enjoyed. After a few years he went to Cheam, a preparatory school and then on to Eton. When he was twenty, just after his father's death in 1899, he joined the Coldstream Guards and was posted to Gibraltar and shortly afterwards to South Africa to fight the Boers. He fought in several memorable battles and emerged unscathed. He fought with the Royal Inniskilling Fusiliers in World War I. He married Lady Beatrice Villiers the daughter of the Earl of Jersey in 1904. He had become the 18th Baron in 1899. The Dunsanys had a house in Derry as well as living at Dunsany Castle.

Whenever he was in Dunsany he hunted with the Meath and was fond of shooting. One day on his return from a day's shooting on the demesne, so as to avoid having to wait for the front door to be opened he shot at the bell.[278]This had the desired effect of a member of staff holding the door open before the party was actually standing in front. He was a keen huntsman and sportsman, and was at one time the chess and pistol champion of Ireland. When his mother died she had left him Dunstall, her family's English property.

---

[277] From Official Papers of the War Office
[278] *Biography of Lord Dunsany* by Mark Amory

Beatrice, Lady Dunsany, was awakened in her Co. Meath home at seven in the morning on the Tuesday of Easter Week in 1916, by a noise outside. From the window she could see a car load of armed men arrive to pick up General Hammond,[279] who was the estate manager. On coming down they heard rumours of a Sinn Fein uprising. Dunsany's son's French governess, who was leaving by train that day, returned from the station saying there were no trains running. Dunsany decided to drive into Dublin to find out what was going on and to offer his services to the military if needed.[280]

Bust of Edward John Moreton Drax Plunkett 18th Baron
(Courtesy Lord & Lady Dunsany)

---

[279] This man continued in his position until he died in the 1940s.
[280] Ibid.

'He set off, driven by his chauffeur and accompanied by a friend called Lindsay who was staying with him. They reached GHQ where Dunsany was told to go to the assistance of an officer in the north eastern section of Dublin. On the way he drove into a rebel road block on the quays near the Four Courts. The car was fired upon and Dunsany jumped out and lay on the road. He was hit in the face. His chauffeur, Cudlipp, held up his hands and had a finger shot off. A man came up and took Dunsany prisoner. Noticing the bullet hole in his face he said 'I am sorry'. He was carried on a stretcher to nearby Jervis Street Hospital and the chauffeur to another hospital. Lindsay was taken prisoner and held in the Four Courts. Remarkably, after the week's fighting the rebels in the Four Courts became very unsure of their situation and asked Lindsay for advice. He examined their plans and found them hopeless. They asked what they should do. Lindsay suggested they should surrender to him. He walked unsteadily out of the Four Courts with four hundred prisoners.'[281]

Edward spent some time in the trenches in France in 1917 but returned home unscathed but on sick leave. During his recuperation he wrote some of his works which were successful in America. After the War he took up a post in the War Office where he remained for a number of years, even touring America, with his wife, giving propaganda lectures. Back in Ireland during 'the Troubles', Dunsany was arrested and accused of having Sinn Fein sympathies. He was a well known Unionist but it took a lot of string pulling before the charges were dropped. They went to London where some of his plays were staged and the following year in 1922 Dunsany went on a Safari in North Africa. Their lives returned to something bordering normality in the late 1920s when the Irish Free State government succeeded in restoring law and order and there was no real fear of Dunsany being burnt. There were worrying signs that their finances were not as healthy as they had been in the past and numerous workmen had to be let off. The family alternated between Meath and London and Edward travelled occasionally to lecture in America, while just as occasionally working at home on some of his plays or poems. Edward and Lady Dunsany still found the time and the money to travel to India in 1929

---

[281] Mark Bence Jones in *Twilight of the Ascendancy*

where they toured for six months.[282]   In 1947 the Dunsanys made the decision to hand over Dunsany and their other Irish properties to their son Randal who had just then returned from India. They did this and removed to Dunstall.

Lord Dunsany continued working on his literary creations, interspersed with holidays and tours until his death in 1957.

Randal Arthur Henry Plunkett the 18th Baron of Dunsany 1906-1999) was educated at Eton. He joined the Army and was posted to India. He rose to the rank of Lieutenant Colonel in the Indian Cavalry. He served in the wars of the North West Frontier and was decorated in 1930 (medal and clasp). He also served in World War II and retired in 1947. He was made Irish Grand Bailiff of the order St. Lazarus.

Randal's wife was Vera the daughter of Dr. Genesio de Sa Sottomajor of Sao Paulo, Brazil a divorcee (formerly wife of Ivor Bryce). They were married in 1938 but that marriage didn't last and they divorced in 1947. He married secondly in same year Sheila Victoria (d.1999) the daughter of Sir Henry Philips and widow of Major John Foley, Baron de Rutzen[283].

Randal had one son, Edward, by first marriage and one daughter Beatrice Mary by his second wife. Beatrice lives in London.

Edward John Carlos Plunkett, the present and 19th Baron of Dunsany was educated at Eton, Slade School of Fine Art and in Ecole des Beaux Arts in Paris. Known as Edward Plunkett in the Art World, he has produced some major works including the famed 'Metropolis'. Edward's wife is Maria Alice Villela de Carvalho, an architect of international repute. They have two sons Randal and Oliver both born in the 1980s.

---

[282] Their eldest son Randal was serving in India at the time.
[283] The Baron, an officer, was killed in Italy in 1944.

Plunkett of Killeen
(Earls of Fingall)

During a period of unrest among the labourers of Meath in the later part of the 19th century a meeting of landlords was called and it was proposed that most of the lands should be left to pasture thus reducing the numbers of labourers needed on the estates. The 11th Earl of Fingall got up and stated 'God did not give me my possessions so that I might oppress my fellow man' and would have nothing to do with the proposal. He was a very frugal man who wore almost threadbare and cleverly patched clothes. In those days it was common practice for poorer people to beg clothes from those who might have decent cast-offs. An Englishman living at the Glebe near the castle was visited by one such beggar looking for 'an auld pair of trousers'. The Englishman nodded towards the castle and said 'why don't you go over to his Lordship in the castle?' The beggar, somewhat offended retorted 'Sure haven't I a character to keep up?'[284]

Because of Lady Fingall's foresight in writing her memoirs posterity has been left an alluring account, not alone of how the aristocracy lived at the time but by inference a revealing glimpse into the lives of the workers without whom no estate could have functioned. Of course the 11th Earl, or simply Fingall as his lady called him, emerges as the most colourful of the Plunketts of Killeen because he is, along with herself one of the central characters in her book.

---

[284] *Seventy Years Young* by Lady Fingall

Just as the Jet Set of the 1960s moved with comparative ease from country to country for holidays or business so it was with the aristocracy of the 19th century in particular. In Lady Fingall's accounts of her travels she does of course mention such mundane matters as seasickness, but only in passing. Such trivial concerns never deterred the Victorians from travelling.

The 11th Earl of Fingall was born in Rome in 1859. His parents had travelled there in the years previously so that his mother who was in poor health could enjoy the warmer climate. His mother was half French and so when she died three years later from tuberculosis, his father, the 10th Earl moved to Paris. The 11th Earl had two younger sisters, Mary Louisa and Henrietta Maria. The children were never sent to school as their father felt they too might be prone to the disease that carried off their mother. They were reared in Paris, in a hotel, where they had a suite of rooms. The 10th Earl employed governesses and a tutor, Fr. McNamara, a Meath man. Fr. McNamara brought the young heir to practically all the churches in Paris as well as to the museums and art galleries.

As he grew to manhood, Arthur, the heir to Killeen, travelled back to his home on many occasions and began his love affair with horses and hunting. He was at Killen for his coming of age, when the butler preparing the great celebrations, 'got gloriously drunk' and set the dining room on fire, damaging the only good pictures there were at Killeen at the time including two Van Dycks of King Charles I and Queen Henrietta Maria.[285] In the same year Arthur was appointed High Sheriff of Co. Meath.

The following year, 1882, he received an appointment, which lasted for three years, as the State Steward to the Lord Lieutenant. His duties included the organization of state banquets in Dublin Castle, which were numerous during the Season (from Christmas to St. Patrick's Day). The Season of course was a time of festivities in Dublin when the gentry and aristocracy of the country flocked to the capital with their eligible daughters on the lookout for suitable partners for them. In many cases the same people travelled to London for their Season which began in May and went on until the end of June. As State Steward, the young Arthur was given the use of the State Steward's house in the yard of Dublin Castle. He brought his sisters over from Paris to stay with him and this also gave him

---

[285] Ibid.

the opportunity of finding suitable partners for them. Both ladies married within a short time of each other in 1884. Mary Louisa's husband was George Murphy J.P.of the Grange, Meath and Henrietta Maria married Robert Gradwell of Dowth Hall, Co. Meath and Carlanstown, Co. Westmeath.

Arthur, too, fell in love. The centre of his attentions was Elizabeth (Daisy) Burke from Co. Galway, one of the young ladies attending the functions in Dublin Castle at the time and they were married in 1883. While the Baron was very much in love Daisy's account of the moment she was asked to be his wife would leave one to believe the love may not have been entirely mutual –'I thought how nice he was and what fun it would be to live at Killeen. And I probably thought it would be fun to marry an earl too. And of course it was exciting to get engaged in one's very first season. So I said, "I think I would like to, awfully". They honeymooned in Paris where Arthur, now the 11th Earl, not quite the romantic, brought his young bride on a tour of the churches, museums and galleries that he had seen with Fr. McNamara.

The Countess of Fingall

Their homecoming was much the same as the homecoming of most young people of their class. This included almost as a matter of routine, the unharnessing of the horses from the carriage at the gate of the estate and the carriage then being pulled to the house by willing tenants. This was usually followed by a prolonged party that included many of the tenants and estate workers who were looked after in marquees while the invited guests dined in the great hall.

Daily life seemed to revolve around hunting and house parties. Lady Fingall had never hunted and appears to have been less than enthusiastic about the sport. However she was determined to be part of the social scene and managed to master the art of staying on a horse while jumping fences and ditches.

Lord Fingall with George Malcomson 1937
(Courtesy George Briscoe)

As her life progressed Daisy became interested in politics and was very close to her husband's relative Horace Plunkett of Dunsany. Horace Plunkett though nominally a Unionist had leanings towards Home Rule and was contemptuously referred to as 'a trimmer' by other members of the Ascendancy. Daisy Fingall was also looked upon as a 'fellow traveller' and was known behind her back as 'The Sinn Fein Countess'.

The 11th Earl, her husband, was known as 'the somnolent earl' as he had a habit of falling asleep almost at will – 'Given a chance, at any moment he will go to sleep, standing on his feet, like a horse.' 'He liked fields at any time better than drawing rooms or dining rooms'. Once the conversation at dinner broached the subject of what constituted a gentleman. Lord Fingall, not noted for breaking his silence too often, ventured his opinion 'A gentleman,' he said, 'is a man who tells the truth and takes a bath every day.'

As the estate finances deteriorated the estate agent suggested that they might vacate the castle for a period with a view to letting it. This was done prior to 1893 and the family went to live in London for a period. While he was there the Earl became friendly with a financier named Myring and with a view to improving his finances he decided to go to Australia with Myring where they were to investigate the possibility of gold mining. While there they were hoaxed into believing that a mine called 'The Golden Hole' was their Shangri La. They appeared to have fun there too. It was reported in a Brisbane newspaper that 'a camel race took place on Saturday, 15th September, between the Earl of Fingall and Mr. R. G. Casey, of Queensland, from Coolgardie to the Londonderry mine. Mr. D. Lindsay piloted the camel ridden by the Earl.'

They arrived back in London with samples and began inviting prospective shareholders to invest. The hoax was soon discovered and all the investors had to be reimbursed much to the dismay and humiliation of the Earl.

In common with many of his peers the Earl heeded the call to arms by the establishment and went off to fight in the Boer War. He was given the title of Major in the 5th battalion of the Connaught Rangers. During one of the battles his horse was shot under him but survived the war as did the Earl. After the war the Earl brought the horse home to Killeen, where it was put out to grass.

The Fingalls spent the Easter of 1916 with Horace Plunkett at Kilteragh. Fingall went with others of the party to the Fairyhouse Races. Plunkett and Daisy and others remained behind. Daisy in trying to telephone the Under Secretary's wife was informed that 'there is a rebellion on'. Daisy hurried to the window and looked out on the lawn where Plunkett and one his male guests were playing 'old man's golf'. 'Horace' she shouted, 'there is a rebellion on in Dublin'. 'What nonsense', he replied, 'someone is pulling your leg'. And he went on with his game. She telephoned the Kildare Street Club and asked the porter there if there was a rebellion in Dublin. 'Never heard a word of it', he said. But he rang back a few minutes later saying 'tell Sir Horace there is a rebellion. They have taken the General Post Office and shot a policeman'.[286]

According to family lore the origin of the name Plunkett is somewhat hazy and Lady Fingall in her very revealing book about the Plunketts claims that the name evolved in the following manner: the first of the family in Ireland came here with white jennets from which the family were called Blanc jenet and in time Planc jenet and so Plunkett. A sixteenth century authority on families, a Mr. Campion, stated that the Plunketts 'possessed special monuments proving that their ancestors came to Ireland with the Danes'. Their first substantial settlement was in Beaulieu in Co. Louth.

Whatever the remote origin it is certain that the Plunkett connection with Co. Meath was begun by Sir Christopher Plunkett, the primal ancestor of the Meath family when he married the daughter and heir of Sir Lucas Cusack[287], of Killeen in the early 15th century. They had two sons John and Christopher. John became the ancestor of the Killeen branch and Christopher the ancestor of the Dunsany family. Christopher married the daughter and heir of a younger son of the 3rd Earl of Kildare and he was settled at Dunsany which is less than a mile distant from Killeen.

According to family folklore the boundary between the Killeen and Dunsany lands was settled by the then wives of the Lords of Killeen and

---

[286] Mark Bence Jones – *The Twilight of the Ascendancy*
[287] The Cusacks were descended from Hugh de Lacy's close companion in arms, Geoffrey de Cusack. His last direct male descendant Sir Lucas died in 1388 and Sir Christopher Plunkett, who had married the only daughter, obtained possession of the vast estates.

Dunsany having a race. Each woman started walking from her own castle and the boundary was put up at the meeting place. For the record the Lady of Killeen was credited with gaining a few yards for her husband.

A private chapel, known as the chantry, was built at Killeen, and continued as a place of worship until the time of King James I. Some of the Lords of Killeen were buried in its precincts. The lands associated with the chantry were granted to the Earl of Fingall in the early part of the 17th century but the chapel was closed by royal command of James I.

Killeen Castle
(Courtesy IAA)

The 10th Baron, known as 'An Tiarna Mor' or the Great Lord of Killeen was elevated to the Earldom of Fingall in 1628. He also benefited from the plantations of 1613 and received considerable estates in Meath and elsewhere. He was granted a licence to hold a fair at Longwood in 1611[288]. He was described by King Charles I as 'one of the ancient nobility of our Kingdom of Ireland and the chief of a very honourable English family planted there since the first conquest'. Despite the statutes of

---

[288] Danny Cusack in *Riocht na Midhe* 1998

159

Kilkenny forbidding intermarriage with the Irish, the 10th Baron took as his wife, Elizabeth, the daughter of Rory O'Donnell the King of Tir Conaill and the 1st Earl of Tyrconnell. This lady appears to have died young and childless and the Earl married again. His second wife was a sister of the Earl of Meath. They had two sons, Christopher, his heir, and George[289] from whom descended the 6th Earl. The 1st Earl was not averse to matrimony and he married twice more.[290] His third and fourth wives were Eleanor Bagenal of Dunleckny, Co. Carlow the widow of Sir Thomas Colclough of Tintern, Co. Wexford and Margaret St. Lawrence of Howth, the widow of Jenico Preston, the 5th Viscount Gormanston.

Sir Nicholas Plunkett 3rd son of Christopher Plunkett, Lord Killeen (1564-1613) was a brother of the 1st Earl of Fingall. Sir Nicholas was one of the most eminent lawyers of his day having studied at Gray's Inn and King's Inn. He played a pivotal role in the turbulent decade of 1640-1650 and was central to all the decision making in the Confederate camp. He lost his lands and his house in the Cromwellian confiscations and was compelled to go to Galway. In the 1660s he was one of the most respected leaders who negotiated with King Charles on behalf of the dispossessed Catholics. He was declared an innocent Papist in 1663 and resided in Dublin where he was employed by many including Colonel Langford in various suits. He had one daughter, Mary, who inherited his wealth in the form of an annuity for life of £700 per annum.[291]

The first Earl died in 1637 and was succeeded by his eldest son Christopher.[292] Christopher the 2nd Earl of Fingall (1612-1649) had to bear

---

[289] George was a Colonel in the Confederate Army of 1641. His son, James, married a Plunkett from Loughcrew, a niece of St. Oliver Plunkett who was martyred at Tyburn in 1681. It is interesting to note that the vestments worn by St. Oliver were preserved in a glazed cabinet in Killeen Castle until the sale of the house in 1952.

[290] Count George Noble Plunkett (1851-1948) the son of a very successful Dublin builder, claimed descent from the 1st Earl of Fingall and collaterally from St. Oliver Plunkett. Joseph Mary Plunkett of 1916 fame was his son. George was a writer and art lover and was director of the National Museum of Ireland for a time. He later occupied several Ministerial posts under the Free State government.

[291] Dictionary of National Biography

[292] Christopher had a younger brother, Edward who was sent abroad during the years of the war. He was captured, as he travelled in Turkey and held captive for

the brunt of the horrors that engulfed the country for the two decades from 1640 onwards. Carte says of his early life: "His father had carried him over very young into England, when he was sent thither as an agent from the Irish; and after bestowing upon him all the breeding which the Court of England could afford, he got him a command in Flanders, where he soon distinguished himself, and was advanced to a better post, being a man of good parts and a pleasant turn of wit, accompanied by a politeness in his behaviour, and a natural civility which flowed towards all men; and these qualities rendering his conversation agreeable, made him universally acceptable to his acquaintances." He took his seat in the Parliament of 1639.

When the war broke out in 1641, he, with other Catholic lords, offered his services to the Government. His offer was rejected and he finally threw himself into the struggle on the Catholic side. He was one of the leading men in the gatherings at Tara and Duleek, commanded the cavalry at the siege of Drogheda, and was seven times indicted and outlawed in the course of his career. He was eventually taken prisoner at the battle of Rathmines, in August 1649, and died from his wounds shortly afterwards in the Castle of Dublin. He had married in 1636 a daughter of the 1st Viscount Barnewall of Kingsland and they had one son Luke, who was only a minor at the time of his father's death and so was able to regain in the Court of Claims the lands forfeited by his father.[293]

Luke the 3rd Earl was born in 1639 and apart from his tussles in the Court of Claims seems to have had a relatively calm life – apart from his marital troubles which seem to have been well known. His wife was a McCarthy from Muskerry, the daughter of Lord Clancarty. She was a sister-in-law of the Duke of Ormonde who seems to have taken up the cudgels in her defence. He wrote to the Queen to 'let her Majesty know what kind of man my Lord Fingall is, and how unreasonable his calumnies against his wife are. From the first three years of her marriage her father and friends were for a separation but she always refused their advice.' Whatever their differences they seemed to be on amicable terms on some occasions as they had one son Peter and three daughters. Luke seems to

---

five years. He managed to escape and made his way back to Ireland. – Randall McDonnell in *The Lost Houses of Ireland*

[293] J.G. Simms in *Riocht na Midhe* 1962

have had to travel to England on occasion as we see by this entry in the House of Lords Journal:-

ORDERED, by the Lords Spiritual and Temporal in Parliament assembled, That Luke Earl of Fingall, in the Kingdom of Ireland, be, and is hereby, authorized and permitted forthwith to repair to any of His Majesty's Sea Ports of this Kingdom, and to pass, with Two Servants, (videlicet) Edmond Barry and Christopher Archbold, from thence to France and Flanders, without the Lett, Stay, or Interruption of any Person or Persons whatsoever; and this shall be a sufficient Warrant on that Behalf.[294]

If his will is anything to go by he seems to have patched up his differences with his wife as he left a will in which he bequeathed £100 a year to his daughters 'until their portions were paid' with an additional £2000 each if his son, Peter, Lord Killeen died without issue. He left the castle and lands of Killeen to his wife Margaret for her life with whatever was required out of the estate to bring her jointure up to £600. He left £100 to his brothers Edward and Nicholas and a £10 annuity to his uncle George. His servant Christopher Archbold was to get £50 and Dame Butler £100. His wife was to manage the person and estate of his son during his minority. His executors were his mother Mabel, Countess Dowager of Fingall, Jenico Preston and Viscount Gormanston.[295]

Peter the 4th Earl (1678-1717), succeeded to the title and estates in 1684. He was as headstrong as his forebears and took up arms on the side of King James II in 1690. He was, predictably, found guilty of treason by the victorious Williamites and his lands confiscated and he was outlawed but by some means or other he managed to have the outlawry overturned in 1697. He was married to a lady of noble birth, the daughter of Sir Edward Hales and they had a son and three daughters. Peter died in 1717. His ghost was reputed to have been seen in Killeen. He had been loyal to King James II whom he had followed on his wanderings and had been with him when he died. His wife and daughters were the only ladies who accompanied Catherine of Braganza to Portugal.[296] *A Light to the Blind* written by Peter the 4th Earl was presented to the National Library of

---

[294] House of Lords Journal Volume 13: 2 December 1678
[295] *Killeen* by Mary Carty
[296] *70 Years Young* by Lady Fingall – Catherine (1638 – 1705) was the daughter of King John IV of Portugal and wife of King Charles II.

Ireland in 1934 by the 12th Earl. It describes the career of James II and contains vivid accounts of the Battle of the Boyne and Aughrim and the siege of Limerick.

The 5th Earl, Justin, who abandoned the Castle of Killeen[297] in the 1720s, died without having had any children in 1734 and the title which was still under attainder, passed to a cousin, Robert , the 6th Earl (1704?-1738), a captain in Berwick's Regiment and a resident of France. Robert's wife was an Irish woman, Mary Magenis from Co. Down and they had one son and one daughter. Their son, Arthur, who was reared in France, became the 7th Earl in 1738 after his father died. He was only seven years old at the time. When he reached manhood he applied to have his titles reinstated but this was not done until 1795, two years after his death.

Arthur the 7th Earl was a young boy when he succeeded. He was placed under the guardianship of the Earl of Aran his nearest Protestant relative but had a second guardian Henry Howard, from Cumberland, a Catholic who appears to have partly managed the estate. The estate was heavily in debt and at least three parts of it were sold off to defray the encumbrances while Arthur was still a minor.[298] The 7th Earl (1731-1793) was careful enough to marry an heiress, Mary Wollascott from Woolhampton in Berkshire in 1755 and by 1780 he felt secure enough to attempt to make his Irish castle habitable. Certain works were carried out to improve the structure. The demesne was landscaped and a lake was incorporated into the whole. The works were carried out over a long number of years by the 7the Earl and his son, also Arthur, the 8th Earl, involving such eminent men as Francis Johnston[299] and Thomas Wogan Browne.[300] While the building works were in progress the 7th Earl and his family lived in a residence at 5 Great Denmark Street in Dublin, known as Killeen House. His wife endowed Killeen with many treasures including

---

[297] The family had a house in Dublin, Killeen House, in Great Denmark St., and they lived there while in Ireland.
[298] *Killeen* by Mary Carty
[299] Johnston was the architect of the G.P.O. in Dublin.
[300] Wogan Browne was a wealthy merchant who had built Castle Wogan (Clongowes Wood College). He was not an architect by profession but his ideas found acceptance with Lord Fingall at any rate.

Queen Anne furniture, silver and an immense quantity of old and valuable books.[301] The Woolhampton estate was sold in 1786.[302]

During the mid 1700s when the Penal Laws were at their worst Randal Plunkett the 13th Baron of Dunsany, a Protestant, began the practice of shielding his Killeen relatives by swearing he was the owner of the Killeen lands. This practice was continued by successive Barons Dunsany until the end of the 18th century. Lady Fingall saw a letter from a later Lord Dunsany written to his cousin at Killeen 'My dear Fingall, I am an old man now and shall soon have to meet my Maker. I do not want to go to Him with a lie upon my soul. Could you not get someone else to swear that the land and property are theirs?'[303]

Arthur, the 8th Earl (1759-1836), was a staunch Catholic and was on very friendly terms with a kinsman, Dr. Patrick Plunkett the Bishop of Meath. He wrote to him in 1795 to tell him that 'on Thursday last my claim to the title of Fingall etc. was established by unanimous resolution in the House of Lords. We shall, I hope, soon become inhabitants of this old Castle'.[304] He was very prominent in the Catholic Committee, the movement that eventually led to Catholic Emancipation. In 1793 following the 'The Battle of Coolnahinch-Moynalty'[305] Fr. Michael Flood from the

---

[301] *Killeen* by Mary Carty

[302] Woolhampton House, now a school, was the main home of the Wollascott family since the mid-16th century. They also owned the manors of Brimpton, Shalford, Shinfield and Sutton Courtenay.

[303] *Seventy Years Young* by Lady Fingall

[304] *The Lost House of Ireland* by Randall McDonnell

[305] The Defenders were very active in the area in 1792-93 and in order to counteract them the gentry from north Meath formed the Co. Meath Association, a secret society also. Their object was to compile information about the Defenders and their activities. On this occasion they got intelligence that a group of Defenders were meeting at a certain house. The Association's leaders, Keady Barnes, a magistrate from Newtown, Mr. Jackson from Lisnabo and Mr. Chandlor from Moynalty applied for assistance from the gentry and military of south Cavan. This formidable well armed force of about sixty surrounded the house. The Defenders inside, realizing they were betrayed, came out and opened fire. One was killed in the exchange of fire and one Donegan was captured. It is not known where he was held prisoner but the Defenders rightly guessed that on the day following he would be transferred to Bailieboro. After midday the next day about one hundred and fifty Defenders had gathered to lay an ambush. A small

Kilbeg area, a chaplain to Lord Fingall, asked the latter to intercede to save the life of one of the Defenders, Captain Geraghty. Lord Fingall was successful and a pardon was issued. The pardon was taken by a relay of horses to Cavan but arrived an hour too late. Captain Geraghty had been hanged.[306]

The 8th Earl was in France prior to the birth of his eldest son but moved to Switzerland in the wake of the French Revolution. His son was born in Geneva. The 8th Earl's brother, Luke, a Captain in the Austrian service, was killed in Italy in 1794 and another brother, William a Colonel in the same Army died in Prague in 1806.[307]

He was definitely in residence in Killeen in 1798 when the Rebellion broke out in May. It would seem that the Plunketts of Killeen and Dunsany had a council of war and decided to try to defend just one of the castles. Dunsany was deserted and was in fact occupied for a short time by the rebels.[308] The crushing of the Rebellion at the Hill of Tara was attributed to Lord Fingall. 'Their rebellion was to end tragically at the 'Croppies Grave' on the Hill of Tara, crushed by an almost uniquely Catholic yeomanry and army led to a large extent by gentry under Lord Fingall, who were anxious to prove their loyalty to the Crown.'[309] The tacit acceptance of the Catholic peers such as Lord Killeen in arms, contrary to

---

party hid behind a wall while the main body concealed themselves on a hill in front of Mr. Tucker's house at Coolnahinch. When the Association party arrived the men behind the wall fired at them and then ran towards the hill. The soldiers and the gentry advanced and fire was exchanged but the firepower and accuracy of the Association party was much superior. The Defenders scattered and many were killed by their pursuers. Some found shelter in Tucker's house where Mr. Tucker saved some by giving them spades and telling them to dig, pretending they were his workmen. Almost forty of the Defenders were killed and as many more taken prisoner, including one 'Captain' Geraghty from Ballymacane, Kilmainhamwood. Geraghty was flogged twice and brutally mistreated before being sent for trial at Trim. The jury disagreed and he was sent for trial to Cavan, before a Protestant jury all drawn from the Kells area. He was sentenced to death despite a plea for clemency from Lord Fingall.

[306] S.O'Loingsigh in *Riocht na Midhe* 1966

[307] Killeen by Mary Carty

[308] See the Plunketts of Dunsany in this book.

[309] Desmond Mooney in Riocht na Midhe, 1987 *The Origins of Agrarian Violence in Meath*

the Penal Laws gives us some indication of the softening of attitudes to Catholics in Co. Meath at any rate. It might be simplistic to infer that there was no opposition to this move as there certainly was but as the century wore on this opposition ameliorated somewhat. There were yeomanry corps at both Killeen and Dunsany.

Killeen Castle was restructured and extended between 1803 and 1813 under Francis Johnston. [310]

In 1821 the 8th Earl of Fingall put forward legislation for Catholic emancipation. This included a veto for the government on nominees for Catholic bishoprics and a modification to the Oath of Supremacy. Bishop Milner, Vicar Apostolic of the Midland District, opposed the bill. However, the Vatican and Bishop Poynter of the London District supported it with reservations. The bill was subsequently passed by the House of Commons but rejected by the Lords.

When King George IV visited Ireland in 1821 he appointed Lord Fingall a Knight of the Most Illustrious Order of St. Patrick. He was the first ever Catholic of Irish descent, to have been given this honour. Although the family had left Berkshire in the previous century he was created a peer of the United Kingdom as Baron Fingall of Woolhampton Lodge in 1831.

The 8th Earl's wife was a Donelan from Galway and they had one son, predictably called Arthur, who became the 9th Earl following his father's death in 1836. In 1841 the 9th Earl (1791-1869) initiated further renovations and remodelling of Killeen Castle and employed the services of James Sheil, a prominent architect of the period. Following these improvements the library became the main living room of the house. It boasted a very fine plasterwork ceiling and housed the family's large collection of books in bookcases specially designed for Killeen and built by Hicks of Dublin. It was also home to the vestments of St. Oliver, as mentioned above. He and his family spent some of their time at least in Killeen as it was noted that in 1858 the Earl of Fingall was in Ireland, as he was chairman of court proceedings in Dunshaughlin concerning a right of way over a bog.[311] The 9th Earl died suddenly at his London residence, 47 Montague Square, in 1869

---

[310] Killeen by Mary Carty
[311] *The Cavan Observer*, 6 Nov. 1858

Louisa Corbally of Corbalton Hall, Co. Meath was the 9th Earl's wife and her son, Arthur, the 10th Earl, was born in Naples in 1819. He had five brothers and two sisters both of whom married English gentlemen.[312] One of his brothers, William, an Army Officer, later became a Catholic priest and another, Francis, who was knighted, was an ambassador to Vienna from 1900 to 1905.

As already mentioned the 10th Earl's wife died young. She was a French woman, the daughter of Mon. Francis Alexis Rio. The 10th Earl who was mainly resident in France only returned to Ireland in 1880. He died in 1881.

The 11th Earl already alluded to at length, had two sons, Oliver and Gerald and two daughters Mary and Henrietta and they lived mainly at Killeen. Their lives were spent in a reasonably tranquil way until the outbreak of the Civil War when they were threatened with being burnt. A pro-treaty politician, John Dillon sent them a warning one day in 1923 and they made some small preparations such as gathering some of their valuables together. But the attackers didn't arrive and the Fingalls, who had waited up all night, simply retired to bed for the day. Daisy, Lady Fingall, mused in her memoirs, about 'how Killeen would burn - badly – that old Norman Castle of stone that had been built as a Pale fortress. Then I remembered the big oak staircase; that would send up a glorious flame. Then I remembered too, how I had often thought that Killeen would make a lovely ruin. And I saw it in my mind, with the light falling through its empty window spaces and its battlemented walls lifted gauntly against the sky'.

The land had already been divided up with the passing of the Land Acts. All that was left was the demesne. Oliver James the 12th Earl succeeded his father. He was educated at Downside and Sandhurst and was commissioned in the 17th Lancers in 1914. Wounded in France in 1916 but having recuperated he was back in France where he got the Military Cross. He married Jessica Hughes of Lynch, Somerset in 1926. He was a formidable jockey and won many National Hunt races including the Gold Cup (on Roddy Owen) and the Champion Hurdle. He was joint Master of the Ward Hounds. He served in the Army again in WWII, mainly in

---

[312] Emma married William Anderton of Euxton Hall, and Henrietta's husband was Thomas Riddell of Felton Park.

England. He sold Killeen in 1951 to Sir Victor Sassoon, but remained there as manager for two years. Sir Victor sold Killeen in 1963.

St. Oliver Plunkett

Oliver and his second wife attended the canonisation of St. Oliver Plunkett in Rome in 1975 where they had an audience with the Pope. Three years later Oliver had a very bad fall while hunting and never recovered properly, being confined to a wheelchair. He died in 1984 when the Peerage became extinct.

Killeen was burnt maliciously in 1981 but not entirely destroyed. It was bought in 1989 by Christopher Slattery.

Preston of Ardsallagh, Bellinter & Swainston, (Kilmessan)

Some confusion still surrounds the origins of the Prestons of Bellinter, who are often claimed as being descended from the younger son of the third Viscount Gormanston. The confusion seems to derive from the seventeenth century association of the Preston name with Ardsallagh, an ancient property near Tara, and the title Lord Tara, which at different times and in different forms was possessed by a Preston.

The first of this family was John Preston, stated erroneously to have been a grandson of Jenico Preston, the 3rd Viscount Gormanston.

Not long after John Pippard gained possession of Ardsallagh in the late thirteenth century it was found to be in the hands of Jordan de Angulo (Nangle), Lord of Kilbixy and 7th Baron of Navan.[313] Descended from one of Hugh de Lacy's ten Palatine barons who had been granted the lands of Ardbraccan and Navan in the twelfth century, the Nangles remained

---

[313] Pippard's lease can be found in E. Curtis, *Calendar of Ormond Deeds*, 1932. For the Nangle connection with Navan see Cyril Ellison, *The Beauties of the Boyne and Blackwater*, 1983; Cyril Ellison, 'Some Aspects of Navan History' in *Riocht na Midhe*, 1963.

resident in the castle at the *Height of the Sallows* until the seventeenth century.

The confusion surrounding the Preston family develops in the sixteenth century when the 17th Baron of Navan, Sir Thomas Nangle of Ardsallagh married Elizabeth Preston, daughter of the 3rd Viscount Gormanston (by his wife Catherine Fitzgerald, daughter of Gearoid Og, the 9th Earl of Kildare).[314] In the eighteenth century *Lodge's Peerage* had implied that an association between the Gormanston Prestons and the Nangles was the basis of the ownership of Ardsallagh by the Preston family in the late seventeenth century.[315] However John Preston, who was confirmed in his possession of Ardsallagh under the Act of Settlement in 1666, reveals no relationship with either the Viscount Gormanstons, a Catholic noble family who had been settled in Ireland since the fourteenth century, or the longer settled Norman family he quietly usurped.[316]

Opinion is still divided on the matter but be that as it may John Preston established himself in Dublin where he became a successful merchant and was Clerk of the Tholsel there in 1650. He was elected to the Corporation and was Mayor of the city in 1653. John Preston did share with his nobler counterparts origins in the same English County. His father is named as Hugh Preston of Bolton, Lancashire. Having established himself as a merchant in Dublin, John Preston, described as an

---

[314] LGI, 1958, p.514.

[315] Lodge, Peerage, Vol. III, p.79, 80 which states that the family descended from Martin Preston 'youngest son of Jenico, 3rd Viscount Gormanston.' The situation is clarified somewhat by Ellison, op. cit. 1963, pp. 38-40. Evidence that John Preston was descended from Hugh Preston of Lancashire is offered in G.E.C Cockayne (ed.), *Complete Peerage*, Vol. XII, p.642, note (c), referring to Preston's funeral entry in Ulster's Office and 'his own statement cited for a grant of armorial bearings, dated 12 Sep. 17 Charles II.' For this see *Burke's Dormant, Abeyant, Forfeited and Extinct Peerages*, 1883, p445, which gives Preston's request 'to assign him such armes and creast as he may lawfully beare without prejudice to any other of that name beinge descended of a family of that surname in ye county of Lancaster'. For the most recent version of the Gormanston genealogy see Burke's *Peerage and Baronetage*, pp. 1178-1180. There is no explanation for the statement contained Burke (LGI, 1958, p.586) that when Mary Preston (widow of Peter Ludlow) died that she left to her Ludlow descendants, along with Ardsallagh, the portraits that she had inherited of Jenico, 3rd Viscount Gormanston and of his wife Lady Catherine Fitzgerald.

[316] Cyril Ellison, *The Beauties of the Boyne and Blackwater*, 1983

'enthusiastic protestant' appears as a clerk of Tholsel in 1650, later becoming a member of the corporation and served as Lord Mayor for 1653-1654.[317] It was about this time that he purchased almost 8,000 acres in Meath, playing his part in creating the development of the estate system that dominated Irish land ownership down to the nineteenth century.[318]

With the Cromwellian conquest having cost more than three times the amount raised through investors under the 1641 Act for Adventurers, a solution to pay dividends to investors and the arrears to some 35, 000 soldiers was found in the confiscation of the lands of 'rebel' landowners. Amongst those displaced in Meath were the Nangles when Thomas, the 19th Baron of Navan, yielded up his Meath acres, including Ardsallagh in 1653; by the end of the century the family appear largely to have abandoned Ireland for the continent.[319] Preston appears to have been one of those who benefited from purchase of debentures. These land vouchers were often quickly and cheaply sold by disbanding soldiers eager to return home. Closeness to the centre of government after being elected an M.P. for Navan in 1661, no doubt assisted John Preston's later confirmation of these lands in Meath along with an estate in Queen's County.[320]

A wealthy man, John was able to pay for the best legal advice and in those turbulent times when Catholic landowners were frantic to regain possession of their lost estates, this was invaluable. In order to preserve some of his lands that were immediately under threat from the

---

[317] Michael Quane, 'Preston Endowed School' in *Riocht na Midhe*, Vol. IV, No. 2, 1968, p.50.

[318] The precise acreage recorded is 7,859a 2r. 22p. to which a further 1,954, in Meath and Laois, was added in 1669. Preston was also busy in Dublin acquiring property leases in Dublin, including the lands of Baldoyle, a plot on the south side of St. Stephen's Green and the ground in Oxmantown (Smithfield) where the Blue Coast School was later erected. Quane, op. cit., pp.50-52.

[319] Cyril Ellison, *The Beauties of the Boyne and Blackwater*, 1983; Walter Nangle, youngest son of Patrick, the 18th Baron, remained in Ireland establishing a branch of the family at Kildalkey and appears later in the century amongst a list of Irish Jacobites outlawed for high treason; and while other family members are also named in this source the absence of the name of the 19th Baron may imply that he had by then left Ireland. See *Analecta Hibernica*, No. 22, 1960, pp.22-25.

[320] These included the lands of Emo, Co. Laois which passed to the Dawson family, later Viscounts Carlow and Earls of Portarlington, through his granddaughter Anne who married Ephraim Dawson.

dispossessed, John made over almost 2000 acres in Laois and Meath for the upkeep of two schools, at Ballyroan in Laois and at Navan. Providing lands for charitable purposes was in effect a precautionary measure designed to secure title where 'the inviolability of the title' of such lands was optimistically considered to extend to the rest of the lands remaining in the grantee's possession. In a further display of generosity and public mindedness, Preston donated the site for the Royal Hospital at Kilmainham.

The school in Navan was called the Preston School and the headmaster was invariably a Preston during the 17th and 18th centuries. The Preston school which survived in the centre of Navan until the late 1960's was established 'for the better promoting supporting and maintaining the Protestant religion and for the better breeding and training up of youth in the fear and knowledge of God.'[321]

The income from the lands allotted to the Preston school in Navan was paid directly to the headmaster. Similarly in Ballyroan in Laois, the income from the lands there went to the Preston nominated schoolmaster. The numbers of pupils in these schools was remarkably small – in Navan the number seldom exceeded 7 students some of whom were on occasion Roman Catholics. The Preston schools were well known as being legal ploys to retain wealth and were so noted by Royal Commissions who held that the trust was being abused. Despite the bad name the schools got the Preston school in Navan continued in existence up to 1969 when it was amalgamated with the Wilson's Hospital school. The actual site of the school became the site of the Navan Shopping Centre, where there is a plaque commemorating the school's existence.

After the Restoration of Charles II, John Preston was confirmed in his lands in Meath and Laois under the Acts of Settlement of 1666. He seems to have established himself at Ardsallagh, but it is highly probable that he continued to live mainly in Dublin.

John Preston's first wife was Mary Morris of Bolton and they had two sons Phineas and Samuel and a daughter Mary. Phineas who was born in the 1640s was settled at Ardsallagh also and the second son Samuel was settled in the Laois lands at Emo.

---

[321] Michael Quane, 'Preston Endowed School' in *Riocht na Midhe*, 1968.

Mary, John's wife, died sometime before 1660 and was buried in Christ Church Cathedral. John married again in 1660 and his second wife appears to have been Katherine Sherlock, a widow, who died sometime before 1675. John married again in that year and his third wife was Anne the daughter of Alderman Richard Tighe of Dublin, a woman who was twice widowed.[322] John and Ann had two sons, John of Balsoon and Nathaniel who according to Mrs. Delaney was 'an old prim beau, as affected as a fine lady: but a very honest man, obstinate in his opinions, but the pink of civility in his own house.'[323] He built Swainston an idiosyncratic country house near Kilmessan where the branch of the family that he established there, still resides.

Phineas, John Preston's eldest son was married to Letitia Hammond of Chertsey and they had one son, Phineas who died at a young age and a daughter Mary. Phineas senior died in 1673, long before his father John. He was a relatively young man and had no opportunity to make his mark on the properties or politically. John senior died in 1686 and he was succeeded in his Ardsallagh estates by his grandson Phineas. He in turn was succeeded in Ardsallagh by his sister Mary who inherited the estates.

The Ardsallagh lands then passed to Peter Ludlow, a grand nephew of Cromwell's trusted general of the same name who fled Ireland in 1660 to escape being hanged.[324]. His father, Stephen Ludlow was a Member of Parliament who had acquired a small estate in Meath in 1703 and settled at Ardsallagh.[325]

Samuel's Emo estate passed after his death to his daughter, Anne. His wife was Mary the daughter of Theophilus Sandford, his stepsister. Anne's husband was Ephraim Dawson of Dawson's Grove, the ancestor of

---

[322] Anne's first husband was Theophilus Sandford, of Moyglare, Co. Meath. Anne married again after John Preston's death and her third husband was the Hon. Oliver Lambart of Painstown, Co. Meath, the younger son the 1st. Earl of Cavan.

[323] LGI, 1958, p.691; Angelique Day, *Letters from Georgian Ireland: The Correspondence of Mary Delaney, 1731-68*, 1991, p.139.

[324] *Swift's Correspondence*, Vol. ii, p. 249, n.7; Johnston-Liik, p.138; Burke's *Dormant and Extinct Peerage*, 1883, p.337 states that Ludlow's uncle was Edmund Ludlow, 'the celebrated republican general' who died in exile in Switzerland in 1693.

[325] Johnston-Liik, p.139. His principal estate comprised 7,954 acres in Cork acquired at the same time.

the Lords Portarlington. Ephraim's son married Mary the last Damer heiress,[326] and it was his son, John who became the 1st Earl of Portarlington.

John I of Balsoon was the ancestor of the Preston family of Bellinter. His wife was Lydia Pratt, a daughter of Joseph Pratt of Cabra, Co. Cavan.[327] John was active politically and was elected an M.P. for Co. Meath in 1709. Originally he settled at Lismullen but having purchased Balsoon from the Usshers he moved there in 1716. Balsoon, on the east side of the Boyne overlooking Bective Abbey had been Ussher property since at least the fourteenth century and in 1590 a castle was erected by Henry Ussher, Primate of Armagh and a founder of Trinity College Dublin, who is buried there.[328]

It was John II, the Preston heir, who was first associated with Bellinter and it was his son John III who is credited with building the house. Richard Castle was the architect. John II of Bellinter was a captain in the Dragoon Guards and later in 1731 after his father resigned (probably due to ill health) he was an M.P. for Co. Meath. His wife, whom he married in the same year he became an M.P., was a daughter of Peter Ludlow and sister of the 1st Earl Ludlow. John II had two sons, John III and Joseph. Joseph found a career in the Army, where he attained the rank of Major and though married to Frances Cuff (nee Sandford), a widow, he died without leaving an heir.

Lydia, the wife of John I died sometime before 1720 and in that year he married Henrietta, the daughter of Sir Thomas Taylour of Headfort. She died in 1729 and he died three years later in 1732.

John II lived until 1753 and was succeeded by his eldest son John III. John lived during the era when political reform was the order of the

---

[326] For information on the Damer family see *The Tipperary Gentry* by Art Kavanagh and Wm Hayes.

[327] There is an extended notice of the Pratts in *The Landed Gentry & Aristocracy of Kilkenny* by Art Kavanagh.

[328] Ibid. p.163. Another member of the family was James Ussher (1581-1656), the renowned scholar, former Bishop of Meath and Primate of Armagh, who is famous for proposing a biblical chronology that placed the date of creation at 4004 BC and whom Oliver Cromwell ordered to be buried in Westminster Cathedral. See LGI, 1958, p. 721; S.J. Connolly, *The Oxford Companion to Irish History*, 1998, pp.575-6; Henry Boylan, *A Dictionary of Irish Biography*, 1998, pp.433-4.

day. The Preston seat in Parliament was held because they controlled the 'pocket' borough. A 'pocket' borough meant that the seat was literally bought out of the pocket of the M.P., who was generally the landlord in the area. The voters were the 40s. freeholders who were Protestants and were tenants of the landlord. During this time of course, the time of the Penal Laws, no Catholic had a vote.

John III married Mary Smyth the daughter of an M.P. in 1758[329]. John had been an M.P. since 1755, when he contested the election. The election results were disputed by Richard Hamilton of Stackallen, who had been defeated in the election. Hamilton alleged that the voters included people who had been dead for years. The allegations were investigated by a Committee of the House of Parliament that found there were abuses. The result of the election was overturned and Hamilton was awarded the seat, much to the chagrin of John III, who had to wait six years before he was able to unseat Hamilton in the 1761 election. After Preston was successfully elected in 1761 he was not considered a supporter of government being deemed 'a constant opposer, sulky and weak.' His younger brother, Joseph, who having been elected for Navan in the same year with the support of his uncle, Lord Ludlow, was described as 'the merest fribble of a man that ever existed.'[330]

John III and Mary had five sons and two daughters, Mary and Eliza who married respectively James Falls of Tyrone and Hon. Henry Forbes a spare heir to the 5th Earl of Granard. Two of the sons, Joseph and Skeffington did what many younger sons of gentlemen did; they took Holy Orders. The family of the Rev. Joseph eventually succeeded to the estate. James the second son of John III joined the Army, and in the course of time was promoted to the rank of Major. He was posted overseas and died a single man in the West Indies. Francis the youngest of the five brothers died unmarried in 1834.

The building of Bellinter House marks an important moment in Irish architectural history; designed in 1750, the death of its architect, Richard Castle, the following year leaves Bellinter recognised as his last major work and brings to an end an extraordinary monopoly of country house design. Castle was the most important (and most prolific) architect

---

[329] Her father held an important official post in Dublin, being the Collector General of the Port of Dublin.
[330] Johnston-Liik, op. cit., p.120-121.

in Ireland in the two decades before his death. As a former draughtsman to the surveyor general, Sir Edward Lovett Pearce, a member of Parliament for Ratoath, this German born protégé of Ireland's first truly Palladian architect undoubtedly benefited from promotion amongst his parliamentary peers.[331] Bellinter constitutes a perfect example of how Palladian villa design was successfully translated for the creation of the eighteenth century Irish country house set piece: a tripartite composition comprising a principal block flanked by connecting pavilions. In this respect the building possesses a design that is at once formal and compact: it has an exerting presence expressed in its massing and architectural detail, symbolising the owner's status and taste, combined with logical and efficient planning to symbolise the position of the house as the focus of the landed estate.[332]

Bellinter House

The cost of building the house must have been burdensome for John Preston and it is recorded that in 1756, when the house was completing or just complete, he borrowed the not insubstantial sum of

---

[331] Edward McParland, *Public Architecture in Ireland 1680-1760*, 2001, pp.14-15.

[332] In 1878, commenting on the stables provided in one of the pavilions, a visitor observed that with 'their Titanic stone pillars and high vaulted roof look as if they had been built by one of the moguls for his white elephants so solid are they and capacious.' M. O' Connor Morris, *Hibernica Venatica*, 1878.

£1,500.[333] By 1772 it was observed that, while he had a large estate, he was constantly in debt but financial embarrassments were normal and shared by many of his peers. This was the cost, not just of sophisticated living, but of the 'improvements' necessary for strong dynastic foundations which reflected the contemporary belief that 'a family is an edifice always in building, but never builded.'[334]

Chimneypiece in Entrance Hall

[333] Johnston-Liik, op. cit. p.120.
[334] Toby Barnard, *A New Anatomy of Ireland, The Irish Protestants, 1649-1770*, 2003, p.67.

The care with which Preston attended to his family's edifice is witnessed in the arrangements made for his son's education in Edinburgh, the Preston family removing to the Scottish city for this purpose, and it was here, in 1781, that that the builder of Bellinter died.

When John III died in 1781 he was considered to have done his country some service when his obituary announced that 'no man ever departed this life more truly lamented; he was…one of those true and steady patriots that poor Ireland must forever mourn, as he was honest even in the worst of times…' [335] He was succeeded by his eldest son John IV who achieved the highest distinction in the family when he was created Baron Tara in 1800. His father had left him a very wealthy man with an income of almost £4000 a year and a town house in Kildare Street in Dublin. John was 17 years old at that time and was attending Oxford. He returned to Ireland in due course and was elected to the Parliament.

During the very disturbed period leading up to the 1798 rebellion, John IV became Captain of a Cavalry troop known as the Navan Cavalry. Like Kildare, Carlow and Wexford, Meath was in a disturbed state.

The United Irishmen had founded cells in many areas and when the call to arms came in May of 1798 the Meath rebels responded by assembling in large numbers at Dunshaughlin. They then moved to the Hill of Tara where they dug defensive ditches. John IV sent scouts from Navan to assess the situation. When they returned they reported that the whole countryside was in a state of insurrection. John IV went to see the officer commanding the regular troops at Navan and succeeded in persuading the reluctant officer to give him three companies of regular soldiers and a cannon.[336] They then moved towards Tara Hill. The defenders, who had very little training and only very crude weapons were no match for the trained soldiers and they were soon defeated, scattering in all directions. The pursuing cavalry slew many of the fugitives and it is said that six of the rebels were shot at Bellinter and buried in a nearby wood, later called the Croppy Wood.[337]

---

[335] Ibid., p.120.

[336] According to other commentators the overall command of the force at Tara was given to Lord Fingall.

[337] Noel French in his booklet *Bellinter House*.

According to the same source, a memorial slab was erected in the area with the inscription 'This is where the croppys of '98 lie'.[338] The memorial was said to have been erected by John IV. It has since disappeared and may have been buried during works carried out on the Royal Tara Golf Club in the 1960s.[339]

John IV eventually voted with the Government in supporting the Act of Union and was rewarded for his loyalty with the title of Baron of Tara in 1800. He married Harriet Powys of Berwick House, Salop, a year later but they had no family. The Baron died in 1821 and his title became extinct. The bulk of his estate passed to his brother, the Rev. Joseph Preston.

Rev. Joseph, a Trinity College graduate, married Mary Anne Massy of Tipperary. He was living in Galbally, Co. Limerick at the time. When he inherited the estate he moved to Bellinter with his family. Rev. Joseph and Mary Anne had three sons and a daughter Mary Jane who married a clergyman, Rev. John Maugham. Two of Rev. Joseph's sons died tragically in the Thames Steamer disaster in 1841 as they travelled from London to Dublin. Rev. Joseph himself died in 1839.

His eldest son was John Joseph Preston of Bellinter who was born in 1815. John Joseph married Sarah O' Meagher, of Kilmoyler, Co. Tipperary, in 1842 when he received title to the estate. They had only one daughter, Helen Maria who married John Joseph Roche-Kelly of Rockstown Castle, Co. Limerick. Helen Maria had two children who died in infancy and she herself died in 1873, probably in childbirth.

John Joseph (1815-1892), 'the Squire of Bellinter', was an outgoing exuberant man and was master of his own hounds. His pack known as the Tara Harriers hunted mainly in Co. Meath. He kept stables of very good hunters and one of his most famous horses was a steeplechaser called 'Brunette' which he himself rode in the Kilrue 'Grand National'. 'Brunette'

---

[338] John Preston was most probably also present at the Battle of Knightstown Bog where many of the Wexford and Wicklow rebels under the command of Anthony Perry withstood numerous rounds of grapeshot and canister until the order was given to disperse. The little army of less than a thousand scattered and fled. They were pursued by the cavalry who showed them no mercy. Anthony Perry and Fr. Mogue Kearns were captured and later hanged at Edenderry. (*Ireland 1798 the Battles* – Art Kavanagh)

[339] Noel French in his booklet *Bellinter House.*.

won the race in 1842 and again the following year. The jockey in 1843 was Allen McDonagh.[340] The Kilrue Steeplechases were notorious. 'A faster, truer, or more severe run race not to be found in the annals of Irish Steeplechasing,' was how one writer described the Kilrue Steeplechase. These races were the antecedents of the Irish Grand National inaugurated at Fairyhouse in 1870.

During the period of the famine changes were effected, probably on the advice of the agent, that were very much to the advantage of the landlord. 'Several tenants with from 20-30 acres on the Preston estate outside Navan worked as labourers for the landlord in lieu of rent in 1847 and 1848. Others despite reduced rents were forced to surrender possession in 1849-50. Several farmers on the estate took advantage of the high number of holdings which became available due to emigration and evictions and acquired additional holdings. The landlord actively promoted this process by letting farms which had been surrendered at reduced rents to tenants whom he regarded favourably. Over 40 per cent of the land that became available was taken by merchants and shopkeepers from Navan. One fifth of the pre famine tenants were 'swept away' during the period 1845-50. Most farmers with holdings over 30 acres experienced little difficulty paying their rents during this time.'[341]

Within the next twenty years the Irish social and political landscape had begun to change. Gladstone's Landlord and Tenant Act, providing limited tenant's rights, had just been passed in 1870 and was soon followed by the foundation of Michael Davitt's Irish National Land League in 1879, presided over by Parnell. This was quickly followed by Gladstone's second land act (The Land Law Act) in 1881 that ensured a fairer system of rents and facilitated land purchase. The Bellinter estate was still very sizeable and was recorded as being almost 7,500 acres in 1876. However the finances must not have been in the greatest of order as in 1878 the Laois and Dublin properties owned by John Joseph Preston had to be sold under the Landed Estates Court. It was around this time that John Joseph leased Bellinter House and demesne to his friend Gustavus Villiers Briscoe, the son of the rector of Kilmessan and a former chaplain to the Viceroy.

---

[340] Ibid
[341] Riocht na Midhe 1985 – *The Famine in Meath* by Peter Connell

John Joseph lived until 1892 and was effectively the last of the Prestons of Bellinter.

Bellinter in modern times

The Prestons of Swainston

This family descended from Nathaniel Preston who was the youngest son of John Preston of Ardsallagh (1630?- 1686) mentioned above, by his third wife, Anne the daughter of Alderman Richard Tighe of Dublin. It is proposed to deal with this family in Volume Two of The Gentry & Aristocracy of Meath.

Preston of Gormanston
(Viscounts Gormanston)

It is stated to be a fact and well documented that whenever the head of the Preston family died large numbers of foxes appeared outside Gormanston. This fact was noted by the Hon. Lucretia Farrell, a granddaughter of Jenico Preston the 12th Viscount Gormanston, who wrote about it in her diary. She stated 'on the day before my grandfather Jenico, the 12th Viscount Gormanston died (in 1860) foxes came in pairs into the demesne from all the country round. They sat under his bedroom window which was on the ground floor and howled and barked all night. They were constantly driven away only to return. We found them the next morning crouched in the grass in front of and around the house. In those days there were many hares in the grass in front of the house and the foxes merely wandered through them and the same among the poultry. On the day of the funeral the keeper saw them all leaving and going across the fields towards the woods where the burial took place, but they did not turn up there but all disappeared.' She also recounted that the foxes came also when her father died but in less numbers. In 1907 the Hon. Richard Preston was waking his father on the night he died in the private chapel when he heard sounds coming from outside the door. When he opened the door he saw a large number of foxes some of which walked straight into the chapel and around the bier. He left the chapel and left the door ajar and during the night he could hear the whining of the foxes which continued until about five in the morning. It stopped abruptly and it would seem that not a trace of a fox was seen thereafter. This account was confirmed by two servants.[342]

The first Prestons to come to Ireland came in the 14th century. Tradition has it that they originated in Burgundy. The first Irish Preston of note was Roger de Preston who was appointed a justice in the Court of Common Pleas in 1330 in the first year of the reign of Edward III. In the account roll of the priory of the Holy Trinity, Dublin 1337-1346 there is the following entry in 1346: 'Also in wine bought for the archdeacon of Dublin, Roger de Preston, Nicholas de Suyterbery, and their retinue, on Sunday (Oct. 1) next after the feast of St. Michael, after dinner, 6 1/2 pence.' From this we can assume that Roger was in the company of both the archdeacon and Nicholas de Suyterbery and their collective retinue when they visited Christ Church in that year.

Because of the depredations of the Gaelic Irish who were in revival mode at this time, particularly the Kavanagh Kings of Leinster, the O'Byrnes, the O'Nolans and the O'Tooles the Anglo Irish beseeched Edward III to send 'a good sufficient chieftain, stocked and strengthened with men and treasure, of which they can live, as a good and noble prince is bound to do for his lieges.' He sent his third son Lionel the Duke of Clarence. Lionel arrived in Ireland in the spring of 1361 with a huge army and equipment and treasure. Lionel's first move was against the Leinster chieftains and in an encounter he captured Art More the McMurrough and King of Leinster and his tanaiste Donal Riabhach who were promptly imprisoned in Dublin castle where they died of the plague.

Roger de Preston's son Sir Robert de Preston (d.1396) was knighted in the field, in 1361, by Lionel, Duke of Clarence, and obtained a grant forever of the Manor of Gormanston in the Counties of Dublin and Meath.[343] He filled the office of Lord High Chancellor of Ireland. He was also possessed of Carbery, County Kildare which he made his chief place

---

[342] Mrs Charles Moseley refutes this account stating that her father would never have allowed foxes into the chapel nor would he have left the door ajar. She also mentions that her father said there were seven foxes.

[343] Mrs. Moseley stated that Gormanston was bought from a Nicholas Armoury de St. Armand and it was then 'smaller and more attractive, on the style of a French Chateau'.

of residence. Sir Robert married Margaret Birmingham, daughter and heir of Walter de Birmingham, Lord of Carbery.

Sir Robert was succeeded by his only son Sir Christopher Preston, Knight. Sir Christopher was imprisoned in the Castle of The Trim for corresponding with the Prior of Kilmainham.[344] The Prior was Thomas Bacach Butler[345] the second son of the 3rd Earl of Ormonde. Thomas's grandmother was a daughter of Sir John Darcy of Plattin, Meath, so it possible that Sir Robert knew the Prior. It is unclear as to the reason for Sir Christopher's imprisonment.

Sir Christopher Preston married Elizabeth Laundres (b.abt.1370), daughter and heir of William Laundres, Baron of Naas, in the right of his mother, Emma Fitzmaurice, daughter of William Fitzmaurice, Baron of Naas (so created by Henry II) and his wife Helen, sister of Richard, Earl of Pembroke, by which marriage the Prestons obtained the Barony of Naas. Sir Christopher was succeeded by his only son Christopher Preston, (b. 1380) Baron of Naas, in the right of his mother, married Jane D'Artois, daughter of Sir Jenico D'Artois, Knight. Christopher was succeeded by his eldest son Robert.

This man must have been a very talented person, who was good at networking. He was appointed Lord Deputy of Ireland in 1478. In the same year he was created a Viscount. As the Lord Deputy he was a

---

[344] Strongbow endowed the Knights Hospitallers with Kilmainham, and this endowment was confirmed by Henry II in 1172. The possessions of the Hospital were augmented in an incredibly short space of time by grants of land and churches in eight counties of Ireland, exclusive of Dublin. In Dublin it enjoyed a mill on the Liffey, the rectories of Kilmainham, Chapelizod, Ballyfermot, and Palmerstown, together with the altarages of these Churches.

[345] Thomas Butler was appointed Prior of Kilmainham in 1403 and held the post down to his death in 1419. He took a prominent part in the wars against the Kavanaghs and the O'Carrolls in 1405-07. He was present at the Battle of Callan in 1407. Thomas was granted manors in Tipperary – Knockgraffon and Kiltenian – as a reward for his participation. He was appointed Deputy to the Duke of Clarence the viceroy in 1409 when that nobleman returned to England. Shortly afterwards he was assailed by the Irish at Kilmainham where he narrowly escaped with his life and was severely wounded. Thomas Bacach, as he was known, brought a small army of 1500 men to England and fought with Henry V in France and his son William acted as his deputy from 1415-18. Thomas fought at Agincourt and was noted for his dash and bravery. He died from wounds received in 1419.

Member of Parliament in Ireland and sat in the Parliaments of 1490 and 1493. His wife was Janet Molyneux, an English lady. The Viscount died in 1503 and was succeeded by his son, the 2nd Viscount, Sir William Preston.

Sir William, like his antecedents and most of his peers, was a warrior. In 1504 Sir William was part of the large force led by the Earl of Kildare, the Lord Deputy, to the famous battle of Knockdoe in the province of Connaught.[346] With Lord Killeen, Sir William led the wings of the bowmen. In 1525 he was appointed Lord Justice of Ireland. His first wife was Anne Burnell a daughter of John Burnell, of Ballgriffin, co. Dublin. He married secondly Eleanor Dowdall a daughter of Sir Thomas Dowdall and widow of John Nangle of Navan.

Sir William's eldest son was Jenico Preston, 3rd Viscount Gormanston, who was unfortunate enough to marry Catherine Fitzgerald, daughter of Gerald the doomed 9th Earl Kildare. Sir William's children included Elizabeth Preston who married firstly Thomas Nangle, Baron of Navan and secondly the 13th Baron Delvin who died in 1559. Three of his sons were Christopher his successor, Nicholas his second son and Martin whom it is thought may have been the ancestor of the Swainston Prestons.[347]

Sir Jenico Preston learned a bitter lesson in loyalty to the Crown as he witnessed the almost total obliteration of his wife's family following the rebellion of Silken Thomas her brother. Thomas and seven of his uncles lost their lives in the Tower of London despite the fact that many of them were not at all involved in the rebellion. A few years later, in 1541, Jenico voted with his peers in Parliament to agree to the title of King of Ireland being conferred on Henry VIII. It was said of Jenico in official circles that he was a man 'of fair possessions, but of mean wit, less activity and keeps no defence'.[348]

Jenico's son, Christopher, the 4th Viscount was no more attractive to the authorities than his father. It was said of him after his death in 1599

---

[346] This was where Gearoid Mor the 8th Earl of Kildare defeated Ulick Burke of Clanrickard, in August of 1504 in a pitched battle that resulted in the deaths of over 2000 men. Burke had taken Galway city and had aspirations to further expand his empire.

[347] This is probably erroneous. See the chapter on the Bellinter Prestons in this volume.

[348] Randal McDonell *The Lost Houses of Ireland*

'the Viscount Gormanston is dead, by whose death Her Majesty is rid of a froward nobleman, contentious and backward in all duties.'[349] He came to the notice of officialdom on at least one occasion when he assaulted his brother-in-law, Lord Slane and was fined £100 for the pleasure. He also got a licence to be absent in England for two years in 1576.[350]

Christopher's second son, Thomas, was created Viscount Tara but this title came to an abrupt end in 1674 when Thomas's grandson and namesake, was killed by the Blundells from Co. Offaly. The Blundells were Sir Francis, William and Winwood.[351] All three received pardons from the King, leading to the conclusion that the Viscount must have been erroneous in his behaviour in some way.

After the Nine Years War and the defeat of the Irish at the Battle of Kinsale, Irish lands of forfeiting landowners was carved up and among the many to benefit was Jenico, the 5th Viscount Gormanston, who got lands in various counties. Following that long period of unrest there was a reasonably long period of calm during which the Gormanstons and their peers could consolidate their holdings. This period came to an abrupt end in 1641 with the outbreak of the Great War as it was called. This was in reality a Civil War where the Catholics sided with King Charles I and most of the Protestant landowners sided with the Parliament. The Prestons, being Catholic threw in their lot with the Royalists, who were eagerly supported by the remaining Gaelic lords also. The 5th Viscount's son, Nicholas, was a Commander in the Catholic forces. He had succeeded his father Jenico in 1630 following that man's death.[352] The first Viscount Tara, his uncle, Thomas Preston, was a Confederate General during the Great War of 1641 and took part in some notable battles including the heavy defeat at New Ross. His forte was siege warfare and he was responsible for

---

[349] Ibid.

[350] Fiants of the Tudor Monarchs

[351] Grandsons of the adventurer Sir Francis Blundell the Secretary for Ireland in the reign of Queen Elizabeth. At the time of the carve up of the Gaelic lands he benefited greatly by being given lands in several counties including Wexford and Offaly.

[352] Jenico's wife was Margaret the daughter of Nicholas St. Lawrence, Lord Howth. They had a daughter also, Mary Preston who was married twice. Her last husband was Simon Luttrell of Luttrellstown.

the capture of many strongholds during the war, including Birr, Carlow and Duncannon.

Sir Nicholas the 6th Viscount, who was married to Mary Barnewall of Kingsland, died during the war in 1643 and was succeeded by his eldest son Jenico, the 7th Viscount who also fought in the war. After the defeat of the Royalist and Confederate forces by the Cromwellians, Jenico chose to go into exile with Charles II. In the meantime his estates were confiscated. He returned to Ireland following the Restoration of King Charles II to the throne and in due course his estates were returned to him.

Jenico the 7th Viscount (1625?-1691) lived quietly and was married on two occasions but none of his wives bore him any sons but he had one daughter, Mary. When the time came again in 1690 to declare for the Stuart King James II or to show that he had learnt the lessons of war by keeping his head down, he chose the former course of action and went off to fight at the Battle of the Boyne and later took part in the defence of the city of Limerick. He died in Limerick in 1691. He was indicted for high treason posthumously and was declared a traitor and his lands and titles were subjected to attainders and declared forfeit.

After his death the Viscountcy passed to his nephew, Jenico, and although that nobleman used the title of Viscount it was not officially recognised. Jenico had no sons and when he died the title passed to his brother, Anthony. Anthony (1670?-1716) exofficio 9th Viscount managed to retrieve most of the estate under the articles of Limerick. Anthony married his cousin Mary, the daughter of the 7th Viscount and their son Jenico, the 10th Viscount married a daughter of the 11th Lord Trimlestown.

Jenico the 10th Viscount (1707-1757) succeeded to the title and properties in 1716 and he and his wife Thomasina had a family, the eldest of whom, Anthony, became the 11th Viscount, upon the death of Jenico in 1757.

The Prestons were still Catholics at this period, as evidenced by the fact that a niece of the 11th Viscount, Mary Frances Preston, became a nun. This of course begs the question of how they succeeded in holding on to their estates during the period of the Penal Laws. It was significant too that Anthony Preston was granted a licence to hold a fair at Nobber in 1784.[353]

---

[353] Danny Cusack in *Riocht na Midhe* 1998

Anthony the 11th Viscount (1736-1786) was married to an English lady, Henrietta Robinson, of Denston Hall, Suffolk. They had one son, Jenico, who was only eleven when his father died in 1786. By the time Jenico, the 12th Viscount reached his majority there were ample funds in the Preston coffers that had accumulated from the huge rent rolls of the Preston estates. Jenico was officially received back into the fold in 1800 when the attainders on his titles were declared void by the Court of the King's Bench.

Gormanston Castle

Jenico, the 12th Viscount (1775-1860) was an active member of the Catholic Committee, a body that worked to secure Catholic Emancipation.[354] This body was active between 1790 and 1811 when it was suppressed. His greatest achievement, from the family point of view and possibly from an Irish heritage point of view was the building of Gormanston Castle.[355] This was done under the supervision of the famous

---

[354] The 12th Viscount, while fighting politically for Catholic Emancipation, was still very much involved in preserving the security of the county. He formed a corps of Yeomen Cavalry in 1797 to combat the growing threat posed by the United Irishmen.

[355] Mrs. Moseley mentioned that 'the family were not pleased when the 12th Viscount razed the building. Explosives had to be used to help the demolition after which the modern day "white elephant" was built.'

19th century architect Francis Johnston. A particular feature of the gardens, possibly added later, was the Yew Walk 'the original appearance and form of which was intended to represent the cloisters of a monastery'. A quaint story goes that one of the Lord Gormanstons had a daughter who expressed the desire to become a nun but he forbade this. As compensation and to allay her disappointment he built the Yew Walk and at the end of the walk a cell like structure also built from yew. Jenico, apart from being an energetic builder was strict in the running of his estate. As was the case on many of the Meath estates tenants who were bad managers and unable to pay the rents were evicted. This may well have occurred over many years but 1834 was recorded as being one such year.[356]

Jenico's wife was Margaret the daughter of Viscount Southwell. They had a large family of seven sons and one daughter. A number of the sons died unmarried and others joined the Army. One of the Army officers was Charles, a Captain in the 24th foot whose descendants are living today in Canada. Another son, Thomas, of Silverstream Co. Dublin was a Deputy Lieutenant and a Commissioner for National Education in Ireland. His descendants who lived mainly in Ireland and in the U.K. have died out.

Jenico's eldest son, Edward John (1796-1876), the 13th Viscount, appears to have become a member of the Church of Ireland and in 1868 he was created Baron Gormanston of Whitewood, Co. Meath. He was at various times Sheriff of Co. Meath and of Co. Dublin. His wife was Lucretia Jerningham and they had two sons and three daughters. The daughters were Margaret, Lucretia and Charlotte who married respectively Vincent Eyre from Leicestershire, John Farrell from Moynalty, Co. Meath and Colonel Richard Donaldson from Hartlands, Co. Meath. The second son, Edward was a career Army officer and was at one time A.D.C. to the Lord Lieutenant of Ireland. He was also a J.P. for counties Meath and Dublin. Although married he had no family.

The eldest son was Jenico William (1837-1907) who became the 14th Viscount on the death of his father in 1876. He was about 40 years old at the time. Like his brother he was a career Army officer who was at various times Governor of the Leeward Isles, British Guiana and Tasmania. He also saw war at its worst in the Indian Mutiny where he was a Lieutenant in the 60th Rifles. Like his uncle Thomas he was a Commissioner for

---

[356] Riocht na Midhe 1989 – *Agrarian Violence in Meath* by Desmond Mooney.

National Education in Ireland, in addition to being High Sheriff of Meath and Dublin and a J.P. for the same counties and a Deputy Lieutenant.

It was during the stewardship of the 14th Viscount that the estate had to be carved up and made over to the tenants under the Land Laws of the period. Jenico William married Georgina Connellan from Coolmore Co. Kilkenny and they had three sons and a daughter Ismay, whose husband was Lord Crichton-Stuart.

The three sons were Jenico Edward, Richard and Hubert who all pursued careers in the Army. Richard rose to the rank of Lieutenant Colonel and was awarded the D.S.O. in World War I. He later embarked upon a career in metallurgy and was President of the Institute of Metals where he acquitted himself with honour being awarded the Platinum Medal in 1945. His modern descendants include Philip, Stephen, Matthew and Anthony, all Downside old boys. His three daughters left him many grand children and great grand children most of whom live mainly in the U.K. These include Mrs. Simon Aldridge, Mrs. David Bull, London, Mr. Simon and Mr. Robert Colledge. The youngest of the three daughters of Richard and Belle was Ursula who married a Corkman, Mr. Charles Moseley. Ursula's children are Dominic, Christopher, Justin, Virginia and Lucy and she has numerous grandchildren.

The 15th Viscount, Jenico Edward (1879-1925) served in the Army and was also a J.P. and Deputy Lieutenant for Co. Meath. His wife was Eileen the daughter of Lt. Gen. Sir William Butler.[357] They had three sons Jenico William who succeeded his father to the titles in 1925 at the age of fourteen and Robert Francis and Stephen and a daughter Eileen who married Peter Lunn.[358]

Robert was educated at Downside and became in due course an Army officer attaining the rank of Captain in World War II. He survived the War. His wife was Jean Shaw from Rugby, whom he divorced in 1955. They have one daughter Jennifer who married Istvan Siklossy von Pernesz and lives in Belgium with her children Georgina and Stephanie.

Stephen, a Lieutenant in the Irish Guards was killed in action during World War II at Anzio in 1944.

---

[357] Lady Butler, Sir William's wife was an artist of note who specialized in painting military objects.
[358] Peter 's father, Sir Arnold Lunn is a well known authority on skiing.

Jenico William (1911-1940) the 16th Viscount, like his military forebears pursued a career in the Army. On the eve of the outbreak of war in 1939 he married Pamela the daughter of Captain Edward Hanly and Lady Marjorie Heath. He was killed in action in France in the following year.

Their son, Jenico Nicholas is the present and 17th Viscount of Gormanston. The 17th Viscount was educated at Downside. He married Eva Landzianowski from Poland and has two sons Jenico Francis and William Luke. Eva died in 1984 and the 17th Viscount married Lucy Fox (the daughter of the celebrated actor Edward Fox) in 1997. She was formerly married to David Grenfell.

Taylour of Headfort
(Marquesses of Headfort)

The elopement of the 2nd Marquess of Headfort, with a rector's wife and the subsequent case brought by the aggrieved husband, Rev. Charles Massy was a cause celebré in its time. The little fun and games expedition cost the Marquess the sum of £10,000 in damages plus the costs of the case which were punitive also. Rev Charles Massy was the second son of Sir Hugh Dillon Massy from Donass, Co. Clare. He fell in love with a Miss Rosslewin, 'who had not the fortune to support the claim of beauty' as Rev. Massy's counsel, Bartholomew Hoare[359], noted during the trial.[360] His father, in fact, disapproved of the marriage and offered to settle £1100 a year on him if he married a lady of fortune from a neighbouring county, but Rev. Charles was determined and married his love. According to their counsel they lived the life of a happy and united couple for eight years and during that time they had a son, 'the bond and cement of their present happiness, the pledge and promise of future multiplied felicites'.

Rev. Massy had a living in Co. Meath for a number of years and his principal parishioner was Lady Bective the mother of Lord Headfort. She was an exemplary parishioner and because of her generosity the living

---

[359] Hoare was instructed by the very famous Counsel, John Philpot Curran. Lord Headfort was represented by George Ponsonby and Richard Pennefather among others.

[360] Miss Rosslewin's sister was married to the Bishop of Limerick.

was most worthwhile. Lord Headfort had occasion to go to Limerick, with his regiment, the Meath Militia and when Rev. Massy heard of his arrival he went to Limerick and met Lord Headfort there. He invited him to his home, Summerhill, little suspecting the devastation to his domestic bliss that lay ahead. Lord Headfort at this time was a man in his fifties who according to Hoare had neither the figure nor the face to give any indication of his intentions.

Lord Headfort stayed there for four days and was introduced to the leading gentlemen of the county who threw their doors open for the noble Lord from Meath. The regiment remained in Limerick for the next couple of months and the Marquess took up residence in the home of Lord Limerick for the duration. During this time he was often visited by the Massys and on numerous occasions by Mrs. Massy alone. One of the reasons given by the defence for the presence of Mrs. Massy in Limerick at this time was that her sister's husband, the Bishop, was dangerously ill. The unsuspecting Charles noticed nothing untoward, but a concerned neighbour wrote to him and warned that Lord Headfort was 'too attentive to Mrs. Massy'. The Rev. Charles took immediate action. He discontinued the visits by Lord Headfort and he forbade his wife to visit Lord Headfort in Limerick. Mrs. Massy succeeded in calming her husband and seemed able to persuade him that there was nothing amiss. However on the Sunday, while the Rev. Massy was in Church conducting the services for the day, Lord Headfort came to Summerhill and he and Mrs. Massy crossed the Shannon in a boat and then went by chaise to Pallas where they spent the night.

From there they journeyed the next day to Roscrea and in the following number of days they made their way to England, where they lived together publicly.

Headfort today is perhaps best known as a magnificent golf course on the outskirts of Kells, designed by Christy O'Connor Jnr. Dominating the course is the huge mansion built by Thomas Taylour the first Earl of Bective. This mansion, luckily, escaped destruction and is currently in use as a private Boarding School for boys. In the late 1940s the 5th Marquess and Lady Headfort, having given much thought to the future of the ancestral home decided to explore the idea of opening a private school based on the English Public School model.

Headfort House

At that time the demesne extended to about 1000 acres and was farmed. Headfort was, like many great houses with large demesnes, a self sufficient entity providing milk, vegetables and meat, not alone for the consumption of the family and the large staff but also for the people of the neighbourhood. When the Boarding School first opened to the public the transition was almost seamless. The Headfort family moved out to the modernized East Wing, which was named "Headfort Court". The staff and boys occupied the rest of the building where they lived in dormitories, dined in the refectory and attended classes. The school kitchens were supplied from the produce of the demesne. Even Lord Headfort's staff moved with ease wearing various hats as required. Bill Kirwan, Lady Headfort's chauffeur, did maintenance work before joining the school on a full time basis. This versatile man mended electrical equipment, painted, mowed the lawns and sports grounds and in winter lit the classroom fires.[361] The first Riding Mistress was Elizabeth Clark, a daughter of Lady Headfort by her first marriage.[362]

Thomas Taylour was an English surveyor who was closely associated with William Petty the famous author of *The Down Survey*.[363] He

---

[361] From an account of the early days of the school at Headfort by Jack Sweetman on the Headfort website.

[362] Ibid.

[363] Most of the Maps of the Down Survey or copies of them are still extant. They are in the National Library of Ireland, The Public Record Office of Northern Ireland (P.R.O.N.I.) and some in the Bibliotechque Nationale in Paris.

was in fact the Deputy Surveyor General from 1660 to 1667. Shortly after the Cromwellian subjugation of the Irish, Sir William Petty was commissioned to carry out a complete survey of the entire country with a view to deciding the lands of the 'rebel' Irish that should be forfeited and made available for distribution to the soldiers and adventurers. Thomas Taylour came to Ireland in 1653 and was in possession of lands in the Kells area before the end of the decade. He got other lands in the country also either by purchase or by grant. In the early 1800s the family owned over 7000 acres in Co. Meath, 14000 plus in Cavan, almost 13,000 in Westmoreland, 4,500 in York and 3,400 in Lancashire. At the time Lord Headfort's rental rolls brought him in a massive £40,000 per annum.

Thomas Taylour made some copies of a number of Baronial Maps, presumably in the Meath area, and these remained in the family until 1837 when they were bought from the then Lord Headfort by the Commissoners for Woods and Forests. These maps were subsequently destroyed in the Four Courts fire in 1922.[364] Thomas occupied some important official post being at various time Deputy Receiver General, Vice Treasurer and Vice Treasurer of War.

Anne Axtell, an English lady, was the bride chosen by Thomas and the nuptials were performed in 1658. They had one son, Thomas, and one daughter Anne, who married Sir Nicholas Acheson. This baronet may well have been the father of Sir Arthur Acheson, High Sheriff of Co. Armagh in 1728. The Taylours took up residence at Bective Abbey, owned by the Boltons (see that family) and remained in residence there until the end of the 18th century.

Thomas Taylour died in 1682 and was succeeded by his son Thomas II, (the 1st Baronet) then 20 years old. Thomas II must have made himself useful to the state also and while we have no record of his services to King William he hardly managed to stay neutral during the conflict of 1689-91. He was created a baronet in 1704 and was a member of the Privy Council in 1726.

Sir Thomas (1662-1736) got married in the same year his father died. His wife was an English lady also, Anne, the daughter of Sir Robert Cotton of Combermere. It is likely that they spent some of their time in England and left the management of their Irish properties to agents. They

---

[364] *The Maps of the Down Survey*

had four sons and three daughters and the fact that the three ladies found husbands in Ireland would indicate that the Taylours were mainly resident in Ireland. This thesis is further strengthened by the fact that while two of the sons died unmarried the other two married ladies from families resident in Ireland. The husbands of the three Taylour ladies were Colonel John Preston of Bellinter (see that family), Bishop Fitzgerald (who occupied the See of Clonfert) and George Pepper of Ballygarth, Co. Meath. The second son, Robert, became the Dean of Clonfert and bought Ardgillan Castle in 1737.[365] He never married and his property passed to his nephew after his death in 1744. The fourth son James married Catherine Meredith but they had no family.

An unusual lot turned up in a Sotheby's auction in 2003. The sale was that of the contents of Fawley House, Henley-on-Thames, Oxfordshire. The lots (14 to 17) were described as 'a set of fine tent-stitched embroidered wall or screen panels, probably Irish, circa 1712 to 1715'. Framed in giltwood, the panels were worked in rich wools highlighted with silks. Each had at its centre a large urn of flowering exotic blooms on a pedestal. This was surrounded by fantastic birds, beasts and stylised oriental figures in flowing robes and turbans, monkeys smoking pipes and small pagodas. Each panel measured 188 by 85 centimeters, and bore the armorials and initials of the original owner Sir Thomas Taylour, Member of Parliament for Kells, Co Meath.

Sir Thomas, the 2nd Baronet (1686-1757), was also a Privy Councillor who had business acumen. 'He bought 10,000 acres of bog in Cavan, much at the rent of only 1s.8d per acre; he drained and improved the bog, though a red one, divided it and brought it to such good land that it is now 15s an acre; part of it was dry rocky land which he divided by walls. '[366] Sir Thomas built a residence there, Virginia Park, which was used mainly as a hunting and sporting retreat.

The 2nd Baronet married Mary Graham of Plattin, Co. Meath. Sir Thomas and Mary had one son and one daughter, Henrietta who married Richard Moore of Barne, Co.Tipperary. The only son was predictably

---

[365] Ardgillan Castle, now owned by the State, was in fact a large country house, the central portion of which was built by Robert Taylour. The east and west wings were added later on in the 18th century by his lateral descendants. The estate was bought from the Ussher family who were wine merchants.

[366] Arthur Young in his *Tour of Ireland*

named Thomas. His wife was Jane, the daughter of a neighbour, the Hon. Hercules Langford Rowley whose spouse was Viscountess Langford. Plans to build a house at Headfort were drawn up by Sir Thomas the 2nd Baronet but he died before any works were begun. After he died in 1757 his son immediately began preparations for building –it was to be another twelve years before the scaffolding was eventually taken down and at least another five years before the famous Adam interiors were completed. [367]

Sir Thomas, the 3rd Baronet (1724-1795), was elevated still further when he was created the 1st Earl of Bective. He too was an M.P. until his move into the House of Lords in 1760. He was actively involved in the defence of the country and was Commander of a force of dragoons in Meath in 1756[368].The Earl and Jane had four sons, Thomas, Robert, Clotworthy and Henry Edward, and two daughters one of whom died unmarried. The other lady, Henrietta, married Chambré Ponsonby Barker of Kilcooley Abbey, Co. Tipperary.[369] It was under 3rd Baronet's guidance that the magnificent house at Headfort was built. Arthur Young in his tour of Ireland in the late 1770s visited Headfort. This is what he had to say about the house and demesne.

'The improvements at Headfort must be astonishing to those who knew the place seventeen years ago; for then there were neither building, walling nor plantations: at present almost everything is created necessary to form a considerable residence. The house and offices are entirely new built. It is a large plain stone edifice. The body of the house is 145 feet long and wings each 180 feet. The hall is 31 by 24 and 17 high. The saloon is of the same dimensions on the left of which is dining room 48 by 24 and 24 high: on the right a drawing room 24 square by 17 high and within that Lady Bective's dressing room 23 by 8. There are also on this floor a breakfast room 23 by 18 and a room for Lord B. of the same size. (He goes on to give the dimensions of the six bedrooms on the first floor which are all 15 feet high) The ground falls

[367] John Harris, *Headfort House and Robert Adam*, 1973.
[368] O.Snoddy *Riocht .na Midhe* 1978
[369] For more information on that family see *The Tipperary Gentry* by Wm. Hayes & Art Kavanagh.

agreeably in front of the house to a narrow winding vale which is filled with wood, where also is a river which Lord Bective intends to enlarge; and on the other side the lawn spreads over a large extent and is every where bounded by very fine plantations. Besides numerous plantations, considerable mansion and an incredible quantity of walling his Lordship has walled in 26 acres of garden and nursery and built six or seven very large pineries 90 feet long each. He has also built a farm yard 280 feet square totally surrounded with offices of various kinds. In the breed of his cattle Lord Bective is very attentive: he sent into Craven for a prime bull and got one which cost him 35 guineas at a year old. This is the breed, which from much experience he prefers, as well for milking as for fattening. In July August and September they have great numbers of Connaught labourers; they are called spalpeens; spal in Irish is a scythe and peen a penny; that is a mower for a penny a day but that was 80 years ago.

The second son, Robert, a career Army Officer never married and died in 1836. The other three sons were the ancestors of the Taylours of Headfort, the Langfords of Summerhill and the Taylors of Ardgillan Castle in Co. Dublin. Clotworthy, the third son married his cousin Frances Rowley Langford of Summerhill and when her uncle Hercules the 2nd Viscount Langford died in 1796 the estates passed to Clotworthy Taylour. Clotworthy was only thirty three years old at the time. He assumed the name Langford and was created Baron Langford in 1800.[370]

Henry Edward Taylor[371] (1768-1852) the 4th son, found a career in the Church. He also found time to marry and his wife was Marianne St. Leger. He inherited Ardgillan Castle which became the seat of that branch of the Taylors. His descendants remained there until 1962 when the estate was sold to Heinrick Pott of Westphalia, Germany. In 1982 Dublin County Council purchased Ardgillan Demesne and it is now managed by Fingal

---

[370] See that family in this volume.
[371] It would seem that the Rev. Taylor changed the spelling of his name from Taylour to Taylor.

Council, as a premier tourist attraction which includes walks through the gardens and the demesne.

Rev. Henry Edward Taylor was the ancestor of some very distinguished men. His eldest son, Thomas Edward (1811-1883) was an army officer for a time, rising to the rank of Colonel of the Meath Militia. He was elected an M.P. for Dublin, a position he occupied from 1841-1883. During the course of his political career he received appointments to high office and was Lord of the Treasury from 1858-1759. In the next decade he was joint secretary of the Treasury and from 1874 until 1880 he was Chancellor of the Duchy of Lancaster. Thomas Edward's brother, Richard Chambré, became a general in the Army and was Governor of Sandhurst from 1883-1886. One of Thomas Edward's sons, Basil, a Navy Commander, was Harbour Master of Hong Kong while Richard's son, Richard Edward was decorated for bravery in the South African Wars, receiving the medal with two clasps.

Thomas Taylour the eldest son of the 3rd Baronet (and 1st Earl of Bective), was born in 1757 and when he reached marriageable age chose as his bride, Mary Quin from Clare, an heiress.[372] Her father was George Quin from Quinsborough, a member of the famous Quin family of Celtic origin, owners of Adare Manor[373]. They were married in 1778 when Thomas was 21 years of age. George Quin left his property to George, the second son of Mary and Thomas. In later life he was known as Lord George Quin[374].

Thomas Taylour (1757-1829) the 4th Baronet and 1st Marquess, already mentioned at the start of this chapter, succeeded his father in 1795. He held various posts including, somewhat ironically, that of Lord of the Bedchamber. He was an officer in the Militia in 1798 and was appointed Colonel in 1804. Sir Thomas was made Marquess of Headfort in 1800

---

[372] Mary's mother was Caroline the daughter of Sir Henry Cavendish of Doveridge Hall, Derby.

[373] George Quin's nephew was the 1st Earl of Dunraven.

[374] Lord George Quin was married twice. He had two sons by his first wife. One of the sons, an Army officer, died at the age of 22. The other son, Richard Robert, who attained the rank of Rear Admiral in the Navy, was married and had three daughters. Only one of those ladies, Georgiana, married. Her husband was George Stewart from Summerhill, Killiney. They had a family so it can be assumed that the Quin fortune was inherited by the Stewarts.

when titles and cash were handed out by government in their determination to put through the Act of Union. Due either to wanton waste or other extraordinary circumstances the family finances deteriorated during the tenure of the 1st Marquess. In 1819 a very revealing article in the Times highlighted the acute state of the family fortunes. An English creditor, Rev.G.Storey, applied to the Courts to have a receiver put in 'for the estates and premises of Lord Headfort'. It would appear that, as far back as 1812 or earlier he had advanced money which was used to pay an annuity but the family expenses outstripped the family income and the loan was not repaid when due. Trustees were appointed in the interim to sell part of the estates and this was done, raising some £60,000 but the plaintiff was not paid. The Court on the strength of the arguments put forward decided that the situation did not warrant the appointment of a receiver.

The litigation didn't appear to have impacted on his social standing as in the same year, in his official capacity of Lord of the Bedchamber, His Lordship attended a Court held by the Prince Regent at Carlton House.

The 1st Marquess died at Lausanne in 1829 and was succeeded by his eldest son, Thomas, the 2nd Marquess. His widow, the marchioness outlived him and survived as Lady Dowager until 1842.

Thomas, the 2nd Marquess (1787-1870) got further honours for the family when he was created Baron Kenlis of Kells, Meath, in 1831. He was also a Colonel in the Meath militia and Lord Lieutenant in Co. Cavan. Thomas became embroiled in some controversy when he acted with the Corporation of Kells, in 1830, in compelling a large number of poor people to leave the Hill of Loyd, where they had gathered because 'the want of subsistence was so intense and so general as to drive a multitude of people to colonize forcibly a tract of land to which they had no shadow of title in law'. The land in fact belonged to the Corporation of Kells. Under the direction of the Chief Magistrate, Lord Headfort, a number of people were arrested and a number of hastily erected huts were thrown down.

Thomas's wife was the daughter of Sir John Stevenson, the celebrated Irish musician who had collaborated with Thomas Moore in the compilation of the internationally famous 'Moores Melodies'. They had three sons and three daughters. Two of the daughters married but only Olivia, who married the Rev. Fitzpatrick, rector of Cloone, Co. Leitrim, had a family. The two younger sons both went into the Army and John

Henry the youngest son attained the rank of Major General. His older brother died at the age of 25.

Thomas the 3rd Marquess (1822-1894) succeeded his father in 1870. He was already a mature man in his fifties. He was also an able man. He was Honorary Colonel in the 5th regiment of Princess Victoria's Royal Irish Fusiliers and until his accession to the title in 1870 he was an M.P. for Westmoreland. He was a member of the Privy Council in Ireland and was Lord Lieutenant and custos rotolorum for Co. Meath. He married Amelia Thompson, an heiress of Underley Hall, Westmoreland in 1842. This beautiful English property became the English seat of the family and was certainly in use as such when the 3rd Marquess's eldest granddaughter was married as she is described as Lady Olivia Taylour of Underley Hall on the occasion of her marriage to Lord Henry Cavendish-Bentwick in 1892.

The 3rd Marquess and Amelia had one son, Thomas who was born in 1844. Amelia died in 1864 and the 3rd Marquess married again in 1875. His second wife was Emily Thynne the widow of Captain Hon. John Patten, and they had a son, Geoffrey and a daughter Beatrix.

The eldest son Thomas (Lord Bective), an hon. Colonel like his father and an M.P. married an heiress, Lady Alice the daughter of the 4th Marquess of Downshire and they had five daughters but no son. Thomas died in 1893 before his father.

When the 3rd Marquess died in 1894 he was succeeded by his son Geoffrey, the 4th Marquess. Geoffrey (1878-1943), was a J.P. and a D.L. for Co. Meath. He was an Army officer with the rank of Captain in the First World War where he distinguished himself, being mentioned in dispatches. He caused something of a sensation when he married the Gaiety girl Rosie Boote in 1901. As one social commentator of the time wrote 'At the old Gaiety in the Strand the chorus was becoming a matrimonial agency for girls with ambitions to marry into the peerage and began in the nineties when Connie Gilchrist a star of the Old Gaiety married the Earl of Orkney and then in 1901 the Marquess of Headfort married Rosie Boote who had charmed London the previous year when she sang Maisie in The Messenger Boy.'

Geoffrey was made a Senator of the Irish Free State and occupied that position from 1922 until 1928. They had two sons, Terence and William and a daughter Millicent who married Henry Tiarks from Kent and had a family.

William Taylour (1904-1989), a Captain in the Derbyshire Yeomen, had a brilliant academic career and was a Fellow of Trinity College Cambridge. Remarkably his studies only commenced after World War II but by the time of his death he had become one of the foremost archaeologists in Britain. He conducted excavations in Greece and Cyprus where he worked with other eminent archaeologists including Kenyon, Ward-Perkins and Blegen. This most talented man was Treasurer of the Cambridge University Catholic Association, President of the Strafford Club and was made Knight Commander of the Order of St. Gregory the Great.

Lord Headfort the 5th Marquess
(Courtesy M. Bolton)

Terence the 5th Marquess (1902-1960) was educated at Harrow and Oxford and was a Captain in the Warwickshire Yeomen. His wife, whom he married in 1928, was Elise Tucker of Devon and Sydney. He was ADC to the Governor of South Australia in 1939-40 and a Staff Captain in the Australian Forces for the next two years of the War. Terence and Elise had one son Thomas and one daughter Olivia. It was Terence the 5th Marquess and Elise, Lady Headfort who took the decision to turn Headfort into a Boarding School as already mentioned above.

Lady Olivia married Victor Waldron of London, and they have two daughters Sarah and Virginia, both of whom are married and have children.

Thomas the 6th and present Marquess was born in 1932 and now lives in the Philippines. He was educated at Stowe and Cambridge and was highly successful academically. He chose a career as a commercial air pilot. His first wife was the Hon. Elizabeth Nall-Cain and they have one son, Christopher and two daughters Rossanagh and Olivia. Both ladies are married and have families. The 6th Earl sold Headfort Estate in 1981.

Christopher the Earl of Bective, born in 1959 was educated at Harrow. He is an estate agent and a partner in the firm of Bective Leslie Marsh of Chelsea. He is married to Susan Vandervell and they have two sons Thomas and Henry and two daughters Natasha and Alexandra.

Tisdall of Charlesfort

Hugo de Lacy granted the Manor of Martry to a knight named Hugh de Turpleton in the late 12th century. Turpleton built a castle and a church in Martry townland. In the mid 14th century the Justiciar for Ireland, Sir John Darcy was granted a number of estates in Ireland including the Manor of Martry. The Darcys managed to stay in continuous possession of Martry until 1668. They had other properties in Meath also, including Plattin where a branch of the family settled. Being Catholic and having taken part in the War of 1641 the Darcys lost much of their lands. Nicholas, a youngster in the time of the War was declared 'an innocent' and managed to retain lands in the Martry area. However he proved to be a bad manager and having run into debt was forced to lease out his lands in the Martry area in 1668. The lessee was Michael Tisdall.

Michael's father, also called Michael, was the first Tisdall in Ireland. He was a tradesman or professional from England. He married a settler woman named Anne Singleton and they had seven sons and two daughters. His eldest son Michael, born in 1637 was sent to school in Dublin where he studied law. While there he met his future wife, Anne Barry, the niece of Sir James Barry (later Lord Santry) the Chief Justice of the Court of the Kings Bench. This fortuitous relationship resulted in marriage and from then on young Michael's star was in the ascendant. He was soon promoted to the position of Secondary of the Court of the Kings

Bench. When the Martry lands came on the market in 1668 Michael seized his opportunity and leased the lands from the impoverished Nicholas Darcy.

The Manor of Martry was quite substantial and included over a hundred cottages, two windmills and almost 2000 acres of land, Irish measure. As Nicholas Darcy's woes continued Michael took the opportunity to acquire the freehold to the property in 1672. Michael's brother, James Tisdall, was appointed the estate manager and continued in that role until 1689 when Michael's eldest son, William, came of age. Michael appears to have built a house in the townland of Bloomsbury. He changed the name of the townland to Mount Tisdall and his house was called Mount Tisdall also and was effectively the Manor House. Nobody is quite sure if there was a house already in existence in Bloomsbury, but if there was it is likely that it was considerably improved by the new owner of the estate. Apart from the townland of Mount Tisdall, the rest of the estate was leased to tenants. Michael himself seldom lived at Mount Tisdall and appears to have lived mainly in Dublin where he continued in his official post. In 1679 he was made a Justice of the Peace and in the same year was conferred with arms by the Ulster King of Arms, Richard St. George.[375] During his time in Dublin he acquired other properties and a brewery.

The Tisdall arms consist of three pheons argent on a shield of sable with a thistle. Above this is a hand erect, charged with a pellet and holding an arrow. The arm comes out of a crown. The motto reads 'tutantur tela coronam'.[376]

Michael II died aged 44 in 1681 and his son William inherited, but the estate continued to be managed by James Tisdall until 1690. James, who must have been a very astute manager, then moved to Ardee, Co. Louth, where he bought an estate at Bawn. James went on to become an M.P. for Ardee and continued in that position until 1713 when he retired from politics due to ill health. His position as M.P. was given to his grandnephew, Michael III.

---

[375] For information on that family see *The Landed Gentry and Aristocracy of Co. Kilkenny* by Art Kavanagh
[376] The darts defend the crown.

Michael II was buried in St. Michan's church in Dublin. From that time onwards the Tisdalls were all buried in the graveyard adjacent to St. Brigid's church in Martry.

The income from the various properties must have been substantial as William was able to pay dowries for his two sisters, Catherine and Elizabeth and was able to pay money to his brother Michael, a barrister, also. In addition he bought another townland in the vicinity of Martry, known as Hurdlestown. During the turbulent years of 1689-90 when the Kings James II and William of Orange were contending for the throne of Ireland, young William Tisdall seems to have kept his head under the parapet. There is no record of any disturbances on his estate.

William, like his father, made sure to marry well and his bride was none other than Frances Fitzgerald, the sister of the 19th Earl of Kildare. Their eldest son Michael III inherited the estate in 1714 when his father retired due to ill health. He represented Ardee, Co. Louth, in parliament, as already alluded to. Michael III had a brother George who entered the church. Michael III left his brother £5 in his will.

In 1719 Michael III married Catherine Palmer, the daughter of William Palmer, an M.P. for Kildare in 1695 and for Castlebar in 1723. He was in very bad health for most of his life and in his will he made provisions for his family, leaving them annuities and of course his estates which went to his only son Charles, who was just seven years of age when his father died in 1726. During his minority the estate was managed by the Rev. George Tisdall, Charles Hamilton of Dunboyne and William Waller of Allenstown.

Charles (1719-1757) received his later education at Trinity College and came into his inheritance in 1740 having spent some time abroad in the year previous to that. Charles, although he didn't live very long either, proved to be one of the most able of the Tisdalls. He was a very meticulous man who kept records of all his dealings. It was he who built the very fine house later known as Charlesfort. In addition to his activities in Co. Meath he spent considerable periods of time in Dublin where he had numerous properties including the brewery, all of which were leased. He lived mainly in a room in Trinity College which he bought from Mr. Napper. According to his papers he occasionally travelled abroad. Like many of the landlords of the time Charles introduced tolls to his area. This must have been as popular then as it is today. Part of the main road from Navan to

Kells passed through his property and it was his duty to maintain the road. In order to defray the costs he erected gates at both ends, which were manned by servants who collected the tolls.

Charles left the running of the demesne to a manager named Hugh Keowan who oversaw the work of the little army of labourers, ploughmen, stockmen, carpenters and masons whose skills were most necessary to keep the demesne productive. It was probably Keowan who saw to the planting the thousands of trees that were introduced to the estate by Charles.

Charles or his manager Keowan collected the various rents from the estate tenants and regulated the letting of lands. One tenant, named Lowther, appears to have been a middleman who rented a considerable portion of the estate and lived at Hurdlestown House. An interesting tenant of the period was Lawrence Balfe, who rented from a Mrs. Fleming, who held lands in Nugentstown and Volvenstown from Charles. According to Tony Coogan, this man may have been a descendant of the Balfes who in times past had been the biggest landowners in Cortown and who lived in Cortown Castle.

Other tenants included the widow Flood, William Waller of Allenstown House, Mr. & Mrs. Pleasant, Thomas Casserly, Patrick Dooley, Patrick Donaghree, Bryan Harford, and James Mooney. Some of these tenants had in turn subtenants such as the Kings, Donaghoos, and Markeys. Labourers mentioned in his documents include Skellys, Taedy Mucklevaney and John Nowlan, who was also a mason. Other important people on the estate were James Holgan, Patrick Doyle who worked the mill, Mathew Leigh, Tady Nall, Mathew Clerkan, Brigid Maglen, John Reilly, the Smiths of Phoenixtown, Leonard Frost and the Caffreys of Nugentstown.

Charles began work on his new house which he decided to call Charlesfort, soon after coming into his inheritance. It was situated about four miles from Mount Tisdall and sited on a hill in the townland of Athgaine Little. It took eight years to build. Robert Castle, the architect was employed to design the house. Much time and money was also spent on laying out the gardens, digging out a lake, planting trees and shrubs and building the avenue road. During this period also, Charles had his portrait painted by Stephen Slaughter, a noted portraitist of the time. This portrait with others of the family is still extant and is in the possession of Anthony Tisdall in Windlesham, England.

Charlesfort House

Hester Cramer of Ballyfoyle, Co. Kilkenny was the lady chosen by Charles to grace the marriage bed. They were married in 1754 and had two sons Michael and Charles II before Charles's untimely death in 1757. Charles II's grandson was Charles Edward (1821-1905), a successful religious who became Chancellor of Christ Church Cathedral in Dublin.

A half brother to the Chancellor, William St. Clair (1831-1892) started a dynasty of his own in New Zealand where he had numerous descendants who contributed to the social, religious and political life of his adopted country. These include Rev. Charles Gordon St. Clair Tisdall (1914-?), a missionary in Persia and West Pakistan in the 1940s and 50s. He has a son Richard and three daughters and possibly grandchildren. His brother, Wilfrid St. Clair was a Major in World War II. Another descendant was Arthur Walderne St. Clair Tisdall who was a War hero. He received the VC for bravery during the landing at Gallipoli. He rescued wounded men lying 200 yards from the enemy lines making several trips under heavy fire. He was killed in action there in 1915. This talented man wrote a book entitled *Memoir and Poems*. Arthur Walderne's brother John was also killed in action in 1916. Their two younger brothers survived the War and one of them Francis, fought in World War II. He later turned to ranching in the U.S. where he has a son Philip. The ladies in the family were heroic too and in 1918 Irene Mary was presented with a gold watch from Trustees of the Carnegie Hero Fund 'for heroic endeavour to save human life'.[377]

Yet another descendant was Arthur St. Clair (1906-1973) an important officer in the British Army who was Control Communications Officer in post war Germany. His children and grandchildren are living in New Zealand. Other descendants that were prominent were Vernon Gordon, Mervyn Cecil and Walderne Norman who all served in the New Zealand defence forces and whose children and grandchildren live and work in New Zealand.

Another grandson of Charles II was Gordon Charles Vernon (1835-1888) who also went on the great adventure to New Zealand. Gordon Charles Vernon's son Charles Archibald became a very distinguished Churchman in New Zealand filling such posts as Canon of St. Mary's Pro Cathedral and warden of St. John's College. Charles Archibald (1868-1933) had one son Gordon who worked in oil and gas exploration in South America and South Africa. Gordon retired to New Zealand in 1970 and had two sons Peter Gordon and Michael Charles (b.1941) a chemical engineer. Peter Gordon (b.1938), a school principal is married and has two sons.

To revert back to the main family of Charlesfort, Michael (1755-1794) the heir and elder brother of Charles II, a Trinity College graduate, was High Sheriff of Co. Meath in 1788. He also attended Oxford and Lincoln's Inn in Dublin. According to local lore Michael was a good landlord who 'set his lands at a moderate rent, gave renewals without raising the rent and had the comfort and welfare of his tenantry at heart'[378]He may also have been something of a bigot as a Fr. Branagan from the area wrote that Michael 'had broken their holy water bottles upon the poor women as they returned home from the chapel' and 'he also burned some of our Catechisms but he did not long survive the conflagration'[379]

---

[377] Burke – *Irish Family Record*
[378] Tony Coogan in *Charlesfort – A Meath estate*
[379] *Charlesfort – A Meath Estate* by Tony Coogan

His wife was Juliana Blennerhassett from Kerry, an heiress. They had three sons, Charles Arthur, James and Archibald and two daughters Juliana and Catherine.[380] Archibald (1786-1854) following a distinguished career became a Rear Admiral in the Navy but died unmarried. James was Rector of Ballinderry and he had a family of four sons and a daughter but his descendants died out with his grandchildren.

Charles Arthur (1782-1835), the eldest son and heir, was educated at Oxford and returned to Charlesfort in 1794 when his father died. He was High Sheriff of Co. Meath in 1811. During his tenure as proprietor of Charlesfort it would appear that his income from the estate amounted to no more that £570 but he also had income from the rents of his property in Dublin. He seems to have made some attempts to proselytise the Catholic by issuing booklets in which he criticised the priests and the Bishops saying they were afraid to let their people read the Bible and interpret it for themselves. [381] In the same year that he died he advised his son to try to consolidate some of the holdings so as to make the estate more profitable.

Charles Arthur's wife was Elizabeth Vernon of Clontarf Castle and they had four sons John, William, Archibald, James and Francis and five daughters.[382] Apart from John and Archibald who have descendants William's descendants died out and James died unmarried. Archibald (1822-1896) got a commission in the Army and rose to the rank of Major-General and his grandson, Archibald James (b.1893) had children.

John Tisdall (1815-1892), of Charlesfort, was High Sheriff of Meath in 1841, and was also a J.P. and a D.L. The famous Meath Hunt was moved to land on John's estate in 1882 when he gave them a lease at Nugentstown[383]. John married Isabella Knox (of the Earls of Ranfurly family) and they had eight sons Charles Arthur (d.1869), John Knox, George Williams, Henry, Vernon, Richard, Arthur and Alfred and three

---

[380] Juliana married Alexander Hamilton a barrister and Catherine's husband was Rev. Francis Gervais from Co. Tyrone.

[381] Tony Coogan in *Charlesfort – A Meath estate*

[382] Three of the daughters married but only one, Juliana, the eldest had any children. Her husband was James Waller from Allenstown, Co. Meath.

[383] *Charlesfort – A Meath Estate* by Tony Coogan

daughters Harriet, Isabella and Anne.[384] Henry and Vernon Tisdall both came back to the area and leased properties on the estate. Vernon, a Vice Admiral, built a house at Martry when he retired.

The heirs to Charlesfort came from the sons of John Knox and from the descendants of Alfred the 8th son. John Knox (1839-1885) was the father of the next two heirs to Charlesfort to follow after John Tisdall's death in 1892. They were Charles Arthur (1875-1914) and William George (1876-1954).

Charles Arthur was less than 20 years old when he inherited in 1892. He had a commission in the Army and rose to the rank of Major. As a result he was seldom at Charlesfort. When he inherited he received almost 4,000 acres of land in Meath, 500 acres in Limerick and almost 600 acres in Kilkenny. Charles Arthur leased the house and garden and some of the lands for ten years to Robert Heuston, a Polo player from Belfast who came to Meath for that sport. It was during Charles Arthur's time as the proprietor of Charlesfort that the tenants began to buy the land they farmed. They were entitled to do this because of the Land Acts of the last decade of the 19th century and the Wyndham Act of 1903 However the demesne of about 1,000 acres was retained. In 1900 on the occasion of the Queen's visit to Dublin the Major organised a trip there for the children of Cortown and Allenstown schools.[385] The children travelled by train and were looked after in Royal fashion by Army personnel who made their day a memorable one.

After the sale of the land to the tenants was completed in 1904 Robert Heuston was asked to quit Charlesfort, which he did most reluctantly. William George, the Major's brother came there to look after the remnants of the estate. The Major often visited and brought friends. One of these was Sir Edward Elgar the famous English composer and violinist. The Major himself had been a pupil of Elgar.[386]

The Major married Gwynneth Adshead and they had two daughters, Judith and Bridget. He was killed in action at Mons in 1914.

---

[384] Harriet and Isabella married. Their husbands were Rev. Arthur Cole-Hamilton from Northants and Arthur Nugent respectively. Harriet and her husband had children and their descendants today are part of the Earls of Enniskillen family.
[385] Tony Coogan in *Charlesfort – A Meath estate*
[386] Ibid.

Judith married William Hargrave-Pawson and had a family. Bridget's husband was Maurice Richardson and they too had a family.

William George took over the reins at Charlesfort in 1914 after his brother's tragic death. He was educated at Malvern and Cambridge. He was High Sheriff of Meath in 1921 and was a J.P and a D.L. He married Elsie Gardiner from Surrey and they had one son, Michael, who died in 1940 as did his mother Elsie. William George married again but he had no further children. After his death in 1954 he was succeeded in Charlesfort by his cousin, Oliver Raphael Tisdall the 5th son of his uncle Alfred.

Alfred (1859-1931) the 8th son of John Tisdall (d.1892), an Oxford graduate became a parson and worked in Buenos Aires. His wife was Evelyn Empson from Northants and they had five sons the youngest of whom, Oliver Raphael succeeded to Charlesfort in 1954 as we have seen. The other sons were Michael, John Denis, Walter and Charles Richard. Michael, an RAF officer, was killed accidentally in 1919 and Charles Richard was a casualty in World War I. A Lieutenant in the Irish Guards he was killed in action in 1916.

Walter (1890-1939) and John Denis (1889-1947) both had families. John Denis had two sons Brian Henry and John Michael and one daughter Judy and they have families. Walter had three sons, Michael Walter, Christopher and Jeremy and one daughter Jennifer and all four have families.

Dr. Oliver Raphael who succeeded to Charlesfort in 1954 was a distinguished medical person who was awarded the Freedom of the City of London. His wife was Christina Corkran and they had one son Anthony Charles and two daughters, Evelyn and Jocelyn. The two ladies married and they have children. Mrs. Christina remained in Charlesfort until it was sold in 1968.

Anthony Charles (b.1932) is married to Jeanne Ford from London. Mrs. Tisdall had a son by a previous marriage, Mark Ian Davis who has been adopted by Mr. Tisdall.

Watson of Bective

With the exception of this one all the other chapters deal with families that have had long associations with Co. Meath. This chapter deals with a very famous man who spent most of his life at Bective, Mr. John Watson (1852-1908), one of the most famous nineteenth century equestrian sportsmen in Ireland.[387]

This writer had the privilege of knowing the last surviving member of the Watson family of Fenagh, Co. Carlow – Corunna North the wife of Captain Gary North who lived at Altamont in Carlow. A fine tall handsome lady, even in her eighties, she worked tirelessly at her beloved Altamont Gardens which, after her death (her husband had predeceased her), she left to the State. These magnificent Gardens are now being well cared for and are open to the public. Whereas the subject of this chapter Mr. John Watson was known to be brusque, vulgar and hasty tempered, Mrs. North was ladylike, calm and measured in her politeness.

The Watsons were a Quaker family; members of the petty gentry who had been established in Carlow by the early seventeenth century after John Watson from Cumberland obtained a lease of lands at Ardristan from the Earl of Ormonde. It is claimed that they were descended from the Rutland based Watson family who were raised in peerage in the early

---

[387]Lord Dunsany, *My Ireland*. 1937, p.127.

eighteenth century to the Marquisate of Rockingham.[388] The family's principal seats in Ireland were in Carlow, at Kilconnor and Ballydarton.

John the first of the family in Ireland died in 1675 so it is unlikely that he came to Ireland any sooner than 1650. He would certainly not have been welcome during the Great War of 1641-49, when Protestants of any persuasion were, to say the least, not encouraged to live in the rural south east. It is more likely that he settled in Kilconnor in the aftermath of the Cromwellian clearance. He may have come to Ireland after the Restoration when the Duke of Ormonde regained much of his estates and some more in recognition of his loyalty to the King, Charles II. The Duke was the titular owner of the lands in the Fenagh area where Watson settled. The family managed to acquire a number of properties in the area including Ballydarton and later Lumclone which became the main family seat.

John Watson, the founding father, was not a Quaker, but his grandson became one. Watson had an only daughter who married Robert Lecky, another post Cromwellian and neighbouring landowner.

It was John Watson III who became a member of the Society of Friends (Quakers) and built the Meeting House at Kilconnor in 1678. The Watsons remained Quakers for the next five generations. As dissenters they would have been prohibited from holding any official posts. Despite this obvious handicap to advancement the family prospered and in due course they acquired two further properties at Lumclone and Ballydarton (Fenagh). This led to three distinct branches of the family, all descended from Samuel of Kilconnor who was born in 1682, the eldest son of John Watson III.

Samuel of Kilconnor had two sons John of Kilconnor and Samuel of Ballydarton. John continued on the Kilconnor line down to John Lecky Watson.

The first of the family to hold any office in Co. Carlow was John Lecky Watson (1801-1870). He was J.P. and a High Sheriff for the county. It may well be the case that it was he who abandoned the Quaker religion. He acquired the name Lecky from his mother Elizabeth Lecky who married his father in 1800. He married his cousin, Sarah of Lumclone and when he died childless his estate passed to that branch of the family.

---

[388] Jimmy O' Toole, *The Carlow Gentry*, 1993, p.198; IFR, pp.1188-1193.

Samuel of Ballydarton (1714-1784), the son of Samuel of Kilconnor had a son John of Ballydarton (1742-1793), who was the great grandfather of John Watson the subject of this article. It was John of Ballydarton who was credited with having killed the last wolf in Ireland at Baltinglass in 1786. His son, another John, John Henry, of Ballydarton, was the founder of the Tullow, later the Carlow Hunt and John Henry's son Robert Gray Watson was one of the most celebrated huntsmen of the day, his fixation such that he in a most unquakerlike belief in karma was convinced he would be reincarnated as a fox. At his burial he was interred in a fox's earth and the mourners are believed to have exclaimed "Gone Away!"[389]

With such fanatical interest in the chase it was inevitable that the passion would be passed on to his son and it seems fair to conclude that every Watson was bred to foxhunt.

John Watson

John Watson was born in 1851 and like many of his young peers he sought adventure and excitement by joining the Army. He got a commission in the 13th Hussars and took part in the fabled march across North Africa from Cabal to Rabat. An expeditionary force made a forced

---

[389] *Seventy Years Young* – Lady Fingal

march across the mountains with a view to effecting the relief of Kandahar. They marched the 331 miles in 21 days, arriving at Rabat. From there they made the shorter journey to Kandahar where they routed the enemy and relieved the siege.

In 1874 Watson travelled to India with the 13th Hussars under the Commander-in-Chief, General Frederick Roberts VC. It was while in India, and under Roberts's encouragement, that he devised the rules that formed the basis of the modern game of polo and he is also credited with the invention of the backhand shot. For these developments in the game he is widely, and deservedly, regarded as 'the father of polo'. He achieved an international reputation when he famously captained the winning All Ireland Polo Club team at the inaugural Westchester Cup final in Rhode Island in 1886. He established a team known as the "Freebooters," a name which survives today in the trophy which he presented to the All Ireland Club, the oldest club in western Europe, and laid out polo grounds for the team within Bective Demesne.

He only remained in the Army for a relatively short time and returned to Ireland to pursue his passion for hunting. Retiring from the army in 1884 after ten years in India he set himself up in Bective; though said to be 'a man of limited financial resources', when it came to his passion 'he never spared himself' and devoted the remainder of his life to equestrian sports.[390]' He was Master of the Meath Hounds from 1891-1908. He took over from the Earl of Fingall. He was also a highly successful breeder of hounds and it is said that he revolutionized the pack. He went chiefly to the Brocklesby, Fitzwilliam, Carlow, and Cheshire kennels, where the best blood of the day was to be found. Later he is credited with being the originator of the excellent packs that were current in Britain and Ireland in the early part of the 20th century.[391] As Master of Foxhounds, John Watson made Bective home to the historically important and renowned Meath Hunt; the kennels, which he had erected within the demesne, survive and remain in use today for their original purpose, now home to the equally legendary Tara Harriers

Many stories were told about this man's behaviour on and off the hunting grounds and it would be amiss not to include some of them here.

---

[390] Muriel Bowen *Irish Hunting*
[391] *Australasian* 1931

The following anecdote tells how he got his comeuppance from a formidable huntress.

"Like all men of action he was lazy with his language, and he did not suffer fools gladly. Heaven help the duffer who crossed his path or unconsciously broke the unwritten but draconian laws of the chase. He was brusque, but business like, and he saw to it that the best of sport be provided as far as circumstances permitted. Big portly and weighty, yet enviably magnificent when mounted, his hard bitten face fringed with early Victorian side whiskers he resented anybody's intrusion in his rightful place- on the tails of his pack. Once to his chagrin, he found that a furious Diana was in front of him. In stentorious tones he shouted "Madam! Come back Madam". The lady took no notice, but went ahead. Watson put on steam, and, eventually came alongside and said, "Do you hear me Madam?" The lady not at all perturbed, turned in her saddle and said "Yes I do hear you, you baldy old County Carlow Scallion-eater!" "Thank you Madam," said Watson raising his cap, and passed onto his desired position- the head of the field."[392]

Lady Fingall had this to say 'I saw John Watson handling horses ruthlessly, almost savagely. He was the cruellest man with a horse that I had ever seen; and I have never seen a man so strong. He had a way of wrapping his great legs around his horse as he rode it at a fence or bank, seeming almost able to lift a tired horse over. He would ride a horse until it dropped, to get to his hounds. A lame or tired horse, he would always get them there. Out hunting he was a dour, silent, unsociable man. He hated women in the hunting field, and hardly ever spoke to them, although he sometimes glared at one if she got in his way. "I wish they'd go home and do their knitting," he used to mutter.'[393]

Lady Fingall had another couple of anecdotes about Watson. 'John Watson's language in the hunting field was notorious. A man who hunted in Warwickshire after Meath and got cursed by the Master, Lord Willoughby de Broke, said to him: "You may save yourself the trouble, my lord. I have just been hunting in Meath with John Watson. Anything you could say sounds to me like the twittering of a bird on the bough!"

'Once I rode some way home with John Watson at the end of a hunting day. It was an evening of grey spring twilight, the quietness

---

[392] Dr. Peter Coutts in an article on the web, quoting Lord Dunsany.
[393] *Seventy Years Young* – Lady Fingal

unbroken except for the singing of birds and the sound of the horses' hoofs on the white road. I think John Watson spoke only once on that ride, and then he pointed with his whip over a low hedge, beyond which there was a field with young lambs playing in it. "Look at those damned lambs," he said. To him that sight only meant that hunting was over.'

Watson in Hunting Dress

On another occasion one of Lady Fingall's acquaintances rode home with a groom who had once served John Watson. 'No one keeps the atmosphere of the past and can re-create it better than those men who have talked and listened all their lives in stables, where the soft warm breath of the horses filling the air makes talking easy, or at some cross-roads where they wait with other grooms to give up second horses or take tired horses home', noted Lady Fingall. Her friend, riding quietly in semi-twilight, content after the hard day, listened. "A terrible man," the groom said of John Watson, and after a pause: "But you could live with him." 'So expressive a phrase that there is nothing more to say, for, after all, the world is divided into those people with whom one may live, and those with whom it is impossible to live at all!' concluded the Lady. The groom told his stories of John Watson. "He liked his horses wise", he said, "and wouldn't have one under ten years old." And "my heels were worn out pushing them along the road. But Mr. Watson had only to come into sight and to call them, and they were all leppin' on their hind legs, like two-year-olds".

Although he was known as the 'father of polo' it was not he, but a Carlow neighbour who was the founder of the All Ireland Polo Club. That honour belonged to Horace Rochfort, of Clogrennan. He inaugurated the Club in Carlow in 1872 and as the honorary secretary he oversaw the move to the Nine Acres in the Phoenix Park in 1873.

It was actually in Meath that the first ever polo game was played in Ireland, believed to have taken place at Gormanston in 1871 when one of the founders of 'hockey on horseback,' Edward 'Chicken' Hartopp, captained the Meath team in victory against a team of cavalry officers.[394] This claim is disputed by other authorities who state that British cavalry officers who had played polo in India founded the Monmouthshire Polo Club in 1872 and in the same year the officers of the 9th Lancers played a team representing County Meath captained by John Watson at Gormanston, the first game of polo played in Ireland.[395]

Within two years of his return he had gained an international reputation as captain of the Freebooters, the winning team of the inaugural Westchester Cup, taking it again two years later and afterwards achieved a hat-trick in the final of the premier English game, the Champion Cup. In all Watson captained his team to victory nine times in the All Ireland Cup; today the All-Ireland cup, which was presented by Watson, is named after the team and continues to be played for on the Nine Acres in the Phoenix Park, home of the All Ireland Polo Club, the oldest in Western Europe.

John Watson's polo career came to an end in 1905 after suffering a heart attack in the saddle at a game in the Phoenix Park. Fortunately he

---

[394] *The Father of the Game* and *An Irish Innovator,* articles from PQInternational.
[395] *The Horse in Ireland* - B. Smith 1991

was saved by an opposing player and managed to return to the saddle to hunt for a further two seasons before his death in 1908.

This indefatigable sportsman's name still remains legendary in County Meath, as much it seems for his abrasive manner in the saddle as for his prowess in the field. In recalling 'forceful men' that he had known, Lord Dunsany was first given to remember Watson whose 'imposing figure, his fine voice, and his tremendous language, awed his field, who obeyed him just as his hounds did.'

His presence lingered long after his death and twenty years after his death Lord Dunsany believed there were still 'old sportsmen sleeping in chairs at their firesides who, if you shouted to them "John Watson wants to know what the hell you are doing there", would hastily back their chairs away from the fire as they waked.'[396]

Watson died at Bective House in 1908; by then the hunt kennels had been established at Nugentstown, on the Charlesfort estate, with a more elaborate complex of buildings that remains home to the Meath pack. The property was sold, and Watson would have been pleased to know that those who acquired it were as obsessive about horses and hunting as he was.

There is a commemorative bookstand in the All Saints Church Fenagh, County Carlow that has the following inscription: "In loving memory of John Henry Watson, Lieut. 13th Hussars who died at Bective 14th Nov. 1908, aged 56 and Robert Watson, Captain, Cape Mounted Rifleman, who died in South Africa Sept. 1900, aged 45 and William Watson who died at Thornhill, East Grinstead, Sussex, 10th Sep 1913, aged 48. The three sons of Robert and Margaret Watson of Ballydarton. 'Till the Day Dawn'"[397]

---

[396] Lord Dunsany, *My Ireland*. 1937
[397] *Fieldcrest Collection of Tombstone Inscriptions County Carlow* 1995

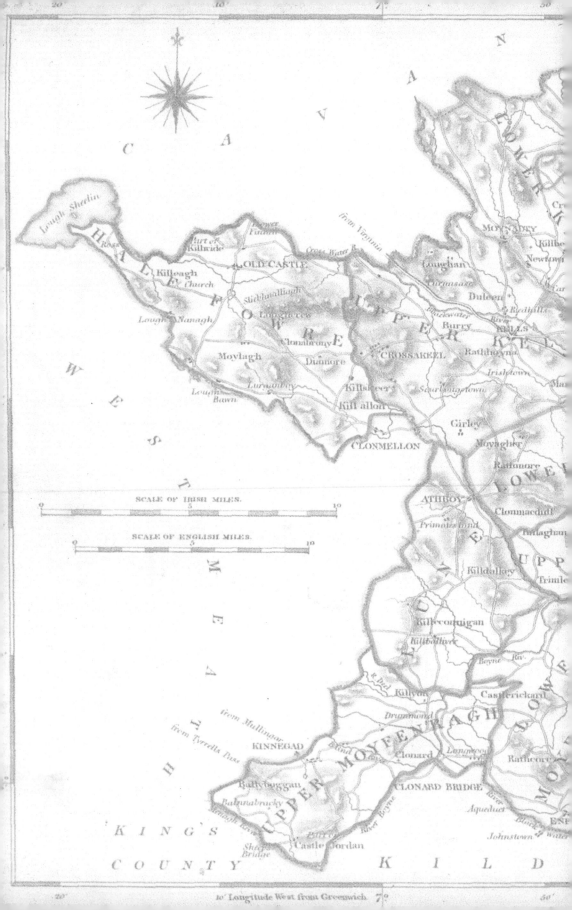

N

C   A   V   A   N

LOWER

Lough Sheelin

Cr

MOYNALTY

Killbe

Newtown

H   A   L   F

Rosa

Killeagh

Ex Church

Port or
Kilbride

Lower
Fuaan

from Virginia

Cross Water B.

Loughan

Turansare

Duleen

Redhills

River

War

OLD CASTLE

U   P   E   R

Slichmallia8h

Lough Nanagh

O

W

Longwees

E

R

Blackwater

Barry

HILLS

CROSSAKEEL

Rathboyna

KEL

Moylagh

Clonabrony

Dinmore

Irishtown

Lurganboy

Lough
Bawn

Killskeer

Scurlangstown

Mar

W

E

S

T

Kill allon

Girley

Moyagher

CLONMELLON

Rathmore

LOWER

SCALE OF IRISH MILES.

0   5   10

ATHBOY

Clonmacduff

SCALE OF ENGLISH MILES.

0   5   10

M   E   A

Primatesfand

Fartaghan

U   P   P

Killdalkey

Trimle

T   H

Killconnigan

Killbaliver

Bayne Riv.

from Mullingar

R. Del

Killyon

Castlerickard

LOWER

from Tyrrells Pass

Drummond

Clonard

Lunnecod

Rathcore

KINNEGAD

MOYFENRAGH

Ballyboggan

UPPER

CLONARD BRIDGE

River Boyne

Aqueduct

Ballinabracky

Castle Jordan

Sha
Bridge

River Boyne

Johnstown

Black water

K   I   N   G'S

C   O   U   N   T   Y

K   I   L   D